The Collected Works of
Byrd Spilman Dewey

BSD

The Collected Works of Byrd Spilman Dewey

Florida's Pioneer Author

Ginger L. Pedersen & Janet M. DeVries, Editors

Cover Image: Byrd Spilman Dewey with cat Billie, 1918 —
Tropical Trunk Line Map, 1894: Courtesy Library of Congress

First Published 2014

ISBN: 978-1494892333

Library of Congress CIP data applied for.

Note: The information in this book is true and complete to the
best of our knowledge. It is offered with no guarantee on the part of
the editors. The editors disclaim all liability in connection with the use
of this book. All works published in the United States prior to January
1, 1923 are in the public domain. All materials written by Byrd Spilman
Dewey meet these criteria with the exception of *Some Bird Notes*, which
appears courtesy of Audubon Florida.

www.byrdspilmandewey.com

This book is dedicated to Byrd Spilman Dewey, for the gift of her writings; they are the descendants that told her story and brought her back to our collective memory. What is found can never be lost again.

Contents

Acknowledgements

Locating all of Byrd Spilman Dewey's known works required detective work in searching databases, used book dealers and archives from across the nation. Numerous people were instrumental in the compilation, transcription, editing and production of the manuscript. We thank all of you for making this project possible to preserve Mrs. Dewey's works in one volume.

Betty Dente, for transcription of the original works.

Jeff Geiger, Jacksonville Public Library, who provided access to the library's Florida collection.

Janis Lydic Hebert and Loretta Lydic Ammerman, Mrs. Dewey's great-great nieces, who provided photographs of Byrd Spilman Dewey from the Spilman family collection. Janis also served as a manuscript reviewer.

Fred Holmstock, who did the wonderful restoration work on the Dewey's portrait and the colorized Ben Trovato picture.

Ron Hurtibise, who produced and directed the documentary on Byrd Spilman Dewey – www.floridalegacyproductions.com

Victoria R. Martin for helping with the cover design.

Debi Murray, Historical Society of Palm Beach County, who provided access to the Society's archives and shared her great knowledge of Palm Beach County history.

Mary Baldwin Woodland, for providing the 1950s pictures of the Ben Trovato house.

Introduction

BYRD SPILMAN DEWEY was born February 16, 1856 as Julia Bird Spilman. The daughter of Jonathan Edwards Spilman and Eliza Sarah Taylor, Mrs. Dewey's ancestry traces back to President Zachary Taylor and other famous early Americans. She grew up in Maysville, Kentucky, along the shores of the Ohio River. Mrs. Dewey's father, an attorney, composer and minister, had his pastorate in Maysville. He composed the famous song "Flow Gently, Sweet Afton." Tragedy took her mother's life in a steamboat accident when Mrs. Dewey was only ten years old.

Mrs. Dewey attended the Maysville Academy, Maysville College and the Sayre Institute in Lexington, Kentucky. As her father moved on to a new pastorate in Salem, Illinois, she met and married Frederick Sidney Dewey, a bank clerk 18 years her senior. The young couple soon caught "Florida fever" as many did in the 1880s, seeking a warmer climate to help Mr. Dewey's tuberculosis contracted during the Civil War.

They arrived in Florida in 1881, and set out to raise an orange grove near Eustis, Florida. Mrs. Dewey began her writing career by submitting articles to women's magazines. Mr. Dewey's fragile health caused him to be unable to work at times, so her writing income was sometimes their sole source of money. They moved on to Jacksonville where their only child, Elizabeth, died as an infant.

Mrs. Dewey's first known published work appeared in the *Christian Union*, published under her pen name of "Judith Sunshine" one of the pen names she used in addition to Judith Ray and Aunt Judith. After their move to the "Lake Worth Country" (today's Palm Beach) in 1887, she became the first columnist for a South Florida newspaper when she started writing her column "The Sitting Room" for *The Tropical Sun*, South Florida's first newspaper. In later years, her magazine writing expanded to national publications such as *Good Housekeeping*, the *Ladies*

11

Home Journal and *Vogue*.

The Dewey home in West Palm Beach, Ben Trovato, was the center point of culture in the pioneer days. Mrs. Dewey hosted many parties and events at the lakeside cottage; its name means "well invented" in Italian. An astute land investor, Mrs. Dewey and her husband founded the Town of Boynton, today's Boynton Beach, with a population of more than 69,000, from land Mrs. Dewey purchased in 1892.

Her 1899 book *Bruno* proved to be her breakthrough work. Published by Little, Brown and Company the book became a national bestseller. She followed that in 1901 with several articles published in *Vogue* magazine that became the basis of her next book, *The Blessed Isle and its Happy Families.* Her third book, *From Pine Woods to Palm Groves,* told of her early pioneering days in the to-be Palm Beach County. This work is unique in South Florida pioneer literature as it is the most complete account written by a woman who was also an accomplished author. She also self-published many of her short stories in pamphlet form, such as *Peter, the Tramp* and *Flying Blossom.*

After husband Fred Dewey's passing in 1919, Mrs. Dewey began a new career in the Florida Audubon Society. She became their field secretary and traveled the state making speeches promoting conservation, bird sanctuaries and humane treatment of animals.

Her last published work was in 1927, after which she retired to Jacksonville, Florida where she passed away in 1942 at age 86.

Mrs. Dewey did not leave behind huge volumes of work, but her writing is unique in Florida literature as an observer of animals and their interactions with the early pioneers. Such stories of kinship between humans and animals are timeless. Critic and reviewer Joseph Leopold Borgerhoff wrote of Mrs. Dewey: "But though dwelling far from the bustle, Mrs. Dewey never knew loneliness. She had her dreams, she had nature, and she had her dumb friends: flowers, birds, dogs and cats. She endowed them with her own cheerful personality and no doubt she is convinced that all possess reasoning and sentient souls."

The Dewey's biography is the focus of the book Pioneering Palm Beach: The Deweys and the South Florida Frontier, *by Ginger L. Pedersen and Janet M. DeVries, published by the History Press.*

Bonus features and photographs can be found at www.byrdspilmandewey.com.

Bruno

Forward to Bruno

Byrd Spilman Dewey's most well-known work, *Bruno*, was published in 1899 and remained in print more than twenty years. Research into the Dewey's lives revealed that the book was autobiographical; Judith is Mrs. Dewey; while Julius is Mr. Dewey. The book opens as the Deweys are in Salem, Illinois. Mr. Dewey is working as a bank clerk at the Salem National Bank, and Mrs. Dewey is keeping house. The household was completed by a large dog they named Bruno, a gift from Fred Dewey's sister Hattie Elder.

In the story, the Deweys begin to "talk Florida." Mr. Dewey had contracted tuberculosis during the Civil War, so they sought a warmer climate for his health. Florida fit the bill. Once the Deweys decided to head to Florida, they could not leave beloved Bruno behind, so he went along to join in the adventures.

The book became a national best seller, and was considered children's literature at the time, but persons of all ages found the story engaging. Critical acclaim for the book is well documented. "A singularly sweet and natural story of a dog" is how the publisher Little, Brown and Company described it. The *Guide for the Christmas Book-Buyer* wrote "*Bruno* is the biography of a pet dog by his admirer, Byrd Spilman Dewey. The army of dog-lovers will find some things to laugh and cry over between its covers." *Donohue's Magazine*, in its review said "*Bruno* is a charming biography of a pet dog. The story is told simply and naturally by a writer who has keen sympathy for animal life. The book is one that will touch deeply readers of all classes, whether lovers of animals or not, and one that will interest young and old. *Bruno* is more than likely to take his place among living dogs in literature." The *New York Times* wrote "It is the story of a dog's life and deeds, and of the faithfulness which made him a genuine companion to his mistress. Not a learned dog like Diomed, not an elegant morsel of refinement like Loveliness, Bruno is a dog whose owners do not think that heaven will be quite complete for them until they can go over to the 'Happy Hunting Grounds' to get Bruno to live with them again." At the conclusion of *Bruno* is a short story which acts as a postscript to the work and provides the background on Rebecca, the Dewey's pet cat in Illinois.

All events described in *Bruno*, happy and sad, did indeed occur. The epilogue after the text of *Bruno* will reveal some of the cities and events described in Mrs. Dewey's classic story.

THIS LITTLE SKETCH

Is dedicated
To all who have ever loved one of those faithful
creatures of whom we, in our ignorance
and vanity, are wont to speak as
"the lower animals."
B.S.D.

Chapter 1

WE DO not count the first half-year of our married life, because, during that time we did not live, we boarded. Then we found we had developed a strong appetite for housekeeping, so we began to look about us for a house.

In the small northern village where we must live, it was not possible to rent anything that suited us; so we decided to take what we could get until we could manage to build what we wanted.

The house we took was one which had originally been built out in the country, but the town had crept around it until it now seemed to be almost in the heart of the village.

While we were furnishing and embellishing this our first home was, I think, the most entirely happy time of our lives.

Julius often said, "I know now why the birds always sing so joyously when they are building their nests."

We were just beginning to feel settled, when a letter came to Julius from his only sister, who lived in a city. It was not unusual for him to have letters from her, but this particular letter stands by itself.

It had a postscript!

The postscript said: "Would you like a nice dog? The children have had a valuable puppy, seven months old, given to them, and we cannot keep him here, in a flat. He is half setter and half water-spaniel; pure on both sides. We call him 'Bruno'."

How our dignity increased at the idea of owning livestock! So far we had only achieved a cat, who had by this time achieved kittens. But a dog! That was something like! It did not take us long to decide and send off an enthusiastic acceptance. Then another letter came, saying that Bruno had started on the journey us-ward.

The next afternoon a car-porter walked into Julius's place of business escorting a shaggy brown dog by a chain fastened to his collar. We have never known just what transpired during that eighteen hours' journey, but something notable there certainly was. He seemed utterly humiliated and dejected when he was led in. Julius looked up from his day-book, and exclaimed,

"Is that you, Bruno? How are you, old fellow?" At the sound of his name, Bruno raised his ears, wrinkled his forehead, and cocked his head on one side inquiringly. Julius stroked and patted him, and Bruno was won.

I was sitting at home busily sewing, when I was startled by a great clatter out on the sidewalk. I looked, and there came Julius leading— puppy, indeed! A dog nearly as big as a calf! I had expected a baby-dog in a basket!

He was a beauty—his hair just the color that is called auburn or red, when humans have it. He sniffed me over approvingly, and let me hug his beautiful head.

We took off the chain, and watched him roll and bathe himself in the high grass of the back yard. He had probably never seen such grass before, and he could not express his delight with it.

There was a three-cornered discussion at bed-time about where our new pet was to sleep. Julius and I did the talking, while Bruno sat upright—I called it "standing up before, and sitting down behind," his ears cocked up, looking from one to the other as we spoke, seeming to understand all that was said. It was finally decided to make him a bed on the floor beside ours, so that he would not be lonesome.

Several times in the night we were startled by his cries. He moaned and whined in his sleep,—evidently having bad dreams. Julius would call to him until he was broad awake, then reach down and pat him till his tail began to thump the floor, and he would rise and wind himself up by going round and round on his bed, then drop, to go off again into an uneasy snooze. We did not sleep much. Towards morning we were awakened from a first sound nap, finding ourselves violently crowded and pushed. Julius sprang out of bed and lighted a candle. There was Bruno monopolizing half of our bed.

It was daylight before we could convince him that his bed was on the floor and that he was expected to occupy it.

The next afternoon, I ventured to take Bruno for a walk. I had tied a broad light-blue ribbon in a big bow round his neck, which contrasted beautifully with his auburn curls. I felt very proud of his appearance, and he also eyed me with a look of satisfaction. Alas! "Pride goeth before a fall, and a haughty spirit before destruction."

As we crossed a street that ran at right angles with the one we were gracing, Bruno, looking down its vista, caught sight of what was probably the first flock of hens he had ever seen.

All the setter in him sprang to the fore, and in a flash he was off after them. Without a thought, I followed. Up and down the street we sped,—he after the one speckled hen he had singled out, and I after him, shrieking to him, and making lunges at him with my parasol, as he and the hen rushed by me.

Finally the distracted Biddy, squawking, cackling, and with outspread wings, found the hole under the fence through which the others had escaped and disappeared, leaving us to view the ruins, heated and disheveled, with smashed parasol, muddy feet, draggled ribbon, and vanished dignity.

After some half-hysterical reproaches from me, which Bruno listened to with drooping ears and tail, we turned, demoralized and dejected, to wend our way homeward, I mentally congratulating myself that the streets were deserted. I shuddered to think of the probable consequences if it had happened after school hours when the small boy was abroad.

So far we had managed to prevent a meeting between Bruno and Rebecca.

Bruno was to us such an uncertain quantity that we feared the result of their first glimpse of each other. So the box containing Rebecca's kittens had been kept out in the stable, and her food carried out to her to prevent the dreaded meeting. I wearied of the daily forced marches stable-ward, though, and longed to have them within reach. So, one evening after Julius came home from the office, we, in fear and trembling, brought in the box, and mounted guard to watch developments.

Bruno looked curious, sniffed, and then drew nearer. I sat down on the floor to be ready to defend them, while Julius stood behind Bruno.

As soon as he spied the kits, his ears rose and he was all alert. Then gradually he seemed to realize, from our way of proceeding, that they were not fair game. His ears drooped forward, his tail began to wag, and I drew back from the protecting attitude I had instinctively assumed. His tail continued to wag, his ears drooped lower and lower, until presently he was licking the little kits and rooting them over with his nose regardless of their ineffectual clawing and spitting.

At this stage of the game, who should arrive on the scene but Rebecca! She came dashing in, having returned from a hunting excursion to find her nest of babies gone; coming, as she always did when anything went wrong, for our help and comfort. As soon as she saw Bruno, her back went up as if a spring had been touched; she stood at bay, growling and spitting.

He started towards her, but Julius grasped his collar. Then Rebecca caught sight of her kits. She darted to them, sprang into the box, and covered them with her body.

Julius loosened his hold of Bruno, who advanced eagerly.

Rebecca received him with a flash of her paw which left a long deep scratch on his nose. He retreated whining and growling. Julius comforted him, while I took Rebecca in hand. For some time we reasoned and experimented with them, until finally we had the satisfaction of seeing Rebecca let down her bristles and begin to purr while Julius smoothed her head and back with Bruno's paw.

After that they kept the peace fairly well, though Rebecca always boxed his ears when she came in and found him licking and nosing her kittens.

We tried to keep him away from them, but he did love them so. He would watch Rebecca out of one eye as he lay dozing, and as soon as she started on a hunt, he would go tiptoeing to the kitten-box for a frolic.

Soon they grew quite fond of playing with his big curly ears, and forgot to spit and scratch.

Chapter 2

ONE MORNING when Julius got up, he could find only one of his slippers. After a long search the other was found under the edge of the washing-stand, but in a decidedly dilapidated condition.

It had evidently been gnawed.

We gravely discussed the misfortune of having our premises invaded by rats, and when on the following morning one of my overshoes was likewise discovered to be a wreck, matters began to look serious, and Julius hastened to procure a trap.

That night I was awakened from my first doze by a sound of gnawing, and on hastily lighting a candle, Bruno was seen with a conscious, shamefaced expression just like a big boy who is caught enjoying a nursery-bottle chewing a shoe!

It was quite a revelation of dog-character to find such a big fellow chewing up things, but we were relieved on the score of rats. Bruno was furnished with an old shoe for his very own on which to exercise his jaws, and we formed the habit of arranging our shoes on the mantelpiece every night before retiring.

We exchanged the trap for some boxes of tacks, which "are always handy to have in the house."

About this time our neighbors, the Crows, became possessed of a large setter dog, by name Leo.

This dog was deficient in morality, and at once developed thieving propensities.

Bruno soon understood that we did not want Leo to come to our house nor even into the yard; still, he personally formed a dog-friendship for him. While this seemed at the time very strange to us, I have since explained it to my own satisfaction.

I think Leo must have confided to Bruno the fact that he was not well cared for by his owners.

Many people seem to think it is unnecessary to give a dog regular meals. They think he ought to "pick up a living." The Crows seemed to have this idea; so Bruno doubtless felt that Leo was not altogether to blame for being a thief, and after fiercely driving him outside of our gate, he would follow, and they would have romps and races until both were exhausted.

Leo was the only real dog-friend Bruno ever had. All his other friends were either humans or cats.

The crowds of dogs that sometimes go yelping and tearing through the streets were to him objects of the loftiest scorn. From front window or porch he would look down his nose at them, then turn, stepping high, to march off and lie down in some remote corner where only the faintest echoes of their din could reach him.

One evening, while Julius and I were at choir-practice, we heard something that distressed me greatly. I felt that I could not stay, so we slipped out and hurried home. As soon as we were inside of our own door I threw myself into Julius's arms with childlike sobbing.

He tried to comfort me, but I could only hear my own heart-throbs. All at once he exclaimed,

"Look, Judith, look at Bruno!"

His tone was so strange, it penetrated even my grief. I raised my head and there was Bruno, standing upright, his head against Julius's shoulder, as close to me as he could get, his eyes full of tears, the picture of woe.

"You see Bruno is crying too," said Julius.

As soon as Bruno saw me look up, he threw back his head and wagged his tail as if to say,—

"Come now, that's better, much better."

My tears still fell, but they were no longer bitter. There was something about the sympathy of that dumb creature which touched a chord not to be reached by anything human. It was so unlooked for and so sincere.

It was wonderful how he entered into all our feelings. In those days I was very much afraid of thunderstorms. In some subtle way Bruno divined this and kept the closest watch for clouds. If the heavens began to be overcast, he would go from window to window, noting developments, coming to me every few minutes to look into my face and wag his tail reassuringly.

When our fears were verified and the storm broke, he would come to rest his head on my knee, wincing with me at the thunders and flashes. When the worst was over, and big scattering drops showed the end of the storm to be near, he would drop at my feet with a huge sigh of relief that showed what a nervous strain he had been enduring.

He also discovered a strong aversion I had for spiders, and went about killing every one he could find. Chancing to be at my side one day when I dodged and exclaimed at the too familiar dartings of a wasp that was flying around me, he from that time made it a rule to destroy flying bugs of all kinds, often jumping high in the air to catch them.

Chapter 3

NOW APPROACHED a troublous time in Bruno's career. He fell into bad ways. We always thought it was Leo who tempted him.

It developed in this way. Soon after dark Bruno would ask to have the door opened for him to go out. He would look as innocent as if he only meant to step around to the well for a fresh drink. At bedtime we would suddenly remember that we had heard nothing of him since he had been let out. Julius would open the door expecting to find him lying on the porch. Disappointed in this, he would whistle, call, whistle again, but there would be no answer. At last we would give him up and go to bed. At gray dawn there would be a sound of scratching on the door, and when it was opened Bruno would come in, muddy, draggled, and exhausted. After drinking with evident relish from his water-bowl, he would curl up on his bed and sleep till noon.

We scolded him about these "tears," as we called them, until he would in spite of his fatigue go through with his tricks on being admitted in the morning : he would "sit up" and offer to "shake hands" with first one paw, then the other; trying to propitiate whichever of us opened the door for him. But he would not give up the "tears." Then we tried chaining him for the night. This kept him at home for nearly a week, until he finally succeeded in pulling out the staple that held the chain. In the morning Bruno, chain, and all had vanished; for it was summer-time and we had chained him outside, under an open shed. The hours crept on towards afternoon, and still he came not. I had heard at intervals all day the distant yelping of a dog, but had only noticed it to suppose that a neighbor some few blocks away had had occasion to tie up his watch-dog.

As evening approached, I anxiously awaited the return of Julius from his office that he might go in search of our missing Bruno. While I was waiting, the milkman came along.

"Where's your dog?" he asked, as he poured out the milk.

Bruno and Rebecca always watched for the milkman and were first to greet him; this day only Rebecca was there.

"I wish I knew," I answered; "he ran off in the night dragging his chain, and we don't know what has become of him."

"There's a big brown dog that looks just like yours chained to the sidewalk over yonder beyond Mr. Black's."

He jerked his head in the direction whence the yelping sounds had come.

Uncle Edwards was then spending a few days with us. He was one of those people who believe that sooner or later all dogs go mad, and that it is as much as one's life is worth to come within ten feet of them. He and Bruno were on the most distant terms of mutual toleration.

But I was desperate. Julius had not come, and I must be at home in case Bruno did arrive hungry, thirsty, and footsore. There was no help for it; I must ask assistance from Uncle Edwards.

He was a gentleman of the old school, always obliging and courteous. He would bow politely and pick up a loaded shell with burning fuse attached, if asked to do so by a lady.

He readily agreed to go round by Mr. Black's to see if by any chance the "big brown dog chained to the sidewalk" could be ours. He shortly returned, leading by the extreme end of his chain a very crestfallen Bruno; tired, hungry, thirsty, his throat raw with ineffectual yelpings.

Delighted and relieved as I was to see him, I still had room for a smothered laugh at his and Uncle Edwards's attitude to each other as they approached. Uncle regarded Bruno out of the tail of his eye, as if he were some infernal machine, liable at any moment to do things unheard of; while Bruno, perfectly aware of his distrust, threw tired, meekly humorous glances out of the tail of his eye. It was comical.

His chain had caught in a cleft board of the sidewalk, and he had been held there, struggling and yelping, part of the night and all day! All who had happened to see him thought he had been fastened there for some purpose or other.

This was a pretty severe lesson for Bruno, and it kept him at home for several nights. At last temptation again overcame him, and at bedtime one night he was missing. When he returned at dawn, his side was peppered with small bloody wounds. He had been shot!

"That settles it," said Julius; "he has been chasing sheep!"

We were extremely troubled at this discovery, and Julius said,

"Our life is too quiet for him. His instincts are all for chasing something. Our little promenades are but an aggravation to a dog who is longing to stretch his legs over miles of country."

We knew he must go at least six miles to find sheep. For the first time we now began seriously to consider the idea of giving Bruno away.

A young hunter, whom we will call Mr. Nimrod, had long been wanting him. He told us it was a shame to turn such a splendid fellow into a drawing-room dog. He would hold forth indefinitely on Bruno's points, especially certain extra toes on his various legs. He said a dog with such toes was built for a "lightning-express" runner, and that it was outraging nature to try to keep him cooped up in a village lot. After many discussions we at last decided we ought to give him up to the life for which he so evidently longed.

We were about to move into the house we had been building, and we thought the best way to make the dog-transfer would be for Julius to take him to Mr. Nimrod's the last day before we moved, so that if he ran away and came to find us, there would be only the deserted house.

It did not occur to us that this would be cruel. We knew we were giving him up for his own good, and we felt sure he would soon get wonted to his new home, where he could live the life for which he was created. So, on the last evening in the old home, Julius took up his hat, which was always a signal to Bruno, who came and sat up before him, with ears at "attention," which was his way of asking,—

"May I go?"

"Yes, Boonie can go," answered Julius.

Then Bruno, who had long since learned to understand the difference between "go" and "stay," went bounding down the walk, leaped over the gate, and began rushing back and forth along in front of the lot, giving short barks of delight. Julius called him back, and he came rather crestfallen, thinking he was, after all, to "stay;" but it was only that I might hug him and tell him, "Good-bye, you must be a good doggie!"

This puzzled him; but his bewilderment was soon forgotten in the fact that he was really and truly to "go." When Julius returned an hour later, he told me he had slipped away while Mr. and Mrs. Nimrod were petting Bruno, and so had escaped a formal leave-taking. I was glad of this, for I had dreaded their parting.

In spite of the fact that I was the one to attend to Bruno's wants,—that he always came to me when hungry or thirsty, and that I never disciplined him as Julius sometimes did,—still he showed in many ways that Julius's place in his heart was far above mine. So I was relieved that there had been no good-byes.

We were both entirely engrossed for the next few days by getting moved and settled. In spite of busy hands, I had many times felt a tugging at the heart-strings for the absent Bruno. I said nothing about it, though; and Julius afterwards confessed that he too had felt longings, but had suppressed them for fear of upsetting me, just as I had concealed my feelings on his account.

On the afternoon of the fourth day Julius could stand it no longer; we must have some news of Bruno. So he looked up Mr. Nimrod.

Before he could ask any questions, Mr. Nimrod began,—

"What did you feed that dog, anyway?"

"Why, the same things we ate," answered Julius, in surprise; "whatever there was on the table."

"Well, he won't eat anything for us. We've tried everything we could think of. What does he like best?"

"Well," said Julius, "he likes biscuit and toast and fried mush,—all sorts of crisp and crackly things; and bones,—little ones that he can bite,—and meats of course."

"We've tried everything except the toast and mush. We'll try him on those. I'll go right home now and see about it."

When Julius came home and repeated this conversation to me, it produced what may without exaggeration be called a state of mind. I was half wild. All the emotions I had been struggling to conceal since Bruno's departure now held sway. Julius was deeply moved too. We could only comfort each other by recalling all the trouble we had had with Bruno, from the anxious night of his first "tear," to that last morning when he had returned wounded and bloody.

We assured each other that he would soon consent to be happy in such a good home, and that it would be wrong for us to indulge our feelings to his ultimate hurt. We dwelt especially on the fact that if he should again go sheep-chasing and be shot at, he stood at least a chance of being fatally wounded.

Thus we talked ourselves into a reasonable frame of mind.

Chapter 4

I KNEW, without anything being said about it, that Julius would lose no time the next day in finding out if Bruno had consented to eat his supper. When he started down town a whole hour earlier than usual, I knew, as well as if he had said so, that it was in order to have time to hunt up Mr. Nimrod before office hours.

"It's no use," began Mr. Nimrod, as soon as Julius appeared; "wouldn't touch a thing. Never saw such a dog. I believe he's trying to starve himself."

"Don't you think," ventured Julius, "it would be well to bring him out to our house for a little visit, to cheer him up?"

"Not much!" answered Mr. Nimrod, promptly "I never could break him in then. He has run away twice already, and both times I followed him and found him hanging around the house you moved from. Lucky the trail was cold. If he once finds out where you are, the jig's up."

When Julius came home at noon, we sat at the table listless and dejected, now and then making fitful attempts to converse. The dainty noon meal had suddenly lost flavor after we had exchanged a few sentences about "Poor, hungry Bruno!"

Were we to eat, drink, and be merry, while our faithful friend starved for love of us!

After Julius had returned to the office, there was such a tugging at my heart-strings that I—well, yes, I did, I cried! How I regretted that I had never cultivated an intimacy with Mrs. Nimrod, so that I might have "run in" to call, and thus have an opportunity to comfort the poor homesick fellow!

Julius saw the tear-traces when he returned towards evening, and proposed a stroll downtown; thinking, I suppose, that if we sat at home we should be sure to talk of Bruno and be melancholy.

We walked through all the principal streets of the town, meeting and greeting friends and acquaintances, stopping to glance at new goods in several of the shops; bringing up at last in the town's largest bookstore.

We were just starting for home, when on the sidewalk there was a sudden flurry and dash, I fell on my knees to hug him; and Bruno, stomach to earth, was crawling about us, uttering yelps and whines that voiced a joy so great it could not be told from mortal agony.

Regardless of the fact that we were on the most public thoroughfare of the town, I fell on my knees to hug him, and could not keep back tears of mingled joy and pain. His poor thin sides! His gasps of rapture! Oh, Boonie, Boonie!

The first excitement over, we looked about us for Mr. Nimrod. He was nowhere to be seen. Bruno had evidently escaped, and was running away to look for us when he had chanced to strike our trail and so had found us.

We were glad he was alone. We both felt that if he had been torn from us at that supreme moment he would have died; he was so faint with fasting and grief, and then the overwhelming joy at finding those he had thought to be forever lost to him! He squeezed himself in between us, and kept step as we went homeward in the gathering twilight.

As soon as we reached home, we hurried him to the kitchen to enjoy the sight of the poor fellow at his trencher. How we fed him! I ransacked the pantry for the things he liked best, till his sides began to swell visibly. He paused between mouthfuls to feast his loving eyes on first one, then the other of us, and his tail never once stopped wagging. Rebecca came purring in to rub against his legs, and even submitted with shut eyes to a kiss from his big wet tongue. He must have felt that such an hour repaid him for all his sufferings.

After he had eaten until he evidently could not take another morsel, we drew him in front of us as we sat side by side, for a three-cornered talk. He sat on end, waving his tail to and fro on the floor, wrinkling his forehead and cocking up his ears, while we explained the situation to him.

We told him how kind Mr. Nimrod meant to be to him, how he would train him to hunt and take him on long daily runs. Then we reminded him how impossible it was for Julius to go on such excursions with him, and of how many scrapes he had got into by going alone,—he seeming to take it all in and to turn it over in his mind.

Then we told him that since he had found our new home he could come often to see us, and he would always find us glad to see him, yes, more than glad I Then Julius got his hat and said,—

"Come on, Boonie; now we're going home."

He seemed quite willing to go. I told him good-by with a heart so light I could scarcely believe it the same one I had felt to be such a burden when I had set off for our walk two hours earlier. I busied myself then preparing a little supper against Julius's return; for we had not been able to eat since breakfast, and I knew by my own feelings that Julius would welcome the sight of a well-spread smoking table; and he said on his return that I "guessed just right."

He and Bruno had found the Nimrods very much disturbed over their dog's disappearance. Mr. Nimrod had just returned from an unsuccessful search, and they were wondering what to do next. They welcomed the wanderer, but were concerned, too, that he had discovered our dwelling-place.

"I'm afraid we'll have to keep him tied up now," said Mr. Nimrod.

Julius thought not, and said,—

"Now that he knows where we are, and can come for a glimpse of us now and then, I believe he'll be better contented than he was when he thought we'd left the country."

Better contented he certainly was, but he positively refused to stay at home. It soon came to be a regular thing for Julius to escort him back every evening.

The Nimrods lived nearly a mile from us, so Julius did not lack for exercise.

Mr. Nimrod finally came to remonstrate with us.

"You ought to shut him out," he cried, "then he'd have to come back home."

For answer, Julius showed him certain long, deep scratches on our handsome new doors, adding,—

"Don't you see? It's as much as our doors are worth to shut him out, and he leaps that four-foot fence as if it were but four inches."

There was obviously no possible reply to such logic as this; so he continued to come,—dragging sometimes a rope or strap, or some other variety of tether, triumphantly proving that love laughs at locksmiths!

The Nimrods at last lost heart. Bruno never would eat there, and he never stayed when he could manage to escape. One night it was raining hard when the time came for him to be taken "home," so they did not go; and that seemed to settle it.

He was our dog.

We had given him away without his consent, and he refused to be given; so the trade was off. He stayed closely at home now, seeming to think we might disappear again if he did not watch us.

Chapter 5

UNLESS THERE were guests in the house, we usually slept with all the inner doors wide open for better circulation of air. One night we were awakened by tremendous barkings and growlings from Bruno. Julius spoke to him, and he answered with a whine. Then we could hear his feet pad-padding on the carpet as he went from our room, tap-tapping on the oil-cloth in the hall, pad-padding again through the sitting-room and the dining-room, then tap-tapping on the painted kitchen floor, with more loud barks and deep growls.

Julius tried again to quiet him, but he refused to be quieted.

"Something disturbs him," I said. "Maybe we'd better let him out."

"No," said Julius, "it is probably that wretched Leo lurking around, trying to toll him off. He's better inside."

I did not think he would seem so fierce if it were Leo, but I was too sleepy to argue; so we dozed off, leaving him still on the alert.

Deep was our surprise next morning to find that a band of thieves had raided the town during the night, and that the houses on both sides of us had been entered! How we petted and praised Bruno, our defender! He was quite unconcerned, though, and seemed as if he would say to us,—

"Oh, that was nothing. I only barked and made a racket!"

Truly, it was only necessary for him to bark and make a racket. There was never any occasion for him to go further. His voice was so loud and deep it always conveyed the impression of a dog as big as a house,—one that could swallow a man at one mouthful without winking.

People were always ready to take the hint when he gave voice to his emotions. They never undertook to argue with him.

After that night we never slept with such comfortable feelings of perfect security as we felt at those times when we were half aroused by Bruno's barks and growls.

For a while the days passed uneventfully in our little home. Julius and I were interested in beautifying and improving our grounds, so time never dragged with us. Rebecca rejoiced in several successive sets of kittens. They and Bruno frolicked through the days, with exciting interruptions in the shape of the milkman's calls, Julius's returns from the office, and occasional visits from the neighbors' children.

For greater convenience we always spoke collectively of Bruno, Rebecca and her kits, as "the cattle."

The milkman's daily calls never grew stale to them. They generally heard his bell before Julius or I suspected he was near, and would all go to the sidewalk to meet him. Bruno would leap the fence; Rebecca and her kits would creep through. As soon as the milk was poured out, they all raced to the back piazza to wait for their share of it. When the dish was filled and placed before them on the floor, Bruno stood back with drooping ears, watching them drink. He seemed to feel that it would not be fair to pit his great flap of a tongue against their tiny rose-leaves. They always left some for him, which he devoured in two or three laps, while they all sat about washing their faces. I don't think he cared for the milk; he took it to be sociable, and seemed to be as well satisfied with a swallow or two as he was after drinking the dishful I sometimes offered him.

He often tried to chew the grain on which the chickens were fed, and would eat anything he saw us taking, including all kinds of fruit, nuts, candies, and ices. Of course the chief of his diet was the various preparations of cereals and meats, but he seemed to want a taste of all that was going.

Once, much to his own ultimate disgust, he coaxed me to give him a sniff of a smelling-bottle he thought I seemed to be enjoying. After that, he regarded all bottles with the deepest suspicion and aversion.

Chapter 6

I T IS hard to remember just when we first began to talk Florida. Then a neighbor went down there on a prospecting tour, and returned bringing enthusiastic accounts of the climate and opportunities. We were greatly interested, and at once sent off for various Florida papers, pamphlets, and books.

Julius had always dreaded the bleak northern winters, having some chronic troubles,—a legacy of the Civil War. It is only in literature that a delicate man is interesting; practically, it subjects him to endless trials and humiliations, so we never gave his state of health as a reason for the proposed change. Instead, we flourished my tender throat. A woman may be an invalid without loss of prestige, so not one of our friends suspected that our proposed change of climate was not solely on my account.

We decided that as soon as our northern property could be disposed of, we would turn our faces southward and try pioneering.

Some children in a neighboring family had formed an enthusiastic friendship with Bruno, and as soon as our plans were announced, their parents asked us to give him to them when we were ready to start south. In spite of our former experience in giving him away, this seemed entirely feasible to us.

In the first place, we thought it would be utterly impossible to take him with us to Florida. Then he was really and truly attached to the children who wanted him; so we readily consented; and we encouraged them to monopolize him as much as possible, so that we might see him comfortably settled before we started. They lived next door to us, and Bruno was always ready to join them in a game of romps. He even ate from their hands. It seemed a perfect arrangement.

Our pretty little home was soon sold and dismantled, and we went to board in another part of town while preparing for the long journey, which then seemed almost as difficult as a trip to the moon. We locked up the empty house and slipped away to our boarding-place, while Bruno, all unconscious of what was going on, was barking and tearing about in a game of tag on the other side of our neighbor's large grounds.

Old Aunt Nancy, a woman who had worked for one of my aunts before the war, and who had been our stand-by in domestic emergencies, had taken Rebecca and her family, promising them "Just as good a home as I can give, Miss Judith." It was a sad breaking up, but we felt that our pets were well provided for, and that we should feel worse for leaving them than they would at being left.

Vain thought!

Two evenings after leaving our home, while I was busy in our room, making ready to begin packing, I heard Julius's step on the stairs, accompanied by a familiar clatter that made my heart stand still. The door burst open, and, before I could rise from my kneeling position, surrounded by piles of folded things, I was knocked over sideways by a rapturous onslaught from Bruno.

"What does this mean!" I exclaimed, as soon as I could speak.

"I don't know," answered Julius. "I found him waiting for me at the office door when I came out. He seemed half wild with delight at seeing me again. I rather think it is a repetition of the Nimrod experiment."

"Poor old fellow!" I cried. "See how his sides have fallen in just in these two days! He has been starving again, and we have nothing to give him!" "That's so," said Julius. "I'd better go and get something for him, hadn't I?"

"Yes, indeed," I answered. "At once, poor old doggie!"

So they went clattering down the stairs again, and soon returned with some promising-looking paper bags.

We spread a newspaper on the hearth to receive his feast, then sat watching him and returning his glances of affection while he ate. When he had eaten to his satisfaction and dropped into a happy snooze, Julius said,—

"Well, I suppose I might as well try to find out if it would be possible to take him with us. I'll see the agent tomorrow. We must either take him, or have him killed; for I see plainly that it won't do at all to try to leave him."

"If we could just have him go along in the train car with us, it would be all right," answered I. "He is such a knowing old fellow he would understand things perfectly."

"That's impossible, I know," cried Julius. "If he goes at all, he must ride in freight cars, and we'll be in a sleeper. I don't see how we can manage it."

I began to think that a way would open, and my heart felt lighter than it had at any time since we first began to talk Florida. If we could have Bruno with us, I no longer dreaded going to a land which, in my imaginings, had appeared to be teeming with unknown dangers.

The next morning Julius went promptly to interview the agent, and found that, after all, it would be possible to take Bruno with us to Florida. It would be some trouble and some expense. Besides his passage as baggage, the porters in each car must be paid; and while we in the sleeper should be in a through car, he would have a number of changes to make,—one of them at early dawn, and another in the night. It would be necessary for Julius to see to these changes in person, in case Bruno proved to be unruly, which was quite probable. We decided to undertake it, and Bruno's outfit for the journey was at once purchased. This consisted of a strong new collar and chain, with a big tin cup fastened to the chain for plenty of drinks, and a lunch-basket full of biscuit.

The memorable day came, and we were escorted to the train by kind neighbors and friends full of good-byes and good wishes for us all, Bruno receiving a full share of their attentions.

We knew well that they considered the whole affair to be a wild-goose chase, and that they expected to see us return, sadder and wiser, in a year at furthest.

As soon as the train was under way, Julius went forward to see how Bruno was taking it. He found him in a state of the utmost excitement, howling and dragging at his chain, probably remembering his other journey on the train cars, when he had left his first home to come alone to us in his puppyhood. When he saw Julius and realized that we were with him, his joy and relief were touching. Julius stayed awhile with him, and got him some water, he was always thirsty after "crying," then came back to report to me.

I felt so relieved to know that we had really got off with Bruno in good shape, it almost made me forget a small ache in the corner of my heart for something that had happened a day or two before. I had gone up by the old home to say good-by to an invalid neighbor, and there, on the sidewalk, by the gate, sat Rebecca. Thin, scrawny, and alert, she sat watching for somebody, easy to guess what "somebody." How glad she was to see me!

I sat down on the gate-step, and took her in my arms, wishing with all my heart that we could take her with us too. Still, I knew we couldn't. She, a sober, middle-aged cat, to be carried all those many miles! Then it might be weeks after we reached Florida before we decided where to settle. A dog, once there, could trot around after us, but what could we do with a cat? She had never learned to follow for any distance, and she was always nervous about being carried.

No, it wasn't to be thought of.

I stayed, petting her as long as I could; then, after urging her to go back and be contented with Aunt Nancy, I bade her a tearful goodbye, and carried away an ache in my heart that I sometimes feel yet.

Dear old Rebecca!

Someday I hope to go across into cat-heaven and hunt her up. Then she can be made to understand why I was seemingly so hard-hearted as to go off and leave her looking mournfully after me on that sad day so long ago. Maybe she knows now; I hope she does.

Chapter 7

IT WAS late forenoon when we set off Florida-ward. Just after dark we reached a big city where we were to take the through sleeper to Jacksonville. In those days there was no Union Depot there, and it was necessary to cross the city in order to get started on the road south.

This transfer had worried us all along, for the time was limited, and there was all our baggage to see to and recheck, and Bruno. We arranged that I was to take Bruno and go with him in the regular transfer omnibus, while Julius crossed with the baggage. We thought that Bruno and I could take care of each other, though I confess I was not willing to have a private cab. In the well-lighted, comfortably filled bus I felt safe enough, even though I was crossing a strange city at nightfall, with only a dog for escort.

Bruno looked wistfully at the door as the bus started, but seemed satisfied when I assured him it was all right. Julius was waiting for us at the other station with tickets and checks.

When he returned from escorting Bruno to the baggage car, reporting, "All's well," we both fairly laughed, in the relief of having passed the most puzzling part of the journey.

I did not see Bruno again until the next morning. It was gray dawn. The train was standing, puffing and snorting like a restless horse, on the track under the shadow of Lookout Mountain.

On inquiry, Julius had learned that there would be a delay of a quarter of an hour or so there, and, as he had to be up, anyway, to transfer Bruno to another baggage car, he had planned to give him a little run; so, as I leaned out of the car window, I saw Julius with Bruno's chain, cup, etc., bunched in his hands, while the happy dog was galloping up and down the roadside. He performed leaps and antics expressive of extreme joy when I leaned out and called to him, saying to me as plainly as possible,—

"Here we are again! Isn't it jolly?"

And I assured him that it was.

After that glimpse I saw no more of Bruno till we reached Jacksonville; but Julius reported, from time to time, that he seemed to comprehend the meaning of our plan of travel, and trotted along from old to new baggage car, so eager not to be left that he tried to enter every one he came to with doors standing open.

Early on the next morning after our stop by Lookout Mountain, we entered the "Florida Metropolis." And now, behold, a great surprise! We had brought thinner clothing in our hand-bags, thinking that, as we journeyed southward, our heavy garments, built for northern winters, would prove to be oppressive. How startling, then, to feel our features pinched by nipping breezes as we stepped from the cars at last in the Sunny South! True, as we passed residences on our way to the hotel, we saw green trees and blooming flowers; but where were the balmy airs that in our dreams were always fanning the fadeless flowers in this Mecca of our hopes?

After leaving the cars, the most welcome sight that greeted our eager eyes was a roaring open fire in the hotel reception-room. We thought this a most excellent joke. They were very good to Bruno (for a consideration) at the hotel, but it was against their rules to allow dogs in the rooms, so he was installed in comfortable quarters outside. Julius went with him to make sure he was satisfied, and to see that he was watered, fed, and in good spirits before we had our own breakfast. On the way down, as ever before, Bruno had attracted much favorable notice. Women and girls exclaimed, "Oh, see that lovely dog!" And a number of men scraped acquaintance with Julius by admiring notice of his "Mighty fine dog!"

Bruno shrank from their attentions. He never made friends with strangers, no matter how much they tried to pet him; and he never ate anything offered to him by others unless we told him to. In fact, he was always very particular about appropriating food. Sometimes at home, when in a brown study, I placed his dish of food on the floor without saying anything; but he would never begin to eat until he had gained my attention by thrusting his nose into my hand, asking, "Is that mine?" by questioning glances directed from me to the dish; then, when I answered, "Yes; that's Boonie's; that's for Boonie," he would fall to and enjoy it.

We were glad of this trait; and we often thought that but for it he would, very early in his career, have fallen a victim to poison, for he was greatly feared by many timid people, especially by various grocer and butcher boys, who approached our premises with so many absurd precautions that it seemed to afford Bruno the greatest delight to keep them in a state of terror.

Chapter 8

WE MADE but a short stay in Jacksonville, then hurried on to St. Augustine, where a former acquaintance of Julius's was living with his family. We had to take a river steamer to Tocoi,—called Decoy by many, for obvious reasons,—then journey across to the coast on a tiny railway.

The steamboat on the St. John's was a first experience of the kind for Bruno, who seemed to enjoy it greatly, for the boat had but few passengers beside ourselves, and we went up and down stairs at will, making him several visits in his quarters on the lower deck.

Things were even more informal on the little railway. There was no one about when we boarded the train; so Bruno followed us into the passenger coach, crept under the seat, doubling himself up like a shut knife, and, totally effaced by the time the conductor came around, rode first-class for once. It seemed such a treat for us all to be together as we journeyed, that our short ride across from "Decoy" to the coast stands out in memory as the pleasantest part of the journey.

We were met at St. Augustine by Julius's friend, and, as he bore a pressing invitation for us from his family, we stopped that first day with them, so that they might have their fill of news from their friends and relatives whom we had seen just before starting to Florida.

They kindly urged us to stay longer, but we thought that two people and a dog made a formidable party to entertain as visitors; so we hunted up a pleasant boarding-house, and settled ourselves for a two weeks' stay.

All three of us found much to surprise us in the old town; but by far the greatest sensation was Bruno's when we first took him out for a run, and he promptly made a dash into one of the creeks as the tide was flowing in, and took a big drink. He was warm with running, and the water looked so inviting that he had taken a number of swallows before he tasted it. Then his antics were most comical. He snorted and shook his head till his ears flapped again, and rubbed at his nose, first with one paw and then with the other. After that one lesson he never again drank from a strange pool or stream without first tasting it very gingerly, then waiting a few seconds to make sure of the after-taste. But if he objected to the taste of salt water, he found no flaw in the feeling of it.

There is no memory of him on which I so much love to dwell as on the picture he made with his tawny curls streaming backwards in the breakers when we took him out to the beach. The green-curling, foam-tipped waves were to him a perfect delight. Even his dashing out in our midst and shaking himself so that we were all drenched in an impromptu shower-bath is pleasant,—as a memory, —though at the time we scolded him, and tried to respond sternly to his waggish glances, as he gamboled about and rolled in the sand.

The salt water was new to all of us, so we spent as much time as possible on the island and the beaches.

On those days when we were confined to the mainland by showers, or by the business we were attending to between times, we used to go, towards evening, to promenade on the seawall. Then Bruno always got down in one of the basins for a swim before we returned to our temporary home.

Although it seemed like northern spring weather, some days being quite chilly, and others warm enough for summer clothes, we awoke one morning to the fact that tomorrow would be Christmas. It had seemed to us, since our arrival in St. Augustine, as if we were in a foreign country, the Spanish element was so large in proportion to the rest of the town, both in the people and their customs and in the arrangement and the construction of the city. We heard of the celebration of midnight Mass in the old Cathedral, and resolved to "assist;" but, as the evening came on crisp and chilly, our enthusiasm cooled with it. The tonic qualities of the unaccustomed salt air had inspired us with a keen interest in food and sleep; so, after fully deciding to sit up for the Mass, we were ready by half-past nine to declare that there was not a sight in the world worth the sacrifice of such a night's sleep as that for which we felt ready. So we embarked for dreamland, whence we were recalled at daylight by Bruno's excitement over a perfect din of tin trumpets and toy drums.

As we dressed, we peeped through the blinds at the processions of small boys marching by in the narrow streets below, blowing trumpets and pounding drums. The daily drills at the barracks in the old city made all the small boys of the town even more ambitious than small boys usually are to be soldiers. Apparently, every one of them had sent Santa Claus a petition to bring him something warlike for a Christmas present.

Julius delighted Bruno by taking him out and buying him a paper of candy, which he ate with much relish; then we three sat on the upper piazza on which our room opened, listening to the music and watching the processions.

It was a very strange Christmas to all three of us. The air was pleasantly warm, and green things, with roses and other flowers, were in sight in all directions.

As soon as Christmas had passed, we, with that feeling of having turned a corner, common at such times, began to hasten our preparations to go on South. We had inspected various tracts of land around St. Augustine, but had not found anything to which we felt particularly drawn. It seemed rather odd, too, to come south intending to pioneer, and then to settle in or near what the old sergeant at the Fort assured us was the oldest city in the Union.

We felt that we must, at all events, see what the wilder parts of the State were like before deciding; so we soon found ourselves speeding away again towards "Decoy," to catch the boat for a little station away down South, up the river, which was then the only route to a small settlement in the mid-lake country, where a relative was living, who had urged us to see his part of Florida before deciding on anything.

It seems odd now to think how remote south middle Florida was in those days. The point we were then trying to reach is now less than twelve hours from Jacksonville by rail. Then we travelled all night by boat, and took train at breakfast time across to a big lake, where a tiny steamer awaited us; on this we crossed the lake, then stopped at a town on the other side, to wait for a wagon which was to come a half-day's journey to meet us.

Our message was delayed, so we spent two days at an English inn, near the big lake, where we made some friends we have kept on our list ever since. And besides these friendships, we have treasured many pleasant memories of this inn. We approached it in the twilight of a chilly, blustering day, and on entering it we were greeted by an immense open fire of lightwood, which glorified the polished floor, strewn with the skins of wild creatures killed in the near-by thickets, called hammocks or hummocks. The firelight gave fitful glimpses of old-fashioned chairs, tables, etc., and lighted up a number of large gilt-framed paintings which adorned the walls; in short, it was a complete picture of artistic comfort. Nor was our satisfaction lessened by the fragrant odor of frying ham and hot muffins, wafted to us as we crossed the hall.

They gave us a ground-floor room in an L opening on one of the side piazzas. This arrangement suited Bruno perfectly, and therefore it pleased us. There was a small lake behind the house, and the next day Julius proposed a row. The boat was quite small, and he was then rather unskilled in the use of oars so we coaxed Bruno to sit on the tiny wharf and see us go by.

He seemed quite willing; so we pushed off. As we floated outward, Bruno lost heart. It was too much like being left behind; so he whined and plunged in after us.

"It isn't far across," said Julius, "and a swim won't hurt him!"

So we went on, letting him follow.

Suddenly he gave a strange cry, and Julius looked around, exclaiming,—

"See, he's cramping!"

We went to him as rapidly as possible, and were just in time. At the risk of upsetting us all in the deepest part of the lake probably about fifteen feet—Julius dragged him into the boat. We then hurried back to the landing, where poor Bruno had to be helped out, and we laid him on the grass in a state of exhaustion which alarmed us greatly.

It was some hours before he was himself again, and many months before he lost a great fear of the water, in fact,—he was never afterwards the fearless water-dog of his youth.

Chapter 9

I SEE us next at the little inland settlement surrounding two small lakes for which we had started.

It had been long years since we had seen the relative who was living there, and childish memories did not tell us that he was the most visionary and unpractical of men. We could not trust our own judgment in such a topsy-turvy country as Florida, where the conditions were all so new to us; so it is no wonder that we took his word for a number of wild statements and decided to buy and settle there. We bought a tract of land from a friend and client of his, who offered us the use of a small homestead shanty near our land, to live in while we were building. This shanty looked decidedly uninviting, but the alternative was a room in the house of our relative, a full mile away from our place; so we decided in favor of the shanty. It was built of rived boards, slabs split out of the native logs. It had one door and no windows. In fact, it needed none; for the boards lapped roughly on each other, leaving cracks like those in window-blinds, so we could put our fingers through the walls almost anywhere. Besides affording a means of light and ventilation, this was vastly convenient for various flying and creeping things. The floor was of rough ten-inch boards, with inch-wide cracks between them. Julius escorted me over to inspect it, saying,—

"If we try to live in this excuse for a house, we shall be pioneering with a vengeance."

After a searching glance around the premises, I answered,—

"The pioneering is all right, if we can just make it clean."

"Oh, that's easy enough!" exclaimed Julius, in a relieved tone. "If you think we can stand its other short-comings, I can whitewash the whole thing, and make it so fresh and sweet you won't know it."

We sent a message for our freight, which we had left at Jacksonville, and Julius took a team to the nearest town to buy a few necessaries. We had brought no furniture South with us, knowing that what we had in our northern home would be unsuitable for pioneering. Our freight, therefore, was mostly books and pictures, with a few boxes of clothes, bedding, etc. The shanty was wonderfully improved by a coat or two of whitewash, and after an old tapestry carpet had been put down to cover the cracks in the floor, extending up on the walls to form a dado, it began to look quite livable.

The bed and a row of trunks filled one end, there being just room to squeeze in between them. At the foot of the bed was a table, used by turns as kitchen, dining, and library table; there was also a box holding a kcrosene stove, with shelves above it for dishes and supplies.

We had two wooden chairs, and a bench which we put to various uses. When these things were all in place, and our books arranged on boards which were laid across the rafters overhead, we felt as snug as was Robinson Crusoe in his cave.

As soon as we were comfortable, Julius got a man to help him, and began to improve our land. A few of the large pine-trees had to be felled, and this performance filled Bruno with the wildest excitement. His natural instincts told him there was only one reason for which a tree should ever be cut, to capture some wild creature which had taken refuge in its top. At the first blow of the axe he would begin to yelp and dance, breaking into still wilder antics when the tree began to sway and stagger, finally rushing into the top as it fell, in a state of excitement that bordered on frenzy.

As he, of course, found nothing there, he seemed to think he had not been quick enough, and that the creature had escaped; so he became more and more reckless, until Julius was alarmed for his safety, and said I must keep him shut in-doors till the trees were down, or he would surely end by being crushed.

I had my hands full. I would coax him in, and shut the door. As soon as he heard the chopping begin, he would whine and bark, coaxing to be let out. I always temporized until I heard the tree falling, then off he would dash, and bounce into its top to yelp and explore.

He never found anything in the trees, but he never grew discouraged. He "assisted" at the felling of every one.

Bruno was much happier in Florida than he had been in our northern home. He had all the woods to stretch his legs in, and for amusement he had the different kinds of wild creatures.

One moonlight night we three had walked over to the post office for the mail. As Julius and I were slowly sauntering homeward, enjoying the night air, while Bruno made little excursions in all directions, he suddenly came up in front of us, and paused in that questioning way which showed he had found something of which he was not quite sure.

"What is it, Boonie?" asked Julius.

Bruno made a short run, then came back, pausing as before, and glancing first in the direction he had started to go, then at Julius.

"It is probably a 'possum," I suggested.

Bruno had shown himself to be very careful about attacking strange animals. He seemed to remember our adventure with the hens, his first meeting with Rebecca, and some of his other experiences.

Julius answered his evident question with,—

"Yes. It's Boonie's 'possum. Go get him!"

Off he sprang, dashing into a little clump of trees, about a bow-shot from us, then with a yelp retreated, throwing himself on the ground, uttering short cries, rubbing and rooting his nose down into the grass and sand. Alas, poor Bruno! We knew what it was. We did not see it, we did not hear it, but we knew. He felt that he had been a victim of misplaced confidence; but we suffered with him, for it was days before he got rid of the "bouquet." Then it was as if by an inspiration. He seemed, all at once, to remember something. There was a tiny lake near our place, that was going dry. Day by day its waters had receded, until it was a mere mud-hole. Bruno went down to it, and buried himself up to the eyes in the black mud.

He lay there until late afternoon, then trotted off to a wet lake nearby, and took a thorough bath. With this, he regained his lost self-respect, but he never forgot the experience. It was only necessary to say,—

"Kitty, kitty, where's kitty?" to make his ears and tail droop in the most dejected manner; then he would creep away, out of sight, till some more agreeable topic of conversation was broached.

It was not strange, after such a trying adventure, that Bruno was rather timid about approaching "Br'er 'Possum" when he did meet him. One night, he was found lurking around outside, sniffing some odds and ends that Bruno had disdained. After a little urging, Bruno was induced to seize him. Finding that nothing unpleasant followed, he became from that moment an enthusiastic 'possum-hunter, and used to bring one in every night or two. I usually cooked them for him, and he ate them with a relish, which we thought was fortunate, as we were about twelve miles from a butcher. Another substitute for beef we found in the Florida gopher. This is a grass-eating tortoise, which digs a house for itself in the sand.

Bruno soon became a most ardent gopher-hunter. Their hard shells make them difficult to handle, as they promptly draw in the head and legs on being approached; so Bruno would nose one over until he could seize the shovel, a protruding piece of the lower shell. Getting this small bit between his side teeth, he balanced the weight by holding his head stiffly sideways, and came trotting in. The shadow of the house reached, he dropped the gopher, carefully turning it over on its back, and lay down beside it, to cool off and rest. Then off he would go for another.

He kept this up day after day, sometimes having as many as a dozen around the place at once. As often as the creatures managed to flop over so they could use their feet again and start to escape, Bruno, yelping and barking, brought them back, and turned them on their backs.

Sometimes, when he returned after a protracted hunt, bringing in a fresh victim, he found several of them escaping at once. Then he would hurriedly drop his latest catch, to speed away, tracking the truants until they were all found and recaptured, to be brought back and nosed over again.

He never wearied of this sport, and after our house was finished, and a well-stocked "chicken-park" was added to our estate, we bought a large camp-kettle, which we arranged on bricks in a secluded place; in this we would heat water and cook Bruno's gophers, so that he and the hens had constant feasts of them and throve apace.

Chapter 10

JULIUS AND I always like to experiment with new articles of food. We have no sympathy with the kind of fussiness that travels around the world with its own lunch-box, disdaining everything strange or new. It is to us part of the charm of changed surroundings to test the native articles of diet.

We had tried roast 'possum and stewed gopher; we now began to long for a taste of alligator steak. We had heard that to be at all eatable the steak must be taken from the fleshy part of the tail of a young animal before the creature grows large enough to lose its shiny skin; so we were quite delighted one day when we found that Bruno had cornered a young one about four feet long. It was in a little glade about three hundred yards from the house; and as soon as Julius found the cause of Bruno's excitement, he hurried to the house for the axe, and soon put a stop to the creature's demonstrations. He was hissing at Bruno like a whole flock of geese, the while snapping at him with his teeth and striking at him with his tail, which he had a most astonishing way of flourishing around.

When the steak was cut the meat looked white and fine-grained, like the more delicate kinds of fish. When cooked it was very inviting, being a compromise between fish and the white meat of domestic fowls.

We enjoyed it very much and were loud in our praises of alligator steak, but—we didn't want any more!

I cooked the rest of it for Bruno, and he ate one more meal of it; then he struck. We have since heard that most people who try alligator steak have the same experience. A first meal is thoroughly enjoyed, but one not brought up on such a diet never gets beyond the second. It is a useful article of food in southern camp-life, because it makes the campers go back to bacon and beans with renewed relish. The same may be said of roast 'possum and stewed gopher,—that is, for the human campers.

Just before our house was ready for us, while we were still living in the little shanty, I noticed one night when Julius came in that he was empty-handed. He had been in the habit of bringing his tools home every evening; so I asked, "What have you done with the saws and things?"

"I left them under the building," he answered, "wrapped in an old coat I had there. They will be perfectly safe, and I am tired of carrying them."

I was always glad when he had discovered an easier way of doing things; so I made no objection to this, and went on preparing the evening meal, for which we three were ready. Bruno had been over at the new house all the afternoon; so I waited on him first, seeing that his water-basin was full to the brim and heaping a plate with food for him. Then Julius and I sat down with keenest enjoyment to such a meal as we would have scorned in our old home, but which our open-air life in the pine-woods made exceedingly welcome.

Afterwards I cleared the table, and we sat down to our usual evening of reading, interrupted with occasional snatches of conversation.

Bruno lay at our feet dozing—when we were quiet, thumping the floor with his tail whenever we spoke. Towards nine o'clock he got up, shook himself, sighed deeply, then asked me in his usual manner to open the door for him. This was the way he asked. He rested his head on my knee until I looked up from my book. Then his tail began to wag, and he glanced quickly from me to the door, then back at me again. I asked, —

"Boonie want to go?"

At this his tail wagged faster than ever, and he went to the door and stood waiting. Julius got up and opened the door for him; standing for a few moments after Bruno had disappeared in the darkness, looking at the stars and listening to that sweet sound the pine-needles make when the wind blows through them.

The night was rather cool, and it was not long before we both began to feel sleepy. Bruno had not returned; so Julius went to the door, whistling and calling to him.

But there was no answer.

We waited a little while; then Julius said: "He will probably be here by the time we are ready to put out the lamp; so let's to bed."

I felt troubled. It reminded me of the old days in Bruno's giddy youth when he was off sheep-chasing. As I brushed out my hair, I was turning over in my mind all those vague fears I had felt when I had formerly dreamed of Florida as a country full of unknown dangers.

At last I spoke,—

"Julius, do you think a big alligator could have caught Bruno?"

"I don't know," answered Julius, slowly.

Then I knew that he was worried too.

When the lamp was out, Julius went to the door again and stood for some minutes whistling, calling, and listening; but no sound came except the pine murmurs and the mournful notes of a distant "Whip-Will's-Widow."

It was impossible for us to sleep. Having always had Bruno at our bedside, we had never before felt uneasy, and had provided no way to lock our shanty. There was just an old-fashioned string-latch with a padlock outside; and here we were, deserted by our protector!

Again and again through the night Julius got up to call and listen.

Towards dawn we both slept heavily, worn out with anxious surmises. We were awakened by a well-known whining and scratching at the door, and when we both sprang up to open it, in walked Bruno, looking just as he usually did in the morning,—lively, glad to see us awake, and ready for his breakfast.

We gave him a welcome so warm it surprised and delighted him, while we vainly questioned him for an explanation of his desertion of us for the night. It was of no use. We could see that he had not been running, but where had he been? We gave it up.

Julius said his troubled night had left him without much appetite for work; but the man who was helping him would be there, so he thought it best to go over to the building, anyway.

He surprised me by returning almost immediately. His face was lighted up and his eyes were dancing. "I came back to tell you where Bruno slept last night," he exclaimed. "You can't guess!"

"No," I answered; "I have already given it up."

"He went back to watch those tools I left over at the building. He dug himself a nest right beside them, drawing the edge of my old coat around for his pillow. The prints are all there as plain as can be!"

We were amazed and delighted at this performance; the reasoning seemed so human. He had watched Julius arranging and leaving the tools, the while making up his own mind that it was an unwise thing to do, and evidently deciding to see to it later. His sitting with us till bedtime, keeping in mind his mental appointment, and then going forth without a word from any one to keep it, seemed to us to be a truly wonderful thing, and so it seems to me yet. From the first, we had made a constant companion of Bruno, talking to him always as if he could speak our language; and we have since thought that this must have been a sort of education for him, drawing out and developing his own natural gifts of thought and reason. He often surprised us by joining in the conversation. He would be lying dozing, and we talking in our usual tones. If we mentioned Robbie or Charlie, the two children who were his friends in his puppy days before he was our dog, or spoke of Leo, or of going somewhere, he would spring up all alert, running to the door or window, and then to us, whining and giving short barks of inquiry or impatience.

Always, after that first time we had tried to give him away, he was subject to terrible nightmares. In his sleep he would whimper and sigh in a manner strangely like human sobbing. We thought at such times that he was going through those trying days again, in his dreams. So we always wakened him, petting and soothing him till he fully realized that it was only a dream.

He had other ways which we thought noteworthy. Although he loved Julius better than he did me, yet he always came to me with his requests. If hungry or thirsty, he would come to me wagging his tail and licking his lips.

Like "Polly," his general term for food was cracker. If I asked, "Boonie want a cracker?" and if it was hunger, he would yawn in a pleased, self-conscious manner, and run towards the place where he knew the food was kept. If I had misunderstood his request, he continued gazing at me, licking his lips and wagging his tail till I asked, "Boonie want a drink?" Then he would yawn and run towards his water-cup, which I would find to be empty.

Often, when he had made his wants known to me, I passed them on to Julius, who would wait on him; but it made no difference: the next time he came to me just the same. He seemed to have reasoned it out that I was the loaf-giver, as the old Saxons had it, or else he felt that I was quicker to enter into his feelings and understand his wishes.

Chapter 11

NOT LONG after Bruno's self-imposed night watch we found ourselves settled on our own estate, ready to carry out our plans for the future. Briefly they were as follows. We had intended to make an orange-grove, and while it was coming to maturity, we expected to raise early vegetables to ship to northern markets. We brought with us only money enough to make our place and live for a year: by that time we had fully expected to have returns from vegetable shipments which would tide us over till another crop. We had plenty of faith and courage, and were troubled by no doubts as to the feasibility of our plans. Nor need we have been, if only our land had contained the proper elements for vegetable growing. It was good enough orange land, but it would be a long time before we could depend on oranges for an income.

All this time we had been learning many things, taking care, as we began to understand the situation, to go to practical doers for advice instead of to visionary talkers.

There began to be serious consultations in our little home circle. The year was drawing to a close, and our whole crop of vegetables would not have filled a two-quart measure. We had gone on with our planting, even after we felt it to be hopeless, because we did not dare to stop and listen to our fears. It is not strange that we felt depressed and disappointed. We could see that our plans could easily have been carried out, had we only known just what sort of land to select. The whole State was before us to choose from, but we had been misled through the romances of a dreamer of dreams. All we had to show for our money, time, and labor was a small house surrounded by trees so young that they were at least five years from yielding us an income, and there was no more money for experiments.

For a while we felt rather bitter towards our misleading adviser, but I know now that we were wrong to feel so. A man can give only what he has. "Out of the fullness of the heart the mouth speaketh." A dreamer of dreams has only visions to offer to his followers, surely landing them either in the briers of difficulty or the mires of discouragement.

One day Julius returned from the nearest large town, where he had been for supplies, with an unusually thoughtful countenance. As soon as his purchases were unloaded and the horse had been attended to, he came in and, drawing a chair beside my work-table, opened the conversation with these memorable words:

"Judith, how would you like to go up to Lemonville to live?"

"What makes you ask?" questioned I. "It depends altogether on the circumstances how I'd like to live there."

"Well, Hawkes bantered me today to come up and keep his books for him, and I have been considering it all the way home. It looks like a way out, and I'll declare I don't see any other!"

"Go back to office work!" I exclaimed; "I thought you were done with that sort of thing!"

"I thought so, too; but after a year of this sort of thing, it begins to look quite different."

We sat up late, discussing this plan in all its bearings. Bruno seemed to know that it was a crisis in our affairs, and sat on end facing us, wrinkling his brows and looking from one to the other as each spoke. We finally decided that Julius was to go back to town in a day or two, and investigate further.

When Julius returned from Lemonville three days later, he brought us the news that he had promised to give the position a trial, and that he had engaged temporary quarters for us in a new house near the office. Moreover, we were to move up there the following week, as Mr. Hawkes was impatient for his help.

While we felt relieved at this decision, there was still something very sad about the breaking up. We had built so many hopes into our pine-woods home, which had seemed to us to be guarded by a "standing army" of giants carrying silver banners, especially imposing on moonlight nights when the wind kept the banners of moss swaying under the immense pine-trees.

We had seen it in imagination blossoming as the rose, a quiet little nest, far from the madding crowd. And now to abandon it at the beginning and go back to village life, it was leaving poetry for the flattest of prose.

The first step towards breaking up was to dispose of our fowls. This was soon arranged, and when the cart came to carry them off, Bruno watched the loading of them with the keenest interest, turning his head sideways, with alert ears, and catching his lip between his side teeth when a hen squawked, as was his way when nervous. At last they were all in the coop. The driver mounted to his seat, and started off. Bruno trotted along after him, evidently not understanding that they were no longer our chickens. He thought it was the beginning of the move he had heard us discuss. He followed along for perhaps a quarter of a mile. All at once he stopped and looked back; he saw us standing and looking after him. It was a dilemma. He looked after the receding wagon, then back at us, then at the wagon again. Then he turned and galloped back, stomach to earth, and bounded up to us, yelping and panting, while we explained that they were not our chickens anymore; they were sold, and had gone away to live in another home.

The poultry disposed of, we began hurriedly to make ready for our own departure. It took a whole long day to pack our books, but we soon stowed our other things, and inside of the agreed time we were transferred and settled in the three rooms Julius had engaged.

There was a sitting-room below, which we used also as a dining-room, with a small kitchen behind it. Over the sitting-room we had a large chamber. The front windows of this room gave on the sloping roof which covered a lower porch. This seemed to meet Bruno's views; he at once sprang through one of the windows, and took possession of it as a lounging-place airy and cool.

Again and again friends we had made in our sylvan retreat, who came up to town to visit us, said,—

"I found where you lived by seeing your dog on the porch-roof."

The house stood on rising ground and could be seen from almost any part of the village; so we found Bruno quite useful as a door-plate in a town where there were as yet no street names nor numbers.

We do not like living in the homes of other people, so as soon as possible we made arrangements for two town lots, and put up a little cottage.

Chapter 12

ONE DAY Julius came home with, invitations for a ball in honor of the Governor, to be given in an ambitious embryo city across the lake. He had learned that the little steamer was to make an extra night-trip across on purpose to accommodate those who wished to attend, and that some of our friends had planned to go in company, and wished us to join their party. We had long intended to take the steamer trip across the lake; the Governor's ball sounded inviting, also the night crossing with our friends. We decided to accept.

The evening fell rather threatening, with flurries of wind and rain. Still we were undaunted, and kept hoping it would clear off.

I filled Bruno's basin and platter, telling him he must take care of the house and be a good dog. He seemed to understand all about it, and stood at the window after we had locked him in, watching us go with perfect composure.

It was still twilight when we started, and we could see his eyes shining through the glass, as long as the house was in sight.

The weather, meantime, had not improved, and had we not promised to go, we should certainly have given it up.

When we reached the wharf, we found that the little steamer's cabin was in the sole possession of our party, all the others having backed out on account of the weather.

We kept up each other's spirits with all sorts of absurdities, and the boat was soon ploughing a foamy track across the big waves.

As soon as we steamed out from behind a point of land that

sheltered the wharf, we were met by a gale of wind that made the little steamer reel and tremble as if from the shock of a collision. The lights were all promptly extinguished, as the doors were forced open by fierce winds, while we huddled together in a corner, and laughingly reminded each other that it was a "pleasure exertion."

I shudder now whenever I think of that night, though at the time we did not know enough about the possibilities to be frightened.

How the little boat pitched and tossed! The waves washed its lower decks, again and again putting out the engine fires; we meanwhile rolling in the trough of the sea until they could be rekindled. We had expected to cross in about three quarters of an hour, and return soon after midnight; but it was along towards the wee small hours when we reached the other shore. Then, when we heard the crew congratulating each other, exchanging experiences, and telling what they had expected to see happen to all concerned every time big waves had washed out the fire, we for the first time fully realized the risks we had taken in crossing.

We were weary enough not to be sorry that the ball was already over. We looked in at its departed glories for a few minutes; and then, finding it would be impossible to start back home before broad daylight, began to look for a lodging-place.

The town was filled with people who had driven in from the surrounding country for the ball, but we succeeded in getting two small top-story rooms in the hotel, which were vacated for us by some sort of "doubling-up" among the good-natured guests. The three men of our party took one, and we three women the other.

It was about three o'clock when we retired to our room, and while the other two slept on the one bed, I sat by the window trying to hurry the dawn; wondering what Bruno was thinking, and how we should look, a party of people clothed in evening array, returning home in broad daylight. As if we had made a night of it, surely! I chuckled to myself as I compared our plight with that of Cinderella.

We met at breakfast in the hotel dining room, a strange-looking crowd. As we laughed at each other's appearance, it was hard for each to realize that he or she looked just as absurd; but an unprejudiced observer would have found little to choose between us. As soon as the meal was over, the three men started out to find a way to get us all home again. Everything seemed to conspire to delay us, and it was half-past twelve at noon when we entered our own gate, the click of the latch bringing Bruno's face to the window with a series of joyful barks.

Poor fellow! His long confinement to the house, his empty plate and bowl, his joyful reception of us, and then his springing out to dash round and round the lot, filled our hearts with compassion.

As soon as his first burst of enthusiasm was over, he came in, and crept up to me with dejected ears and tail, which in his language meant "mea culpa." I asked,

"What is it, Boonie? What's Boonie been doing?"

Still lower sank head and tail, and his knees began to weaken. I made a hasty survey of the sitting-room, and then I understood. He had slept on the lounge, a thing he was strictly forbidden to do.

"Oh, Boonie!" I cried, "you naughty dog! Judith thought she could trust you!"

At this his knees gave way, and he sank to the floor utterly dejected. He would not rise, nor even look up, until I had forgiven and comforted him.

The next time we had to leave him alone in the house, I built a "booby-trap," with two light chairs on the lounge, which left him looking so utterly crushed that I never had the heart to do it again. But he never more transgressed in that way, so I felt that I had dealt wisely with him.

It was a hard necessity which forced us to shut him up when we were going where it would not do to take him. At first we had tried leaving him outside; but we found that after we had been gone awhile, his heart was always sure to fail him, and he would track us, turning up invariably just in time to cover us with confusion, his own dejected mien saying plainly,—

"I know this is against orders, but I just had to do it." He had a wonderful development of conscience. We sometimes thought that this, as well as the other mental gifts of which he showed himself to be possessed, were due to the shape of his head. His nose was very short, and his forehead unusually high and well-rounded. Of course his life as a close companion to humans and as a full member of a family circle, was calculated to foster these mental gifts; but they were surely there, to begin with. We might treat dozens of dogs just as we treated Bruno, without developing another that would compare with him. He was unique; and I shall always glory in the fact that he loved and trusted us. His was a love not to be lightly won, nor, once given, ever to be recalled.

Chapter 13

IN SPITE of our snug little home in Lemonville, we never felt quite settled there. We were not built for village life. Country life is good, and city life is good; but in a village one has all the drawbacks of both, with the rewards of neither. So it was not long before we resolved on another change.

We sold our little home furnished, packed up our books, with a few other personal belongings, and turned our faces towards St. Augustine, to investigate several openings there, of which we had chanced to hear. We were so fortunate as to be able to rent a small cottage, and at once took possession, furnishing it from our trunks, only buying a few necessary articles of the plainest kind.

Just as we had settled ourselves in these temporary quarters, a matter of business came up, making necessary a return to Lemonville for a day or two. The trip was both tedious and expensive, so after some discussion we decided that Bruno and I should stay and keep house, while Julius made the trip alone "light weight."

I had some trouble in persuading Julius that I should be perfectly safe in Bruno's care. He wished us to close the cottage, and go to some one of the many pleasant boarding-places, where we had friends or acquaintances stopping. This I should certainly have done, had I been alone; but I reminded Julius how more than able Bruno was to take care of me, and how much trouble he always gave in a strange house. So he was finally persuaded that it would be best for us to stay in the cottage.

Julius left on a noon train, carrying only a small hand-bag. When he said good-by to us, he impressed this on Bruno's mind, "Take good care of Judith."

Bruno stood at the door with me, watching him out of sight, then breathed a deep sigh, and crept off under the bed to have it out with himself alone and unseen. I busied myself picking up the articles which had been scattered in the confusion of packing, then sat down to drown thought in a book.

Towards evening I had a caller. One of our friends, who had seen Julius, bag in hand, at the station, and had thus learned that I was alone, sent a message by her little son that I was to "come right around" to their house for the night. I sent our thanks, with further message that Bruno and I had agreed to take care of each other. The child went home; then his mother came. She thought I "must be crazy" to think of staying alone. She "wouldn't do it for any money." I assured her I was not staying alone, and had some trouble to convince her that I could not possibly be more safely guarded than by Bruno. I assured her, further, that nothing would now induce me to lock up the house and leave it, for it would be impossible to know just when Julius would return ; he would be sure to catch the first boat and train after his business was finished, and I would not for anything have him return to find his nest deserted.

I succeeded, at last, in quieting all of her kind objections, and was left in peace.

Darkness came on, and then Bruno lost courage. As I was preparing his evening meal, he ran to meet me as I crossed the room, and raising himself to an upright position, he rested his paws on my shoulders and gazed with mournful questioning into my eyes. I knew what he would say, and sitting down, I drew his head to my knee, and told him all about it, —that Julius would only stay a "little, little while," then he would come back and "stay—stay—stay always with us." His ears rose and fell, his forehead wrinkled and unwrinkled as I talked to him. Then he seemed comforted, and ate a good supper.

I sat reading far into the night, until the letters began to blur. Bruno sat beside me, sometimes with his head on my knee while I stroked his silken ears,—which always suggested the wavy locks of a red-haired girl,—and sometimes he lay at full length on the floor, with his head against my feet.

As midnight tolled, I closed my book, covered up the fire, and tried to go to sleep, with Bruno lying on the rug beside my bed. Whenever I stirred, he got up, and putting his forefeet on the side of the bed, reached his head over for me to stroke it. It was the first time I had ever spent a night in a house with no other humans, and Bruno seemed to enter thoroughly into my feelings.

I lay listening to the breakers booming on the outer bar, wondering how far on his journey Julius could be. Dawn looked in at me before I fell asleep; then I knew nothing until aroused by Bruno's barks, to find that someone was rapping on the front door.

After hastily putting on a dressing-gown, I investigated through a crack made by holding the door slightly ajar, and found that the same kind friends had sent to see how I had spent the night. I gave a glowing account of our comfort and security, for my morning nap had thoroughly rested and refreshed me; then I hastened to prepare some breakfast for Bruno, meanwhile letting him out for a run in the lot.

After the small household duties were attended to, I had sat down to finish some souvenirs I was painting for one of the shops, when I heard a great din and clatter outside. Bruno, who was sitting beside me, gravely watching my work, while now and then he gave a disgusted snort as he got a good whiff of the turpentine I was using to thin my paints, started up, barking and bounding towards the closed door. I sprang to open it, and was met on the very threshold by a trembling, half-grown deer. The gate was open, showing how it had entered, and there, hesitating at the sight of Bruno and me, was a motley crowd of boys and dogs. I at once grasped the situation. Many people in St. Augustine had such pets, and I was sure this one must have escaped from the grounds of its owner, to fall into the hands of the rabble.

I hurried out to shut the gate. Most boys are more or less cruel; but these boys were intensely so. When I returned to the porch, Bruno and the deer were regarding each other with mutual doubts. I settled Bruno's at once by laying my hand on his head while I stroked our gentle visitor, saying,—

"Pretty deer, Boonie mustn't hurt it!"

The deer seemed satisfied too, and to feel that danger was past. I brought water, and everything I could think of to offer it to eat. It was too warm with running to want food, though, and only took a few swallows of water. It's lovely, deep eyes suggested all sorts of romantic thoughts. Of course I quoted, "Come rest in this bosom," and "I never nursed a dear gazelle." I was sure its name should be Juanita, after the girl in the sweet Spanish song.

All day the pretty creature roamed about our little enclosure, Bruno and I attending to its wants as best we could, having had no experience in catering for such guests.

It turned quite chilly towards evening. When I had shut all the doors and built up the fire, I heard a clatter of small hoofs on the porch floor, and there stood Juanita, looking wistfully in through the window. Bruno and I looked at each other, thoroughly perplexed. We were not prepared for such a hint. I thought afterwards it must have been taken as a baby-deer, and raised indoors "by hand."

We went out and prepared a warm bed for it in the woodshed back of the house. It seemed quite satisfied with this arrangement, and settled down cozily as we left it and returned to our fireside. We spent this evening and night as we had the previous one, and were aroused very early in the morning by the sound of Juanita's impatient little hoofs on the porch floor. I had just finished feeding her and Bruno, when I heard the gate-latch click. I looked out. A little girl was coming up the walk.

"Morning, Lady," she said; "I heard our deer is here. That's you, you good-for nothing ole runaway! Thank you, Lady. Come on, Billy!" And hitting him a resounding slap on the back, she went off, accompanied by our romantic Juanita, transformed into meek and prosy Billy.

Thus perish our illusions!

Bruno was inclined to resent this unceremonious taking off of our pet, and began to growl; but as soon as I recovered from the mingled emotions which at first had rendered me speechless, I realized from Billy's actions that he and the little girl were old friends; so I silenced him by saying,—

"Never mind, Boonie, it wasn't our deer; it only came for a little visit, and now it's going home." Then we stood watching graceful Billy and his companion till they disappeared through the old City Gates.

Late that evening, Bruno having had his supper, I sat by the fire sipping a cup of chocolate, and thinking those tender, half-melancholy thoughts we are apt to have at twilight when separated from those beloved.

All at once I heard the gate click. Bruno sprang up, thrilled and alert. A footstep on the walk—ah, Bruno knew it, even before I did, and was so eager to get out that he almost held the door shut in his excitement. We finally got it open, and there, weary, eager, and travel-stained, was Julius! Before his lips reached my face, I mentally exclaimed,—

"How glad I am that Bruno and I have stayed here, instead of leaving a shut-up house, where he would have to drop his bag and start out to look for us!"

That moment, when I felt his arms around me and heard his words of joy mingled with Bruno's ecstatic yelps, paid for all of our endless, lonely hours. I dare say there was not in all the world a happier group of three than sat before our open fire that night. Every time Bruno dozed, he would awaken with a start, and go to sniff and paw at Julius to make sure it wasn't a dream, that he really had come back to us. Julius reported his business successfully concluded; a change in one of the time-tables had enabled him to get back sooner than we had dared to hope.

The next day I received his letter, telling me to look for him by the train on which he had come the night before!

In those days our mail not infrequently took an ocean voyage on its way from one Florida town to another quite nearby, so we were never surprised at anything in the mail line,—except a prompt delivery!

Chapter 14

I T WAS shortly after the events related in the last chapter that we came to a final decision against the various business openings we had been investigating in St. Augustine, and concluded to go on to Jacksonville. We disposed of the few things we had bought for our little cottage, and when we again found ourselves on the train with our household gods, I gave us both a fit of merriment by quoting the words of poor little Joe in "Bleak House,"—

"Wisht I may die if I ain't a-movin' on."

It was by this time mid-season, and Jacksonville was full of tourists. It was then very popular as a winter resort, Southern Florida was not much known; so we had some difficulty in finding a place to live.

We decided to get just one room somewhere, and board at a restaurant till the city emptied so we could secure a cottage.

The first room we found that would do, was too far from the business part of town; so we took it for only a month, and kept on looking. We heard of one, at last, which seemed close to everything. It proved to be large, lofty, and pleasant, with a glimpse of the river from its front windows.

The house was well recommended to us by the few business acquaintances Julius had made, though they all confessed that such places were constantly changing hands and inmates and that it was hard to keep up with them. Time pressed, and nothing better offered; so we moved in. It was entirely bare; so we bought some furniture, and, as it was rather a long room for its breadth, we managed, with a screen or two, to make it seem like three rooms.

When all was in place, it was really quite inviting. I had a small lamp stove, so we need only go out for dinners. We began to feel more settled than for a long time, especially, as Julius had in the meantime found a business opening which was entirely satisfactory. We saw nothing at all of the other lodgers; but this did not disturb us, as we were in no hurry to make acquaintances. We felt that it was best to be circumspect in a city of this size and make-up.

Our evenings were our pleasantest times, sitting on either side of the reading-lamp, with Bruno stretched at our feet; so I was inclined to object one evening, when Julius announced at dinner that he had promised to give a few hours to helping a young friend of his to straighten out his accounts. He had promised, though; so I had to yield. He set off betimes, so as to be home earlier. I locked the door after him, as I always did, and began to make myself as comfortable as possible for a quiet hour or two, with a new magazine.

Before I had finished cutting the leaves, I was struck with surprise at Bruno's actions. He crept in a very stealthy manner to the door, and stood there in an attitude of listening, with every nerve and muscle tense.

I watched him a minute, and then asked, "What is it, Boonie?"—

He did not look around; he waved his tail once or twice, then resumed his tense pose. Thoroughly surprised, I went softly to him, and stood also listening. I could hear nothing but a faint rustling, a suppressed whispering, and the soft click of a latch. I touched Bruno's head; he looked up at me, and I saw he was holding his lip between his side-teeth, as he had a way of doing when he was very much puzzled or excited.

I tried to coax him away from the door, but he refused to come. I made sure the bolt was shot, and then sat down at a little distance to watch him. There was a door in the middle of one side of the room, which, when we took possession, we had found to be nailed up. We utilized the recess with the aid of some draperies, as a place to hang clothing. Bruno went to this door, thrusting his head in among the clothes.

He listened there for a long time, probably ten minutes; he returned again to the other door; then he gave a low growl, followed by several half-suppressed barks, and lay down against it.

I forgot all about my book, and sat watching to see what he would do next. The evening seemed endless. At last I heard Julius below in the hall; Bruno sprang up when I opened the door, and went clattering down the stairs to escort him up. It was not late, only about ten. I at once told Julius of the queer evening we had spent, and had the satisfaction of seeing him as thoroughly puzzled as I had been. We sat until a late hour discussing it, then gave it up as something quite beyond us.

About three o'clock in the morning we were awakened by an alarm of fire. The room was full of light, and when we looked out of the window we found that it was close by—only about two squares away. It was a big blaze and, as it was on the opposite side of the street, we had a fine view of it. I was terribly frightened. My uneasiness earlier in the evening had unnerved me, and this terrible fire so near us upset me completely. A fire fills me with horror, especially if it breaks out in the night: it always reminds me of the burning of a big steamer that happened one awful night in my tenth year.

I watched the flames, fascinated by their lurid splendor,—imagining that the three white pigeons which had been awakened by the light and were circling around the tower of smoke now hidden by it, and now silhouetted against it—were the souls of those who had perished in the flames. Overcome by horror, I finally exclaimed:—

"Suppose it had been this big building that had caught fire!"

"But it wasn't," said Julius.

"No: but it might have been. I don't like his at all. I want to be in a little house by ourselves, close to the ground." "Yes, it would be better," said Julius, who saw by the light of the flames how pale I had become, and noted how I was trembling. "It will not do to have you so terrified: we'll make a change at once. But it will be difficult to find a house until the tourists begin to scatter."

We thoroughly discussed the situation, and by breakfast-time had reached a decision.

I was to return to Lemonville for a stay of a week or two, and while there to see to the packing and shipping of a piano we had left in storage. Julius meanwhile was to find a cottage, and have our belongings transferred to it. We did not like the arrangement very well, but it seemed to be the only thing we could do.

Thus ended our experience as lodgers.

I was gone two weeks. It was pleasant to meet old friends, after a separation long enough to have plenty of news to exchange, without having had time to lose interest in each other's affairs, but my heart was back in Jacksonville.

Julius and I wrote to each other every day, but the mails were so tedious and uncertain that we usually got each other's letters by threes or fours, with days full of anxiety and heartache between. I still have the package of letters received then. I have just been reading them over again. Bruno pervades them all. It is -

"Took Bruno with me to the office today, he begged so hard when I started to leave him; it's lonely for him, poor fellow!"

And—"While I ate breakfast, I had the waiter put up a good lunch for Boonie; he's getting tired of biscuit, and I don't like to give him raw bones."

On Sunday,—

"I took Bruno a long walk in the suburbs today. It did him a lot of good."

A letter written just before I returned says,

"Bruno seems down-hearted tonight; I think he misses somebody."

I returned as soon as Julius wrote that he had procured a house. The welcome I received told me that Bruno was not the only one who had missed "somebody."

Chapter 15

ALL THAT season we lived in a rented cottage, but before the next summer came we were planting roses in our own grounds. We had been renting just about a year, when we bought our little home in one of the suburbs; so we could fully appreciate the joys of being on our own place again.

We found a kitten, the "very moral" of Rebecca, striped black and blue-gray. She was a dear little thing, and she and Bruno soon became fast friends.

The only creature we ever knew him to bite—except, indeed, wild animals, which he considered fair game—was in defending Catsie.

His victim was a handsome coach-dog, following some friends who one day drove out to call on us. He was a thoroughbred dog, but he had not Bruno's gentlemanly instincts. The first thing he did was to go trotting around to the back porch, where he spied Catsie enjoying a fine meaty bone. He sneaked up behind her, and snatching it in his teeth, made off with it.

Bruno could not stand that. It seemed to make a perfect fury of him. I think he felt that the fault was worse, because the coach-dog was so sleek and plump; there was not even the excuse of hunger.

Poor fellow! Bruno sent him howling and limping from the yard.

The call came to an untimely end, our visitors declaring,—

"That great savage brute of yours has almost killed our beautiful dog!"

I am afraid we did not feel very contrite. We never took our "great savage brute" anywhere to visit, except when he was especially invited; and besides, we had our own opinion, which was similar to Bruno's, of big dogs that robbed little cats.

It took a great deal to rouse Bruno, so much that we sometimes mistook his amiability for lack of courage.

We had often watched him chasing the animals that lax town laws had allowed to roam the streets of the only two villages we had ever known. He would go dashing after a pig or a cow. If the creature ran, he would chase it until he was exhausted; but if it stood its ground and calmly returned his excited gaze, he would stop, look at it for a minute, then turn and come trotting back, with an air that said plainly,—

"I was only in fun; I wanted to see what it would do."

There was a big watch-dog which lived in an enclosure we had to pass on our way to town. When we took Bruno that way for a stroll, as soon as he reached this lot, he and the other dog would greet each other through the picket fence with the most blood-curdling growls and snarls. They seemed fairly to thirst for each other's life-blood. Then, each on his own side of the fence, they would go racing along, keeping up their growls and snarls, till they reached a place where there were half a dozen pickets broken out, so that either could have leaped through with ease.

Then what a change!

Their ears would droop, and their coats and tempers smooth down to the most insipid amiability. But at their next meeting they were quite as savage, till they again reached the opening in the fence. It was the same program, over and over. Bruno liked to play at anger just for a little excitement, but when he found anything really worth a spell of the furies, it was quite another story.

The butcher-boy, who came every other day, took Bruno's tragic demonstrations for the real thing, and was terribly afraid of him. He used to shout to me, "Come out and hold the dog!" until he could run to the kitchen and get safely back outside the gate.

It was all in vain for me to assure him there was no danger. He thought I did not know what I was talking about. His terror was so real, I pitied the child—he was not more than twelve or fourteen—so I used to shut Bruno up in the front hall on butcher-boy days until after he had made his call.

Our maid used to spend her nights in the bosom of her family, coming back every morning in time to get breakfast. One morning she failed to appear. It was butcher-boy morning, and the weather was quite chilly. When I called Bruno in to shut him up, I noticed that the house next to ours was closed. Our neighbors were off for the day. There were two vacant lots opposite our place, and on the other side, a church. So when our neighbors went off for a day's jaunt, as they frequently did, we were quite isolated.

After I had shut Bruno in the hall, I sat down by the kitchen fire to toast my toes and wait for the butcher-boy. I was impatient for him to come, so I could release Bruno, who did not like being shut up. He was perfectly willing to lie in the hall—in fact, it was a favorite dozing-place with him,—but, like some people, he did not enjoy the idea of being forced to do even what he liked best. I was glad when I heard a step on the back porch, and sprang eagerly to open the door. There stood the dirtiest, most evil-looking tramp I had ever seen. He was so taken aback at the way the door flew open, that I had slammed it and shot the bolt before he recovered. I hurried in for Bruno, who had heard the strange step and was eager to investigate. As soon as I returned and unfastened the bolt, the tramp threw his weight against the door to force it open. Bruno sprang to the opening with a whole volley of barks and growls. I caught his collar, saying to the tramp,—

"You'd better run; I can't hold him long!"

I never saw a man make better time. I gave him a minute's start, then loosed Bruno. He reached the fence just as the tramp had fallen over it without stopping to open the gate. When I saw all was safe, I felt so limp I fell back in a chair weak and nerveless. Bruno watched the tramp around the corner, then returned to look after me. He was much exercised to find me in such a state, and relieved his feelings by alternately trying to lick my face, and dashing out to bark again after the vanished tramp.

After that, Bruno seemed to feel more than ever responsible for me. He had all along been my especial protector, but seeing me overcome with fright seemed to make a deep impression on him.

Chapter 16

JULIUS AND I had been in the habit of taking evening walks, and as Bruno stayed with me through the day when Julius was gone, it was his only chance for a run.

One evening, when Julius came home, it had been raining, and I felt that it would not do for me to go out. "You'd better take Boonie for a little run, though," I said; "he has been in the house all day."

"I have an errand down at the corner," answered Julius, "and he can race around the square while I am attending to it. You won't be afraid?"

"Not for that little while; you will be back again before I have time to miss you." Julius went into the hall for his overcoat and hat.

"Come on, Boonie," he said; "Boonie can go."

Bruno bounced up, all excitement, showing how he had felt the confinement. He dashed into the hall, where Julius was putting on his overcoat, then came trotting back into the sitting-room and stood, ears erect, looking at me and wagging his tail. I understood him, and answered,—

"No, Boonie; Judith must stay. Just Julius and Boonie are going."

He knew us only by the names he heard us call each other.

He sat down at my feet, all his excitement gone.

"Come, Boonie," called Julius from the door. "Come on, Boonie's going!"

Bruno looked at him, wagged his tail, looked at me, and refused to stir.

"Don't you see?" I said; "he thinks I ought not to be left alone."

Then to him, "Go on, Boonie; Boonie must go. Judith isn't afraid." He looked gratefully at me, and wagged his tail, saying plainly, in his dog-fashion,—

"Thank you, but I'd rather not."

Julius waxed impatient.

"You Boon! come along, sir! come on!" he thundered. Bruno's ears and tail drooped. He looked up sideways in a deprecating manner at Julius, then came and laid his head on my knee. It was of no use. Neither threats nor coaxing could move him. Noble creature! His ideas of chivalry were not to be tampered with, even by those who were his gods, his all!

The next morning at breakfast I said to Julius,—

"I am afraid Bruno will be ill staying indoors so closely. Can't you take him for a little run before you go to the office?" "Yes," answered Julius, "I'll take him if he'll go." "Oh, he'll go fast enough. Dinah is here, and he will think it safe to leave me."

Bruno was delighted at the invitation, and went tearing around the square four times while Julius walked it once; then came in, hot and happy, to tell Catsie and me all about it.

There was something so peculiarly tender about our feelings for Bruno and his for us. He was at once our protector and our dependent. It is not strange that we never failed to be thoroughly enraged when dog-lovers tried, as they sometimes did, to coax us to sell him. Sell our Bruno! True, we had tried to give him away, but that was for his own good. But to take money for him! To sell him!! Unspeakable!!!

Three times we had nursed him through trying illnesses,—twice the blind staggers, and once the distemper; and when either of us was ill, he could not be coaxed from the bedside. No matter who watched at night, Bruno would watch too, and no slightest sound nor movement escaped his vigilance.

How often since he left us have I longed in weary vigils for the comfort of his presence!

Chapter 17

IN LOOKING back at that winter, most of its evenings seem to have been spent before the open fire, the room lighted only by its blaze.

Sometimes Little Blossom lay across my knees, the firelight mirrored in her thoughtful eyes, her pink toes curling and uncurling to the heat. Sometimes she lay cradled in Julius's arms, while he crooned old ditties remembered from his own childhood.

Bruno never seemed to tire of studying this new-comer to our home circle. He would stand with ears drooped forward, watching me bathe and dress her, so absorbed in contemplation that he would start when I spoke, as if he had forgotten my existence.

He had always before seemed intensely jealous when Julius or I had noticed children, but with Little Blossom it was different; he seemed to share our feelings, she was our baby.

At first he showed a disposition to play with her as he had long ago romped with Rebecca's kittens, but after I had once explained to him that she was too little and tender for such frolics, that he must wait till she could run about, he seemed quite satisfied, and constituted himself her guardian, as he had always been mine. While she slept, he would lie beside her crib. When she took an airing, it was his delight to walk proudly beside the carriage. When I held her, he sat at my elbow; and when she laughed and cooed in her romps with Julius, he would make short runs around the room, barking his delight.

Happy hours, all too short!

As spring advanced, our Little Blossom drooped. Her brain had always been in advance of her physical development. She had never the meaningless stare seen in normal babies. Instead, there was a wistful, pensive expression as she gazed into the fire or through the window, with always a quick dimpling smile when either of us spoke to her. There was much sickness in town, especially among young children. We decided to spend the summer months at the seashore. A cottage was leased, and trunks were packed full of summer clothes, draperies, and other joys and comforts.

When the time came to start, the cry arose,—

"Where is Bruno?"

No one knew. None remembered seeing him since breakfast. It was now half-past ten. The train was to go at eleven, and we were three-quarters of a mile from the station! We felt utterly lost. It was impossible to leave Bruno, and yet we must go.

Julius looked in all directions, calling and whistling. No answer. Our baggage had gone, a wagon full of it. The tickets were bought, and everything was arranged.

Julius came in from an unsuccessful search, a look of desperation on his face.

"There's no help for it," he said; "we must start, Bruno or no Bruno."

We locked up the house and set off. As we drove along, I kept looking out, hoping to see the familiar form come dashing after us, but in vain. Julius was to come into town each morning to the office, returning to us at the seashore on the afternoon train. I began to think I could not know Bruno's fate (for I feared something serious must have happened) until the afternoon of the next day. We had been so delayed it was necessary to make all speed.

We hurried into the station, and there, standing beside our heap of luggage, one eye for the packages and the other on the lookout for us, stood Bruno!

He greeted us with such extravagant delight, and we felt so relieved at seeing him, that we found no reproaches ready. Besides, although he had so delayed us, it was quite evident that he had thought we had our hands over-full, and that by keeping his eye on the things he would be helping us. So he had followed the wagon, overlooked the unloading, and evidently had kept tally of every package. Our man who had driven the wagon was to go on with us to help in the transfer at the other end, and to make all ready for comfort in the cottage. He told us that Bruno had mounted guard over him as well as our effects, and while rather overdoing it, had been quite helpful.

It is hard to write of the weeks that followed.

I see Bruno racing up and down the beach and swimming out through the breakers, while Julius and I sit on either side of a little wicker wagon drawn up beyond the reach of the tide, watching him.

I see him chasing crabs and sea-birds, or limping up to show us his foot stung by a stranded jelly-fish.

Then—darkness. It is night in a long white-draped room. One end of it is lighted by a lamp having a rose-colored shade.

In the middle of the lighted end stands a crib. A little white-robed form lies within.

The pink light so simulates a glow of health that the mother, sitting beside the crib, bends low, thinking the little breast heaves.

But no. The waxen cheeks chill her lips.

Still she bends and gazes on that loved little form.

Bruno lies at the mother's feet. When she moves he rises, looking mournfully into the crib, then turns to rest his head on her knee.

On a lounge, in the end of the room where shadows lurk, the father lies asleep, exhausted with grief.

The curtains sway in the open windows, as if the room were breathing. All else is still.

I see all this as if it were a scene in a dream or as a picture,—something in which I have no part; and yet I feel that my heart throbbed in that mother's bosom.

I know that after she had sent away all kind friends, to watch alone that last night, it was literally and truly a "white night" to her.

She felt neither sorrow nor grief.

Yesterday her heart was torn with anguish, when those heavenly eyes grew dim with the death-glaze.

Tomorrow it will be rent again, when the little form is hidden from her in its white casket; and again—at that bitterest moment Life can give—when the first handful of earth makes hollow echo above it.

But tonight there is the uplifted feeling of perfect peace.

Although it is the third sleepless night, there is no thought of weariness. All through the short hours she sits and feasts her eyes on the angelic face with its look of joy unutterable.

And Bruno watches with her.

* * *

The next day Bruno does not ask to join the sad procession leaving the cottage.

He has no thought for self at such a time.

As it turns the corner, his mournful eyes are seen at the window, gazing after his little playmate who is being carried away. Or does he realize it is only the beautiful body they are taking, which was all too frail for the bright spirit now flown these two days since!

Chapter 18

AGAIN THE mother is in the city home. No crib stands by the fireplace; no tiny garments are spread out to air. All is orderly as in the years that now seem so far away.

She sits with book or needle.

The book falls to her knee, the work slips to the floor; tears steal down her cheeks.

Bruno presses near, his head against her arm. With his uplifted, pleading eyes, he seems to say,—

"Don't cry, Judith, please don't cry."

Oh, matchless comforter! After a time we notice that Bruno is growing old and feeble. Do we grieve at this? Far from it. We feel that life is over for us; our only thought is to escape its grasp and join our Little Blossom.

We could never leave Bruno alone; he would grieve himself to death, and meanwhile, perhaps, be abused as a stupid brute for refusing to be comforted. So it is with a feeling of sad resignation that we realize how his hold on life is weakening. At least he will die in comfort, ministered to by his loved ones.

We sit alone, we three, in the twilight,—Julius and I, with Bruno at our feet,—talking of the future. We speculate on the Beyond, hoping it will not be the conventional Heaven, with harps and crowns.

We long for a sheltered nook, near the River of Life, where we and Little Blossom can resume the life so happily begun here, going over to the Happy Hunting Grounds to get Bruno, and to the Cat Heaven for Rebecca and Catsie.

Then, our family circle complete, we would settle down to an eternity of HOME.

Can Heaven itself offer anything sweeter than home,—the wedded home, where love abides!

One morning Bruno seemed not to care for his breakfast. He sniffed daintily at it, and turned away, though I tried to tempt him with everything he liked best.

He rested his head on my knee, looking gratefully into my eyes, while his tail waved his thanks.

Then he went to his bed, and lying down upon it, he fell asleep, not a short uneasy nap, with ears open for every sound, but a deep, dreamless sleep.

There was a beautiful young fig-tree in our lot. Under this his grave was dug. His bed was laid in, he on it, with his blanket wrapped around him.

> "Arise against thy narrow door of earth,
> and keep the watch for me!"

The End

Epilogue

Several of the city names and characters mentioned in *Bruno* were identified through our research. The town called "Lemonville" was actually Eustis, Florida, located northeast of Orlando in the heart of the citrus belt. The "relative" she mentions as living nearby was Mrs. Dewey's maternal cousin Richard Goldsborough Robinson, who co-founded the town of Zellwood, Florida, where the Deweys bought twenty acres to raise oranges and where the vegetable crop failed.

The character of "Little Blossom" was their lost infant, Elizabeth Dewey, born about 1885. She is buried next to her uncle, William Magill Spilman, in Jacksonville at the Greenlawn Cemetery, about 150 feet from her mother, Byrd Spilman Dewey.

The following story, *Rebecca: A Postscript to Bruno* will complete the story of Mrs. Dewey's cat who appeared early in the story of Bruno.

Rebecca
A Postscript to Bruno

THE STORY of BRUNO, being simply the story of Bruno, did not go into details about any other personality, except when it was necessary in order to bring into prominence some characteristic of its hero.

In the letters that have come, from the friends that Bruno has won out in the big world, there have been many inquiries about the other characters of the book. Rebecca has the lion's share of these; and no wonder. She was a dear kitty. Some of the readers who wish to know how she got her name. Others inquire about her kitten-hood; and several tender-hearted little people write to ask if we ever had tidings of her fate after we left her to come to Florida.

This postscript is written to answer these questions.

In talking over our home-to-be, when Julius and I first planned to go to housekeeping, he said, in glancing at some of the minor details of the prospective ménage:

"Well, I'll tell you one thing, Judith: We never want to own any cats."

Oh, why not?" I cried, distressed at the thought of a cat-less hearth.

Then I learned that Julius considered the cat to be a cold-hearted, selfish creature, destitute of real affection—choosing always the best of everything for herself, and getting possession of it by hook or by crook. He added, when he saw how surprised I was at all this, that he had inherited his antipathy for the whole feline race because of a stray cat which had frightened—and then had persisted in annoying—his mother in her early days of home-making.

Such a feeling is not easily overcome; and so, like a dutiful wife, I did not try to argue the matter.

We began housekeeping with no kitty.

After a few weeks, Julius said to me, one evening:

"Judith, I believe you get moped here alone all day. How do you amuse yourself while I am at the office?"

"Oh, with various things. It is a little quiet after the houseful we always had at home; but I don't think I ever 'mope'."

"Well, maybe not; but you find the days pretty long; now, don't you?"

"Sometimes: but I don't want anyone else in the house. Only..." I paused, hesitating; and Julius said:

"Only what?"

"Nothing. Except that, sometimes, I wish you did not hate cats."

"Is that all?" asked Julius, in a relieved tone. "Well, let's have a cat. By all means!"

"Not if it would make you unhappy," objected I.

"Oh, that's all right. If I don't like the little beast it will soon learn to keep out of sight when I am at home."

The next afternoon Julius came from the office earlier than usual because he could not wait to tell me that my kitten would arrive on the following day. A man who lived in a town some five miles distant had driven to our village that morning and had come during his stay, to transact business with Julius. This man was celebrated as possessing some fine cats; and, on hearing that Julius wanted a kit for his young wife, he said:

"Yes; our old Malty has some kittens she is just weaning; and Mrs. Judith shall have the prettiest one in the lot; unless Wife has promised him to someone else." He explained that these kits were three-quarters Maltese—the mother being half-bred and the father a thorough-bred.

When Mr. Othertown arrived with the kitten, next day, he

explained that during his absence, the day before, his wife had been tempted by the offer of a most excellent home for the pretty blue Tom he had intended to bring me; and so he had brought Tom's sister—a kitty having the blue Maltese fur, it is true; but having also, bands of black marking her coat at regular intervals. I paid no attention to his apologies. In fact, I scarcely heard them, so delighted was I at the first glimpse of the beautiful soft ball of fluff whose starry eyes radiated answering affection, while two velvet paws reached out in the vain endeavor to grasp my cheeks, as I held the little creature off to admire its many charms. Mr. Othertown laughed heartily at us both; and took his leave, doubtless convinced that the apologies were not needed.

Kitty scampered around, just like a child; exploring all the rooms—jumping up to peep out of the windows; and, in all ways, showing herself to be a most intelligent and observing puss.

Several days after her arrival a neighbor who came in one chilly morning, before the sitting-room fire had been kindled, was taken into the dining-room. After a glance around, she turned to me, saying in an undertone:

"I didn't know you had visitors. Who is here?"

"No one," said I. "We are alone, Julius and I, except for the neighbor who has just come in."

She smiled. Then said:

"Yes; but these toys," pointing to a big soft ball; a spool tied to a string; and a doll scattered on the carpet; then a tiny brass bell hung by a string to the knob of the door leading into the pantry; and a small mirror leaning against the door-jam; "What child have you here?"

"Oh, those are the kitty's playthings."

"Well I never!" cried Mrs. Neighbor. "The idea of making all that to-do for a cat!"

"Why not? She likes it; and so do we."

Just then there was an insistent "Me-ow-wow" outside; and, when the door was opened, in dashed kitty; who ran at once to tinkle the bell; giving a passing slap at the spool; then rolled over holding the ball with her front feet while she vigorously kicked it with her hind-claws; and, lastly, bounced over to the mirror, dancing stiff-legged and bushy-tailed back and forth before it, daring the lively kitty in its depths to come out and have a tussle.

"Well, she is cute," admitted my caller; "but I never should have thought of getting playthings for a cat!"

We had pondered and discussed, trying to find a suitable name for our cat. I say "our" advisedly; for Julius could not long hold out against the allurements of such a fascinating little creature. When I tried to rally him about his sudden capitulation to her charms, he took refuge in:

"I never said I didn't like high-bred cats; and this is no common, back-fence yeowler!"

Our kitty had come to us in the days when Mark Twain's charming boy-story had been distributed over the country by enterprising book-agents; and was being widely read and discussed. A young girl neighbor had a big Maltese cat she had named for its hero—Tom Sawyer.

One day I noticed this cat playing out in the street, in full view of our windows. He sprang up in the air again and again, leaping higher each time, snatching at imaginary butterflies; then made a flying leap to the top of the gate post. There he sat, under pretense of making a most elaborate toilet, until he had regained breath after the exertions of his gymnastics. Then, down he leaped, and began over again.

Our kitty sat on the window-sill, sometimes watching him with the most absorbed attention; then, when she met his glance, looking away with a disdainful expression that seemed to say:

"Pshaw, any cat can do that!"

The whole performance was so much like the scene in the story of Tom Sawyer, where Tom goes to "show off" in the street before the house where Rebecca Thatcher lives, that the question of a name for our kitty was then and there solved. She was Rebecca. Like the little girl in the story from whom she got her name, she was not obliged to answer the more formal title. It was usually "Becky" or "Becca"; and, sometimes, "Tebec" in memory of an old school-mate, Rebecca, who was always addressed by our foreign music-master as "Mees Tebec."

Our little pet was two months old when we got her; and, at eight months a cat considers herself to be "grown up." Rebecca was just about that old when she asked for a larger bed. Soon after it had been made ready, she found four baby-kits to occupy it. Three of them were blue—the real Maltese color—and the other was like Rebecca, blue with black marking.

All kittens are pretty and graceful; but there is something especially fascinating about the little Maltese kits. They are much more nervous than ordinary cats. The least sound or movement, that takes them unaware, makes them bounce up in the air as if the floor had spurned them; and they are in a perpetual state of surprise and enthusiasm.

A young relative—a boy in his teens—came to pay us a visit while Rebecca's kits were in their second month—just at the most enchanting age. He used to amuse himself by the hour with their antics.

One day he sat on the edge of the couch trailing a walking-stick back and forth along the floor for their entertainment. Each time all the little noses fastened themselves with fascinated attention to the moving stick, he gave it a jerk, startling the youngsters so that all bounced into the air at once as if a spring had been touched that lifted them. This sent the boy into fits of laughing. He kept repeating the performance until much laughter had made him breathless; then, throwing the stick to the floor, where it scattered the kits in a panic, he fell back exhausted on the lounge, crying:

"Oh, when I get rich, I'm going to have a thousand cats!"

Naturally, such beautiful kittens as Rebecca's were in great demand. They were always promised; and there was a "waiting list" which was always increasing.

This first family's owners sent daily inquiries, as soon as it was known that the kits were out of the nursery-box, to ask when each pet might be fetched to its waiting home.

Finally, it seemed as if they were really weaned. They ate bread and milk; gnawed bits of tender meat; and for several days I had not noticed that Rebecca called them to her for nature's supplies. They had learned to wash their own faces; and in all ways, they seemed to be quite independent, and self-sufficient. So I sent word to their new owners that the time had at last come when they might claim their little pets.

As it happened, all came on the same day.

The first arrived right after breakfast.

The second came along about lunch time; and the third right after luncheon. It began to look pretty serious, and I said:

"I do hope the other kitty-owner will not come today; for I don't know what Rebecca would say."

But, in spite of hopes, the last one was called for just before dark. I objected to letting this last baby-kit go; but the messenger had made a long trip purposely, and it seemed a pity to disappoint him.

I called Rebecca and explained it to her.

She did not seem at all excited; but peeped in the basket which was ready to receive her baby—climbed in and arranged its lining with much treading and nestling; then curled up on it experimentally. We put the kitten in with her, and she jumped out.

"She doesn't seem to want to cuddle it," said the messenger; and it did look that way. So I picked up Rebecca, holding her over to kiss the baby "good-bye"; then the cover was fastened snugly, the basket placed under the buggy-seat; and the last baby-kit was gone.

Rebecca came back into the house with me. As soon as I sat down she sprang into my lap and curled up in my sewing-apron just as she had used to do in her youth before family cares came to absorb her attention. This was reassuring; and, though I did miss the lively youngsters, it was pleasant to have Rebecca all to myself again.

After a short snooze in my lap, she got up, stretched herself with most elaborate yawns, then jumped to the floor and asked to have the door opened. After letting her out, I heard her mewing outside in the same tone she had always used to call her babies. She made the circuit of the house, pausing on the galleries, where the kits had loved to play, calling louder and louder. Presently she came around to the outside door nearest to where she knew me to be, and cried to be let in. When the door was opened she came in and went from room to room searching and calling. While she was looking in the store-room Julius came, it being the hour of his usual return from the office. Rebecca heard him and came running in. She sprang up in my lap looking into my face and mewing plaintively. Then she dropped to the floor and went to look up anxiously at Julius with still louder mewings.

94

"What's the matter with Becky?" asked Julius.

"She is hunting her kits," said I; "they all left us today, and she has only just missed them."

"What made you let them all go at once?" asked Julius.

"I didn't mean to. It just happened so. Everybody was impatient to possess them, and they all rushed to get them as soon as the news spread that they were weaned."

"Poor kitty!" said Julius, lifting her to his knee. Rebecca looked up in his face mewing eloquently; then leaped to the floor and running to the door looked back at Julius, and then up at the door-knob, still mewing.

"She thinks I can get them for her." Said Julius. "Where is the nearest one?"

"At Mrs. Simon's. It's nearly a mile, isn't it?"

"About three quarters," said Julius, reaching for his hat.

"Surely you are not going out there this time of the night! It's quite dark."

"No matter. We can't have Rebecca crying this way all night. Where's the lantern?"

I ran to get it; and lit it while Julius was putting on his overcoat. When he was all ready he said to Rebecca:

"Never mind, Kitty, I'll soon bring you one baby to cuddle."

Rebecca seemed to understand, and sat down on the edge of the hearth, no longer mewing; but keeping an alert watch on the door, listening with both eyes and ears.

In about half an hour we heard the gate click. Rebecca got to the door before I did, and when Julius entered, she looked up with eager, questioning mew, then sprang with fierce joy to receive the little bundle of blue fur that leaped from a pocket in his overcoat and sprang to her clasp.

As soon as I could speak, I asked Julius:

"What did Mrs. Simon say?"

"She laughed at me for taking a cold night-tramp to humor what she called a 'cat's whim'; and she did not want to let the kitty go. I had to promise to bring it back tomorrow."

95

"That's all right," said I. "You can promise what you please; but the kitten doesn't go back again until Rebecca is willing."

"I would have promised anything rather than come back without it," said Julius. "If she had refused to give it to me, I would have tramped on after one of the others. Nothing would have induced me to come back empty-handed. Almost anything would have been easier than to face Rebecca's disappointment."

"Yes, indeed!" said I; "and this is the last time I will ever scatter a kitten-family in such a hurry."

Bruno had come to join our family circle while these first kittens were still very young. He had accompanied Julius on the kind errand of bringing back the kitten; and now sat with lolling tongue, panting with the fatigue of racing up and down the streets, having made the trip about four times while Julius walked it once. While he rested, he beamed on happy Rebecca, and her joyful kitten who were purring together on the hearth-rug—the little one having promptly responded to the mother's invitation to enjoy a hearty meal—equally welcome to giver and receiver.

The remainder of Rebecca's history is lightly sketched in the story of Bruno.

She was not a remarkable cat—just such a pet as any ardent cat-lover may have. Her strongest characteristics were daintiness of ways, affection; and a marked disinclination for giving trouble.

In cold weather she liked to sleep indoors with us—dozing on the warm hearth, or in a cushioned chair. Sometimes, in the middle of the night, she wished to go on a little prowl. I have always been a light sleeper; and many a night I have been awakened by her efforts to get out without disturbing anyone. I pretended to be asleep while I listened to see how she would manage. Each window was in turn visited, until one was found to be a little way open. Then, if the opening proved to be too small to admit her body, she poked her paws in, following with her head and shoulders, to push it further open. The windows were well-hung, so that she could easily lift them when they were far enough open to push in a paw. That much accomplished, she began on the fastenings of the blinds. Sometimes she found a catch that she could manipulate; then it was easy to throw her weight against the blind to push it open, and leap down on the lawn underneath. Sometimes the catch resisted all her efforts; and, after trying all the windows, she had to admit herself defeated.

Then she came to me and sprang up on the bed to hook her claws in my sleeve and give a gentle pull to awaken me; at the same time making an imperative little sound in her throat. It was impossible to mistake her meaning; and there was real pleasure in attending to the wants of such a gentle, considerate little creature.

Usually Rebecca was not troublesome about her food; but would accept whatever was offered. If tempting morsels were given her she enjoyed them with evident gratitude and enthusiasm. If there seemed to be nothing available except simple bread-and-milk, this was taken without protest, and eaten with a docile air of content; but now and then she came to me with a coaxing manner as if trying to say she was hungry for some little extra treat. At such times I spared no pains to please her. It was not an uncommon thing for a tiny omelet to be made for her with one egg and a spoonful of milk. This was greatly appreciated. Rebecca watched the whole performance, from breaking the egg, to cooling the finished omelet by holding the little pan over cold water. Then, purring against me to express gratitude, she sat down to enjoy her feast, always saving a little taste of it for Bruno, who had looked on from the beginning and had waited patiently for his share.

Chapter Sixth of Bruno tells of our parting with Rebecca. After we left her, old Aunt Nancy tried to make her feel at home; but Rebecca was not happy as a member of a strange family. Though she was not a cat to give her affection to a mere locality, as she had proved by moving with us when we went from our first home to the one we later built, she went from Aunt Nancy's house back to the home where she had been so happy with us, and finding a family settled there with two gentle little children, Rebecca adopted them as her friends and protectors and settled down to live out her allotted days in peace and happiness. We were glad when we learned of this happy home for her old age, though of course we have often wished we could have prevented the separation from her. It had to be that way; and now there is no longer that pain in thoughts of her that we used to feel before we knew what had befallen her when she found herself to be left behind.

From Pine Woods to Palm Groves

Forward to
From Pine Woods to Palm Groves

Byrd Spilman Dewey's third book, *From Pine Woods to Palm Groves*, was her last book and was published in serialized form in 1909 in a journal called the *Florida Review*. As she notes in the forward, this work tells the Dewey's story between *Bruno* and *The Blessed Isle*, hence its placement between the two works in this volume.

She had started writing this book ten years earlier in about 1900, but had put it aside for other writings. It was never published as a book on its own, and was discovered through a chance finding in a Kentucky newspaper clipping from the Maysville *Daily Public Ledger* that noted the running of the serial story.

No South Florida historians had any knowledge of the work, and its discovery brought to light a delightful tale of pioneering in the nascent Palm Beach County, Florida while it was still a part of Dade County. The book describes the Dewey's first homestead in Palm Beach County, located about one mile inland from Lake Worth, the twenty-one mile long lake that borders Palm Beach and several other barrier islands.

In the book, pioneering in the wilds of South Florida is told from a woman's perspective—the difficulty of keeping house with the insects and wildlife, being forced to hunt for quail and squirrel, and doing mundane tasks such as laundry in a humid climate where everything rusts. Living more than a mile from the nearest settlement in Palm Beach also meant Mrs. Dewey was alone most of the day, having encounters with Seminole Indians on their way back to the Everglades.

The work presents a South Florida that is forever lost, a wild paradise that was tamed to today's landscape of manicured lawns, concrete and asphalt. Mrs. Dewey's South Florida of 1890 was one of sand pines, wooden cottages and waterways. Let this story offer a glimpse into that forgotten paradise.

Author's Note: On the appearance of the first edition of BRUNO, ten years ago, this record was begun, then was laid aside in response to a request from the editors of VOGUE for short sketches dealing with animal life. The first chapters of THE BLESSED ISLE, which appeared singly, as short stories in that publication, excited so much interest, it was thought best to complete that book first, and to let this chronicle appear later.

The reader who is familiar with BRUNO; and the BLESSED ISLE, will see that FROM PINE WOODS TO PALM GROVES is intended to bridge the interval between them. —B. S. D.

Chapter First
Beginning a New Life

H E WHO has eyes to see, and who regards events with an understanding heart, finds it interesting to study how all the facts of the material world correspond with the experiences of the heart and spirit. Everything visible and tangible has its unseen and intangible parallel. It is well to comprehend cause and effect as they swing to and fro over the barriers which separate the material from the immaterial. Some of these laws are already grasped with full understanding of their workings. Others are still only divined. A most fully accepted and comprehended law is that of the effect of surroundings, acting through mind and spirit, on the bodily health. When all else fails, Wisdom commands: Seek changed environment. Go somewhere and begin anew. Change affects the spirit through every sense. Hope and courage follow revived interest. Body and mind are made whole. Life begins again from a new starting-point, and there appears a new Heaven and a new Earth. The fabled Phoenix, arising from its own ashes, is no fable. It is one of Nature's strongest laws; else her plans could never mature, and this world would have ended ere it was scarce begun.

In the closing chapters of the story of Bruno, it was related how Julius and I felt that our emptied home seemed to leave us nothing more to hope. Then were we constrained, by the god of things as they must be, to seek new scenes. The Lake Worth Country, then but little known, beckoned with alluring hands. All Southern Florida bordering the Ocean had ever seemed to us a land of romance, fanned by mysterious, spice-laden breezes. Thus when those who had boated in its waters gave Fate's message, it seemed as if a door had been opened to invite us to enter a new world and find new interests in exploring a land hitherto existing only in our dreams. Then we gathered up our household gods and journeyed southward. The Lake Worth Country was then almost as remote as the moon. The railroad ended at Titusville, and, from there, we sailed in a schooner large enough to carry both us and our effects. The voyage consumed seven days. The wind was dead ahead most of the way, a double-reef breeze. During the brief intervals of fair winds, we were stuck on some of the numerous sand-bars which make sailing over Indian River so full of events for the venturesome mariner. On the seventh day from leaving the city, which, in its early history, thus saith the Old Inhabitant, was christened "Sand Point," we sailed into Lake Worth Inlet from white-capped Seas to a ruffled Sound bordered with shores of primeval forests and thickets. There was a semi-occasional clearing where toy houses, tip-toed to peep over what looked like immense bushes of red roses; but which proved later, on closer inspection, to be the glorious, ever-blooming hibiscus.

It was a new Florida we had discovered. True, there were already a few families living there; but we felt ourselves to be, none-the-less, real discoverers. This was partly because much that we found existed only for, and to us. The elect will understand this. To others, it will seem only a riddle to which there is no answer. All the country was practically an Island; because its only highway was the water.

An isle of charm, mosquitoes, sandflies, redbugs, makeshifts and charm. The charm predominated. It was first and last; but all the other things were just as real.

After a short rest on the East Side Peninsula, we took possession of the homestead, back from the water on the West Side, which had been already secured, "unsight, unseen," at the Land Office in Gainesville. There we literally pitched our tent, and began to make a home in the heart of the pine woods.

There was a wooded hill overlooking a Lake which bordered our Western shores; on the further side of this Lake, we had a fine view of the cypress trees which guard the entrance to the famous Everglades. By climbing a tree on the wooded hill we also had a fine view of the Atlantic Ocean, with its passing sails and smoke-stacks. After exploring the seventy six acres of our homestead, this hill was chosen as the best building site. Here the sleeping and cooking tents were pitched; and a chicken park was staked off and fenced with woven-wire netting before our own dwelling was begun.

As a child I had delighted in boy-books like *Robinson Crusoe, Swiss Family Robinson, The Young Marooners on the Florida Coast*, and all such tales of adventure. Many times I had thought how delightful it would be to live over such situations—far from civilization—exploring, and struggling with nature at her wildest and sweetest. And here these dreams had come true. We were as isolated, and as much on our own resources as were any of those who took part in the beloved and fascinating dramas of childhood.

From the beginning of this new departure there were many long hours when I seemed to myself like a sole survivor of a depopulated world. These hours absolutely alone with wild nature, where there was not one single familiar sound except the various noises made by the fowls, were so full of strange new experiences that I began to wish for something more companionable than were the busy occupants of the fowlery, and the offer of the pair of kittens was hailed with delighted enthusiasm. Never was the arrival of Santa Claus, in childhood's eager days, more impatiently awaited than was the coming of these two little chums. The words "two kittens" had given me an immediate mental picture of gentle, purring little pets that would creep into my arms and snuggle there long enough to get acquainted, then spring to the ground for amusing and wildly exciting games of tag with one another. Later, I found that their career had begun in a tool house back on the clearing of our generous neighbors across the water, and that they had never seen any humans except an occasional workman. They had been caught and literally "bagged" after a most exciting chase. When they arrived, we, all unsuspecting, untied the confining string, and the result was as utterly surprising as is the average child's first acquaintance with that toy called a Jack-in-the-box. There was a wild scramble—a furry flash—and they vanished in opposite directions, swallowed up by the forests that surrounded our home.

We looked at one another in dismay. The saucer of "tin milk"— the dish of nice bits—"There was the sandwich; but where was the mouth to put it in!"

We called, and called. There was no response. No faintest sign that there ever was a cat anywhere.

"If it were not for the water to cross" said Julius, "I'd think they had gone back home."

What a disappointment! After all those eager and impatient anticipations there was only the empty bag, lying limp on the porch-floor; and the memory of that brief scramble to assure that the little savages had ever arrived.

It seemed like abandoning the kittens to a cruel fate, to go indoors and shut up the house for the night. We knew the forest to be full of wild creatures which, though not dangerous for humans, were quite ready to gobble up two plump young kittens. Still, we knew it was useless to try to follow and catch them after their flight to cover in the tangled undergrowth where they could creep and climb through and over places utterly inaccessible to us. So we had to give it up, assuring one another that we should never see them again—that before morning their tragic fate would doubtless be decided.

All through the night our dreams were haunted by visions of the two helpless little creatures struggling with the dangers of the wilderness, and the first thought in the morning was to go out again to call them, which I did with no real expectation of a response; but, first from one side, and then, from the other, came the sound of mews so very faint we thought, at first, it was only imagination prompted by our eager longings. The sounds came again—still faint—no nearer—but ever from the same quarters. We concluded that the little creatures had been so crazed with terror from the effects of being chased—bagged— boated across, then carried the long tramp, and released among strange sights and sounds, that they had fled to the first available hiding-place, and had only just begun to realize that there were such things as hunger and thirst; and that they were also beginning to wonder what had become of one another.

Repeated calls brought the sound of their mewing no nearer; and I felt sure that, although we could hear both kittens, being apparently about midway between them, the poor lonely little creatures could not possibly hear one another. Then it occurred to me to imitate their mews; and almost immediately, the sounds began to approach on both sides. They kept coming closer and closer until it was no longer necessary for me to play at being a kitten—they could evidently hear one another's mews. Then they came to a standstill, and no coaxing would bring them into the open space about the house. We then placed food and water in the edge of the wood where it could easily be seen, and went indoors to our own breakfast; after which Julius set out for a day over on the peninsula, and I busied myself, as usual, about various household affairs.

It would hardly be stretching the truth to say, of this woodland home that it was "two miles from nowhere." To reach the sparse settlement we had to walk a mile, or more, through the winding woods path to the shore of the Sound. Then row, or sail, more than another mile to the little "store" where, in its primitive post-office, in one corner, mail was distributed sometimes twice a week, and sometimes once a month, according to the wind and weather. Beside the post-office both "stores" which were three miles apart on the East shore of the Sound, carried stocks of merchandise which ranged in variety from groceries to hardware and the more necessary kinds of dry goods and notions. Julius went over almost every day, usually leaving right after breakfast, and not returning until nightfall. Some days he was helping with the post-office and "store" accounts, or giving some other sort of a "lift" to the friendly settlers who had so warmly welcomed us to our new life. Incidentally, he did the errands, watching eagerly for the irregular mail-boat, which was our only "wire" to the outside world; doing our small buying and a little hunting or fishing to vary the primitive bills of fare.

Fishing, hunting and roughing it are joys in which the feminine woman is apt to feel only a vicarious interest; but, it was such a pleasant change to see Julius interested and ready to make new plans, that I cheerfully accepted the isolated life. There were long days which averaged the full ten or more hours of being absolutely alone. The small household tasks were usually done by half-past nine or ten. The rest of each day was devoted to reading, sewing, writing and attending to the wants of a yard of fowls, occasionally varying the monotony with the "pleasures of the chase" to rout some wild creature that wished a plump hen to carry home to his family lying perdu somewhere in the forest. In no direction could people be reached without a mile, or more, of tedious thicket-threading. There was no passing except an occasional Indian, or a semi-occasional hunter on the way to the fresh-water Lake, West of us, which was the gateway to the romantic Everglades. With the kindest of feelings existing among all the dwellers on both sides of the Sound, there was very little visiting because distances were great, and the men of all the families were too busy to cease the necessary toil of pioneer life to escort the women to make social calls, which involved rowing; or sailing; or long lonely tramps, and often all three to make a single brief visit. Now and then there was a neighborhood picnic; or a Sunday spend-the-day visit, with long weeks between during which the housekeeper having no daughters never saw a woman's face except the reflection of her own when, for very loneliness she carried her sewing to sit before the dressing-table where she could lift her eyes now and then and "play" that the reflected image was a busy companion.

Such a complete change in all the conditions and associations of life began to heal our wounds. We spoke almost constantly of Bruno, wishing for his presence in this wild, free life so exactly to his taste, and longing for his protecting companionship for me in the endless of utter isolation. Of our Little Blossom we never spoke. That was a pain too deep; and each hoped that the other might succeed in the impossible task of forgetting.

As one step toward the forming of new heart-interests, we had welcomed the offer of the pair of kittens. During the day which followed their arrival, I went often out of doors hoping to find that hunger had impelled them to surrender; but they were nowhere in evidence. About mid-afternoon, I heard one of our squirrels scolding violently; and, on peeping cautiously through the transparent window-draperies, I saw him on a low bough just over where I had placed the cat-lunch, and there, greedily eating, the while casting frightened glances from side to side, with an occasional nervous lift of the eyes to the angry squirrel overhead, were the two famished kits! They cleared the dish of food, and, after drinking long from the water-bowl, again disappeared in the woods; this time, together. Their departure was viewed with evident satisfaction by the squirrel, which was one of a pair that had appeared on the scene as we were taking possession of our woodland home and had stayed by us ever since, making daily trips from their nest in a near-by pine tree to thrust their thirsty little tongues in our rain-barrel.

Chapter Second

ON HIS return home that evening Julius was immensely pleased to hear that the kits had found the way to their lunch table.

"It is only a question of time now," he said. "If they can live in safety through one night in the woods, each one alone, there is no reason why they cannot survive a few more nights now that they are together; and their dependence on us for rations will soon enable us to tame them."

They came again the next day, about dusk, for the dish of boiled grits and gravy I had placed ready for them; so, the third evening I moved the dish of food and the water bowl to a place a little nearer the house. As that seemed, in no way, to embarrass them, I moved them still nearer on the fourth, fifth and sixth evenings; and, by the end of the week, they came to eat beside the steps. Then their supplies were moved up a step at a time each evening, until, before they had realized it, they were eating on the porch, we meanwhile watching them from behind the window draperies, noting, with great satisfaction, their growth, and their pretty graceful ways. The larger one was snow white, handsomely marked with dark gray ankles and cap. The other one was a glossy jet black, except for a white button on the tip of her tail, and a tiny white star, like a brooch, under her chin. Having coaxed them up on the porch, we prepared for a climax. The next evening the screen door was propped open and a cord was tied to its outer edge. This was long enough to reach to the other side of the room. We placed the dishes of food and water on the floor inside then seated ourselves in the shadows where we kept as still as two statues. Soon the little cats appeared, coming from their usual haunts in the wood, as truly wild creatures as any beast born therein, except for their inherited taste for what old Nancy used to call "city folkses vittles."

When they reached the top step and saw that there were no dishes on the porch-floor, they turned to one another making soft little throat-sounds of disappointment and inquiry. Then they saw the open door and approached cautiously. We did not move an eyelash. They paused on the threshold, sniffing, with outstretched necks—then they saw the food. Again they looked hesitatingly at one another, making little questioning throat-sounds, then advanced and began to eat.

Julius jerked the cord.

The door slammed, and the kittens were trapped.

With arched backs, and fur all a-bristle they sprang for the door. Baffled there, they turned—apparently all tails, eyes and claws,—and took refuge, one behind the book-case, and the other far back under the corner table.

We sat perfectly motionless.

The twilight deepened.

After what seemed like hours; but was probably only about twenty minutes, first one kitty, then the other crept out and moved toward the dishes. Seeing that nothing happened, they came nearer and nearer until both were soon busy absorbing their longed-for and much-needed evening repast.

By the time their feast was ended the room was almost in darkness. They turned from the emptied dish and started to the oblong of grey twilight falling through the screen-door. Just as they reached it; and had begun to push and claw at the wire, I made a quick, noiseless dash and caught the little black kit by the back of her neck as a mother-cat had accustomed it to being grasped and carried. It struggled wildly for a few seconds then relaxed its tense muscles. I sat down, holding it closely and stroking its silky fur. Before many minutes it began purring; though, at every sound or movement it ceased singing and began to struggle. After awhile I handed it over, with some protest on its part, to

Julius, and succeeded in catching the other one, from which I also coaxed a little purring sound—weak and tremulous; but still a purr. For some time we petted and talked to them, then I took both in my arms—Julius opened the door—I went outside and sat down on the steps holding both kits in my lap. Pretty soon I relaxed the clasp. They hesitated a few seconds—leaped down and scampered off to the woods where they disappeared.

The next evening we repeated the program with a like result, except that the kits were scarcely frightened at all when the door banged shut after they had begun to eat; and that they seemed quite willing to be caught when their feast was ended. After that their surrender was complete. They were house-cats, and it was time to christen them.

"Catty" and "Kitty" were the names we chose.

"Kitty" was soon lengthened to "Kitty-Winks" and she suggested the name herself.

It happened this way:

One day two or three house-flies from the chicken-yard managed to get into the house and the kittens undertook to catch them. Around the rooms they chased them from window to window.

Our little home consisted of four rooms below; a living-room and a bed-room in front connected by a large archway, and back of these were the dining-room and the kitchen. There was an attic above the two front rooms where we stored various odds and ends; - the piles of papers and magazines that are always with us; also, spare sails; and other boat-tackle, dry herbs some of which we had already discovered growing wild in the woods, and the low places near the water; seeds and so forth. The little attic served another most important purpose—we found that, as the summer waxed warm and yet warmer, our attic, with its open window, drew up the heated air and kept the lower rooms always pleasantly cool, even when there was a fire in the kitchen stove.

Below, the doors which connected the four rooms were always open, or practically so. The draperies in the archways—the ones between the two front rooms, and also those between the dining-room and the kitchen—offered no obstacle to the eager scamperings of the kittens. They galloped around as freely as if there were not walls between the rooms.

To return to the flies. The kittens soon caught all but one, and this one had been stalked untiringly from window to window. I had gone into the bedroom to do some cutting-out on one of the beds, and sat beside it with my sewing spread on the coverlet.

The fly had been chased to a window near where I sat, and then the kits had lost sight of it. Being so near, it occurred to Kitty to leap up on the bed and see how the sewing was getting along. Then her ears pointed at attention—she crouched for a spring—her tail lashing back and forth. I looked to see what it was, and understood at once.

The bed had a white coverlet. My work was also white; but among the scraps there was a tiny bit of black—a small knot from a skein of black zephyr which had been in the basket with the cloth. It was quite evident that Kitty mistook this curled wisp for the lost fly. Cautiously, with narrowed eyes, she crept nearer and nearer—then she pounced, covering the supposed fly with her paws. With one triumphant glance at me she began to investigate her catch. First one paw, then the other was gingerly curled sideways and peeped under. Yes; there it was! She grasped it again—smelled it—scraped at it with her paw—then lifted her eyes to mine in a shame-faced way and winked. When I began to laugh she leaped to the floor, scampering around to escape from the embarrassment of the situation. As soon as I could speak, for laughing, I cried:

"Oh, you funny little "Kitty-Winks!" and from that time she had the double name. And, as we could not show partiality, Catty's title was also hyphenated, and he learned to respond to "Catty-Meow."

These dear kittens added much to the home-feeling of our new abode. We had saved only the simplest things from the wreck of our city home; but these we had chosen with much care.

There were white draperies for the windows; red rugs for the floors, which we had oiled for a hardwood effect; a few pictures for the walls; many books; comfortable chairs; tables of convenient sizes; two single beds; a couch for the living-room and a good-sized wood-stove for the kitchen.

Our rooms were really attractive.

It was so much of an undertaking for me to go visiting, that I was seldom off of our own land, which consisted of more than seventy acres.

Julius went over to the settlement almost every day, so an occasional storm which confined us both to the house and to one another's society, came as a delight to us both—a day welcomed, and dated from. I always missed him during his long hours of absence; but I knew it was mentally healthier for us both to have him stirring around keeping us in touch with our neighbors and, so far as was possible, with the outside world. He was always on the lookout for anything that would interest me. Beside the semi-occasional mail, and the news from the small community across the Sound, he brought home many things which were full of interest and that gave us subjects for conversation and lively discussions. Sometimes a wild flower; or a strange plant; often a bright feather dropped by some unknown, or little-known bird of passage. And, now and then, the young of some of the forest denizens he had caught; or had rescued from some other creature which had captured it. Sometimes he came back with thrilling tidings of a wreck over on the Beach and with samples of the cargo which the tide had brought ashore. Even things so prosaic as bags of flour or boxes of candles were full of romantic interest as trophies from a wreck. As the Summer-weather came on, he often came home laden with bags of turtle-eggs, or a piece of the captured turtle, together with directions given by some friendly "Old Settler" for the palatable dishes to be made of these strange new edibles.

After the little cats came I seemed to be less alone when Julius was gone. They were almost as much company as two children would have been. I kept a loaded gun always within reach, and was constantly on the alert—a state of mind that is not conducive to rapid increase of health and strength, as I soon realized.

Julius delighted in the free outdoor life. The beauty and the healthfulness of country and climate, and the pleasures of fishing, hunting and boating, were giving him new life, and bringing back those boyish enthusiasms which he had left behind him years ago. He knew that I had always enjoyed a quiet, simple life, and that there was no real danger for me in the lonely woods; and, as I never felt the isolation except when he was gone, it was a long time before he discovered why I did not grow strong and rosy. The fears that haunted my lonely hours were due to that state of nervous collapse which often follows a bereavement or other severe shock.

One morning Julius turned back after he had started and asked me to hand him the gun from its place behind the door.

"I can bring back some ducks with me" he explained; "I saw so many yesterday I was wishing all the way that I had brought the gun along."

Without a word of protest I gave it to him, inwardly condemning myself for tremors.

It required some mental arguments to bring about a reasonable state of tranquility after Julius had disappeared from view down the woods-path, serenely unconscious of my tragic frame of mind.

The only way to combat baseless fears is to smother them with absorption in some interesting occupation.

I hurried through with small daily tasks and sat down to books with the two kittens in my lap for company.

That year I re-read *Vanity Fair* six times, always with increased interest. And some parts of *Martin Chuzzlewit*—the "Pecksniffs at Todgers," and the vagaries of "Mrs. Gamp"—more times than I can remember.

If spirits do return to make sure their earthly friends have not forgotten them, I hope the shades of the two enchanters who are responsible for the sweetened solicitude of my endless days, were often near to see the effects of their magic.

Completely lost to all surrounds in the fascinating recital of Mr. Jos. Sedley's conquest, all at once I was disturbed by that indescribable feeling of being stared at.

On lifting my eyes it required great self-command to repress a start.

The screen-door was shut and hooked; but the inner door was fastened open.

On the porch, close to the screen-door, and staring through it at me, stood the wildest-looking Indian I had yet seen.

Chapter Three

H IS LONG black hair hung from under a projecting turban. The remainder of his costume consisted of a gay calico shirt. There was no mistake about the first impression of him. He was a genuine primeval American.

"Where man?" he asked, as soon as he saw that I was looking at him.

The two kits sprang to the floor and scampered away to hide, at the sound of the strange voice.

I 'rose, and approached the door with an air of calm security which hid feelings akin to terror.

"Man outside," I answered; not daring to tell him I was all alone.

"Want man;" he insisted.

"Man busy."

"Good Indian want man's boat."

"Boat busy, too."

"No! Other boat. Me see um," he protested, with a majestic wave of his hand toward the West.

Then I knew he meant the skiff which was owned and used by hunters to reach the points and further shores of the straits and sheets of water lying west of The Hermitage, which formed the Indian highway to their Everglades home.

Though I had no right to lend the boat, I felt that this was a case where authority might be stretched, so I asked:

"Will good Indian bring back boat?"

"Mh-hm; bring him back tomorrow."

"Then good Indian take boat."

"Me take him;" was the answer, with a satisfied grunt.

I supposed that this would end the interview; but not so. He stood calmly regarding me with the unwinking stare of a child. All the stories of Indian horrors I had ever read or heard galloped through my mind as he stood there, his big red limbs knotted with muscles—a king by right of his strength and fearlessness.

It seemed ages that we stood regarding one another. I racked my brain for a way to terminate the trying situation. All at once an inspiration came to me to say to him:

"Goodbye."

Apparently that was just what he was lingering to hear. He answered:

"Goodbye;" and turned from me, going down the steps—down the hill—and disappeared among the trees and undergrowth. As he was lost to view, I felt like a stopped clock. Something gave way; and the next I knew the kits were clawing at my shoulders and licking my cheeks with their rough little tongues. I found that the sun was nearly down, and they were evidently trying to say:

"It's time to eat again."

While their dishes were being filled, the sound came from away down the hill in the woods, of the "Bob White" whistle with which Julius always announced his approach.

Though I was still all a-tremble as I ran to the welcome shelter of his encircling arms, I could now laugh at my fears, and could see the humor of the situation. Poor Lo, anxious and desirous to be off on his way across the waters to where his own people were in the camp; and I, equally eager to have him go, neither of us knowing the rules of etiquette necessary to terminate the scene.

"But," I finished the laughing recital by saying, "never, never leave me alone again without the gun!"

"I won't," answered Julius. "The Indians are friendly and as harmless as the other creatures here in the woods; but there is real danger in the helpless feeling and the fright."

All the same, we enjoyed the ducks he had brought, and the kits picked the bones with great satisfaction.

Up to this time, I had used the gun only as a means of defense— to scare away wild-cats, 'possums, hawks and other creatures which came to rob the fowlery; but one morning Julius failed to relish his breakfast. He had been over-doing for several days—preparing a place to set out some pineapple-slips. His evening meal of the day before had disagreed with him; because he was too weary to assimilate the simple food of which he was growing rather tired. It had so delighted me to see his vigorous appetite, that I felt a sense of personal loss at its failure. Right after breakfast, he left for a day across the Sound in the Settlement, carrying, by way of luncheon, only a bread-and-jelly sandwich. I was just wishing there was some little surprise delicacy I could prepare against his return when I heard a covey of quails out in the edge of the woods. It had always seemed to me like murder to shoot a quail, and nothing would induce me to kill one for my own enjoyment; but the Eternal Feminine would shoot a Cherubim to nourish the invalid dependent on her care!

I got the gun, which was always loaded, and "drew a bead" on the quail nearest me. The recoil of the discharge stunned me for a second or two; but when I had found myself, I saw the little bird in its death-struggle, and it was quite dead when I reached it—the head gone, being as neatly taken off as if done by a sharp blade.

When Julius sat down to dinner that evening and found that his plate held a delicious young quail, done to a turn, and served on a crisp square of brown toast, it was delightful to see his surprise; and also his pride in the fact that I had done it all un-aided—had shot, "peeled," and cooked it all so deliciously for his pleasure. Seeing how refreshed and strengthened he was with this little surprise-treat, I often went out for squirrels during my long days alone, taking great care to go some distance from our clearing to make sure of not killing the pair that had nested near the house, and had, from the first, been such interesting neighbors.

I very seldom wasted a shot. No matter how high in the tree a little creature might be, I had such a horror of maiming and leaving it to die alone, that I was always careful to aim so that the head or neck was pierced, and so death was instantaneous. Julius became so proud of my skill as a Diana, that it added greatly to his enjoyment of our game dinners.

Meanwhile, the little cats were growing rapidly. Kitty-Winks, though the younger and smaller of the two, seemed to mature earlier than Catty-Meow. He had a long period of hobbledehoy awkwardness as some human boys have between youth and maturity. The two youngsters were fuller, even than are most kittens, of coil-springs; and they galloped and bounced around most divertingly. All small children delight in a game they call "playing bear." Our kits had a similar game, of which they never tired. One would hide; while the other assuming a most distrait air—hands in pockets, so to speak, —head held high— sauntered by. Then out sprang the hidden one to leap on the other, slaying it with great slaughter—the two rolling over together—biting; kicking; scratching and growling—in the death-struggle. Then they changed places, and went through the same program, playing with the greatest fairness, first one and then the other consenting to be "it."

Another favorite game was "playing mouse." This was a livelier scramble than the other—a continuous performance, without climax. It was played by one getting on each side of the portières and catching one another's paws under the folds. One usually began the game by playing with the edge of the curtain. Then the other slipped around on the other side to snatch at the feet as they

"Like little mice peeped in and out."

These games were always played to exhaustion; then they curled up in one another's clasp for long sleeps. Their favorite bed was my lap; but, if they saw it was not convenient for me to take them, they were quite philosophical about contenting themselves with another bed. After these long sleeps they always awakened in a state of enthusiastic hunger. I never liked to give them hot food; so it sometimes happened that they began to clamor for what they smelled cooking—fish, or some sort of game—and, in order to keep them satisfied to await the coming feast, I gave them some cold bits from the safe. This used to enrage Kitty-Winks. First she dashed at the dish offered, thinking it was what she had smelled cooking, and when she found it to be something quite different—something less tempting, left over from a previous meal—she was so angry she always turned on Catty-Meow and soundly boxed his ears! He, poor fellow! though enough larger and stronger to avenge this unfair treatment, always shut his eyes, flattened down his ears and submitted as meekly as "Mr. Henry Peck." Then when Kitty-Winks had relieved her feelings, they fell to and enjoyed their repast together as amiably as if a blow or a cross word had never been thought of by either.

Now came a second fright that was funnier than the interview with the wild son of the Everglades. This time Julius had his share of it, and so learned, by experience, that even where there is no danger, a serious scare is not an impossibility.

One night I was awakened from as sound asleep as I ever had there at The Hermitage, by hearing voices. I 'rose up on elbow, and reached over to Julius. His bed stood so near that I could touch him without stepping on the floor. I awakened him in that noiseless way, learned from those who were taught by forest guides who have need of it in their life among hostile Indians and other wild-wood dangers, by laying a stealthy hand on his forehead.

"What is it?" he whispered. Then he heard the voices too, and lifted himself on elbow to listen.

"Do you think it is the Indians?" I asked; for there had been rumors of an Indian up-rising over in the Glades, to "wipe-out" all the settlers, and take possession of their belongings.

"No. Listen!" he whispered.

My teeth began to click together in a nervous chill, and I reached to the floor for my shoes, with a vague idea of dressing.

The voices came nearer.

Then we heard footsteps. They approached, passed under the windows of our sleeping-room; but kept on without pausing. Presently, there was a tremendous crash; then, some very unprintable words, and a rattlety-bang clatter, as if some sort of animals were trying to extricate themselves from a pile of mixed planks and tinware. Then we knew what had happened. Julius had been painting a skiff, which he had built for a fishing-boat in the waters west of us. For convenience the skiff had been placed on two boards resting on trestles, to bring it up to a height which made stooping unnecessary. The boards were very much too long; but Julius had not sawed them off, because he wished, later, to use them for another purpose. The owners of the voices, well-laden with hunting and camping-out "plunder," had tripped on one of these boards, and had gone over in a heap, too startled to restrain their feelings or their language. When we heard the crash and clatter, it was such a relief from fright and bewilderment; then, the swift vengeance to those who had disturbed us was so funny, that we both went into fits of uncontrollable laughing.

Finally the outside clatter and language ceased. They were evidently gathering up their belongings, and loading themselves for a fresh start. They were just in time to strike the board at the other end of the skiff, and down they went again, all in a heap, and this time the boat jumped on top of them. The clatter was almost deafening, and, as soon as it began to subside, we heard remarks which were something awful. As they were gathering up the fragments, we heard one voice ask something about "How many more blamed deadfalls," and we smothered in our pillows a succession of laughs which left us both weak. As soon as the voices and footsteps had died away in the distance, Julius struck a match, and we found it to be midway between three and four. A glance outside showed that it was one of those dark murky nights, when the clouds hang thick and low, so that he who fares forth must "walk by faith; and not by sight;" and we marveled that anyone should be willing to start out in such darkness without a lantern. Also, we wondered greatly the whys and wherefores of the night-march through our place, which was on the way to no-where. The only logical conclusion was that the owners of the voices were fugitives of some sort making a night-flitting to hide in the trackless Everglades.

A day or two later Julius met those men on their way back to the settlement, and they told him how they had made an early morning start to go into camp on an Everglades island for a few days of hunting and fishing. Also they said they had conversed loudly in passing through our place so that if we were awake, we would know it was not some marauding animal and be tempted to fire at them. Julius explained, in turn how our "booby-trap" happened to be set, with no idea of a catch; as it was the first time there had ever been any humans passing during the hours of darkness; though we had often been wakened by the tramp of passing herds of deer and other creatures of the woods who have eyes constructed for night-travel.

All sorts of wild creatures lived in our thickets, making us feel as we imagined our first parents felt in their Heaven-made garden with dominion over bird, beast and creeping things. Sometimes an osprey, sailing prey-laden from the salt-water to his mate and their younglings in the top of some tree in the far Everglades, met an eagle bent on robbery, and during the struggle in the clouds over our heads a big fish was dropped at our very door-step. One day this happened just as Julius had said he would like a chowder for our noon meal; but did not wish to take the time from his work to go fishing. I answered that we had everything to make chowder—potatoes, onions, bacon, and pilot biscuit—everything except the fish; and had laughingly quoted: "First catch your hare;" when the quarreling birds of prey overhead came to a climax and the big fish, still alive and squirming, was dropped, with a thud, within twenty steps of the out-door workbench where Julius was tacking sheet-copper strips on a pair of oars, and I was sitting close-by with darning basket!

Julius dropped his hammer to scale the fish, while I went indoors to put on the kettle and prepare the other "fixin's" for our chowder. The place teemed with romance and adventure. The weather was usually so perfect that we lived out of doors. I used to carry my writing-things out and arrange them on one end of the work-bench; and, one day when I was there alone absorbed in a long letter which was describing our wild-woods life to a friend in the frozen north, I had a fright that left me all a-tremble. Lost to surroundings, I was, all at once, seized by the hair, and thought for one terrible second, that I was gone; but it was only a blue-jay whose curiosity to see what I could be at, had overcome his discretion. He had alighted on my head, clinging, with all his claws to the unstable hair-ripples, and was leaning over to cock his eyes at pen and paper; while his mate, perched on a twig overhead, also leaned as far down toward my busy fingers as she could without falling on her bill. I shoo-ed them away and went on with the letter; but the pen seemed tipsy, and the flow of thought struck snags. Sub-consciously an old picture of Robinson Crusoe standing horrified at sight of the foot-print in the sand came up from oblivion and obscured the paper. It is strange how nervous one can be at the most ordinary things when one happens to live in a world emptied of his kind!

After a few months of life at The Hermitage, we had some weeks of continuous North-East winds. All the freight was brought to our little world by water. Schooners built for freighting made usually about two trips a month to Jacksonville, going out through the Inlet—a narrow strait connecting our Sound with its mother-Ocean—and sailing by what was called the "Inside Passage" to Jacksonville. This "Inside Passage" was that portion of the Ocean which flowed river-like, between the shore and a chain of reefs which broke the force of the Ocean swell. When the winds were North-East, it was dangerous, and well-nigh impossible, to pass through the Inlet. Sometimes the schooners were kept out-side, tacking up and down for days, waiting for the wind to change or become gentle enough for them to enter. Occasionally such heavy squalls arose, that they were forced to fly before the wind and take refuge in the wide-mouthed Bay nearly one hundred miles further south. Once a schooner loaded with groceries was kept dodging back and forth until the exasperated crew had eaten all the cargo; so, instead of making further effort to enter the Inlet, they signaled to the anxious shore-watch the nature of their plight, and sailed back to Jacksonville for a fresh cargo. At this time, of North-East squalls, the little settlement was all out of several necessities. The principal lacks were flour and kerosene. Salt and butter were also exhausted at the "stores" so those who had salt shared with the rest, and vegetables were boiled in the salt-water of the Sound for economy's sake. Butter was replaced by a dish taught us by the Old Settlers, who called it "scorch gravy," made by thickening bacon-fryings with browned flour, then thinning the mixture with boiling water. This was not so bad as it sounds; for open-air life gives a flavor to even the coarsest food that choice viands often lack in an indoor artificial life.

The butter which was brought South in the schooner-holds, was of good quality. It was sealed in air-tight tins, with Spanish labels, being prepared for the Island trade—and that, with the evaporated cream, made life a hundred or two miles from a dairy, quite livable.

It seemed a dramatic co-incidence that, at this time of no boats coming in, we should have a wreck which supplied the most important of our wants. All the settlement was wearying of corn-meal bread. As for lights, we were going to bed with the chickens. One evening, after ten days of no mail, Julius came home just at dusk with the mail-pouch over his shoulder full of letters, and a rope he had borrowed "Lassooed" around a big bundle of newspapers and magazines. It was too dark to make out a word; and the evening was warm. Anyone who has been ten days without news from friends, relatives, and the world in general, can imagine how we felt with all this mail and no light. We built up a fire of fat-wood knots, and sat down on the floor in front of the stove, with its fire-doors open, our treasures of mail in our laps, devouring the words until the backs of our heads began to feel cooked. Never before had we fully appreciated the blessing of artificial lights— the help they are to civilization, and the joy they give!

The very next day Julius came home from a trip over to the settlement with a bundle of candles and a package of flour. A ship loaded with supplies had been caught on its way to South America, in the same gale which was preventing our schooner from reaching us, and its crew had been obliged to throw over-board the very supplies that we needed! So we had candles to burn and flour for bread which lasted until the gale ceased and our own ships came in.

Much of the romance in all these things lay in the memory of stories we had both read in days of youthful enthusiasm for adventure. All sorts of delightful dreams, long since forgotten, came back to us in these strange surroundings. Julius was happy; the cats found it a paradise; our fowls crowed and cackled and clucked, surrounded by their broods in scratching-grounds which yielded a never-failing supply of bugs and worms. I was content to live this dreamy, romantic life, in touch with the outside world only through letters, papers, and books. It seemed to us to be simply a question of time that such a beautiful country of delightful possibilities should become known and settled. We often looked into the future and talked of a day when the world should come to us, and our wilderness forget it had ever been wild and deserted. It was pleasant to believe this in days when often for weeks and even months at a time I never saw a woman's face. When one of the busy housekeepers from the settlement did get out for a long-expected visit, she always amused me by asking if I were not afraid of snakes, bears; panthers; wildcats and so forth. Also if I did not get "awfully lonesome." The innocent animals had no terrors for me; and I was too much interested in the new life ever to feel bored with the isolation; but the several frights that had proved to be for nothing at all, had given such moments of real terror that whenever I was left alone I found myself starting at every little sound—even the snapping of a twig under a squirrel's lively scamper was enough to make my heart stand still, and then begin to gallop. After another baseless scare, which really made me ill for several days, we began to discuss a plan which those in the settlement had long been urging us to try. This was to make a temporary abiding-place over near them, only going from time to time for picnic days of work on our own land. This to continue until we could have some nearer neighbors at The Hermitage so I need not be left so much alone. It seemed a good plan, especially as there was no trouble about taking the "live-stock" consisting of cats and fowls, with us. In order to try the experiment of living "in town," with as little labor as possible, we took only two or three camp-chairs from The Hermitage, beside the live creatures and a hand-bag of clothing. Over at one of the "stores" we bought a small camp-stove and two cots.

The door was locked on The Hermitage and its contents, with the feeling that we were only going for a picnic, and that this, our real home, would be ready to receive us again whenever we chose to return to it.

Chapter Four

THE CAMPING-PLACE, which we had chosen from several that had been offered, was an elaborate boat-house on the East shore of the Sound, which had been built by a man who afterwards changed his mind about "making a home so far from everywhere" as he expressed it. He had means to do things well, so the boat-house was strongly built, commodious, neat, and comfortable. There was a large room, which had the water of the Sound for its floor, and had been planned for a boat-shelter. Big double doors opened and shut between it and the outside waves, manipulated by ropes that worked on cleats and pulleys. There was a railed gallery overlooking this enclosed water-room, like an indoor verandah. This made a pleasant living room. Of one end, we made a cooking-corner; a little further along, we placed a primitive dining-table, then another table also improvised from a packing-box, and white-draped, which held books, papers, and my work-box. In the most protected corner of the gallery, the one nearest the shore, there was a little enclosed room which just held the two cots. We hung a pocket-mirror by its one window, and placed our toilet-articles on a small towel-draped box which just fitted in between the heads of the two cots. It all recalled the "play-houses" dear to childhood, and added another chapter to our fascinating pioneer experiences, which had already included three weeks of tent-life while we were building the house at The Hermitage. This brief period of tenting had been an experience always longed-for, and very satisfying; for we had moved from the tents—one for sleeping, and the other for cooking and dining room—to our only-partly finished house, with a lively appreciation of solid walls, and roofs which did not "cup" to gather huge bowlfuls of wetness to seep down on beds, clothing or groceries!

The boat-house life was now to satisfy another dream; for it was in many ways like house-boat living. The ceaseless lap-lapping of waves, the aids to easy housekeeping in the ability to throw or sweep overboard every sort of trash or "clutter," and to watch at ease the movements of fish, or other water-creatures while busy at indoor tasks.

There were to be six days out of each seven passed in the boat-house camp. Every Saturday afternoon we went over to The Hermitage to remain until Monday morning. As soon as we arrived there we washed the garments worn during the week and hung them up to dry over Sunday. At bedtime I "set sponge" and the next day had a week's supply of bread ready to go into the oven by noon; so, on Monday morning, we had fresh bread, cakes, and refreshed garments to take back to our camp.

Though the camping-place was comfortable, and we were there surrounded by an atmosphere of kind friendliness which was delightful after our long months of isolation over at The Hermitage, every time we went back to our pine-woods home we found it more attractive. The spicy woods-breath was more invigorating than ever after a sojourn in the edge of the Peninsula's jungle-growth. The land lay higher on the West Shore, and there was much less moisture in the air.

As soon as we had arranged our belongings in the boat-house, after taking possession of it as a temporary home, the first thing I did was to drop a baited hook from between the railings of our indoor gallery and catch a mess of pan-fish for the noon meal. I soon found that it was an easy matter to tie hand-lines there and let them do the fishing for me while I was attending to the little daily tasks of this primitive housekeeping. The shut-in water proved to be full of small fish which took shelter there to escape the larger ones wriggling around outside the water-doors on the lookout for small fry.

I enjoyed these experiments in the "gentle art;" for, in our life over at The Hermitage the only fishing I had done was after Julius had made the Everglades skiff and we went for occasional half days to troll in the fresh-water for black bass. We would take turns in rowing, while the other held the line, baited only with a streamer of white cotton cloth. The bass snatched eagerly at the hook as it glided through the water hidden by the white scrap, and we usually carried back so much fish that we both had to make several trips from the boat, up the hill, carrying, each time, as much as we could lift.

These bass were rather coarse, and only a very fish-hungry human would relish them; but they made royal feasts for the cats and the fowls. We did not try to cook them indoors; but emptied the baskets into a huge iron kettle which stood on bricks in the corner of the chicken-park. Then the kettle was filled with water, and a fire built underneath. As soon as the fish had boiled, the fire was put out. It was amusing to see how well both cats and fowls understood the whole process, and how eagerly they awaited the climax. The kettle was tipped over to spill its contents on the ground to hurry the cooling and for convenience of access for the feasters. Cats and fowl all gathered around; and, every few seconds, some impatient member of the "invited guests" tried a taste. Of course tongues were burnt. When a fowl had taken a too hot morsel, it shook its head to flip the bit away, then wiped its hot beak on the ground. Kitty-Winks was the more impatient of the two cats; and, whenever she had burnt her little tongue, Catty-Meow at once shut his eyes and flattened his ears to take the drubbing he knew was coming. Her invariable habit of visiting the wrath of every disappointment on his meek head was a most striking example of the kinship of the cat with a certain type of woman. I have seen her human sister figuratively spit at and scratch the man at her mercy because the weather was disappointing; or for any other uncontrollable circumstance which had thwarted her wishes. We call such a woman "catty." It would not be inconsistent to call a cat like Kitty-Winks "as unreasonable as a woman!" She gave us occasion for many good laughs; and we always tried to make up to poor patient Catty-Meow for the unmerited punishments she gave him.

In all our trips to and fro between The Hermitage and our East Shore camp, we took the cats with us, and they soon learned to follow us like little dogs; stopping from time to time to rest and cool off; then up, and scampering on ahead again. We soon found it best to dispose of the fowls until such time as we should again be settled in one home; for on both sides of the Sound the wild growth was full of their natural enemies, and it made too much hard work to take them to and fro with us in the weekly migrations.

In those days we had only semi-occasional religious observances. The Home Missionary Society (what a joke it seemed to us to require the attention of the Home Missionaries!) had a clergyman engaged to travel up and down the East Coast of the State stopping in every settlement to hold services. He usually came to us at the end of each trip, as this was then the "Jumping-off Place." Two Sundays he rested among us, and then started back to make another circuit. Wind and tide made these trips irregular; but, on his arrival, word was sent from house to house, and, on Sunday morning the faithful worker usually found every man, woman and child, including the babies, gathered in the school-house for the purpose of "assisting" at a religious service which generally lasted two, and sometimes three hours! In this way, it once happened that Julius and I were prevented for two Sundays, from making our usual weekly pilgrimages to The Hermitage; and, at the end of the third week, we had a very severe North-East storm, with such heavy rain-squalls, that it was out of the question to venture forth. Luckily, we had heard through the mail-carrier, that the clergyman who had us on his conscience was approaching our settlement, and we had brought over from our home an extra supply of fresh garments. For bread, I had found a good neighbor who was willing to change work, and would bake for us in return for some fine stitchery of the sort I love to do. So we had done very well, though kept by circumstances in our simple camp for nearly a month.

At last, when we started back home, so eager were we to find ourselves again in the beloved rooms, we almost ran up the hill. In fact, the kits and I did have a race to the front door, while Julius followed with long strides, laughing at the eagerness which he plainly shared.

As soon as we entered we were struck with the "cluttered" appearance of the floor. It was strewn everywhere with ravellings and bits of yarn. Investigation showed that the yarn had been taken from the rugs, where it had ornamented the edges in the form of fringe.

The white ravellings proved to be of flax, and suggested an examination of our store of table-linen, which was kept in a home-made side-board Julius had built into the dining-room walls. Two of our best tablecloths had been tunneled through, and the fringe had apparently been neatly sliced from a pile of fruit-napkins.

"Can it be squirrels?" I asked.

"No. It's wild mice," said Julius. "They came in to find something soft to line their nests."

When he started out to the pump for a bucket of water, he noted that a corner of the outside kitchen-door had been gnawed off, then we understood how they had entered.

The cats prowled around, sniffing at everything, and showing an unusual interest in the edges of the rugs, the furniture and all the corners. It was quite evident that they "smelled a mouse;" but whether past or present, we could not determine.

Julius busied himself with kindling a fire in the cooking-stove and filling the kettle, while I mixed and cut out a pan of biscuit.

I found a table-cloth that was not all holes, and proceeded to set the table. This done; and finding that the biscuits were beginning to take on a handsome brown, I climbed on a chair to reach a pot of guava jelly from the top shelf where we kept our store of sweets. Next to the rows of fruit-jars were some empty tins which had contained coffee. Over the rim of one of them, from which the cover had been pushed aside, I noticed a flax ravelling hanging. Tip-toeing, I peeped inside, and met the startled glance of four beady black eyes. Carefully, I lifted down the tin, just as Julius entered the room with the armful of wood he had gone to seek.

"Look here," said I, "here are the little villains that played smash while we were gone!"

The two mice did not try to escape, because—faithful little parents!—nestled under their bodies were six naked baby-mice.

"Miserable little wretches!" cried Julius. "Here!" and lifting a red-hot lid from over the roaring fire, he dropped nest and inmates on a bed of white-hot coals, then clapped the cover back so quickly there was not a single squeak heard.

For a moment, it seemed to us both that the swift execution was perfectly just. Then, there was a sudden revulsion of feeling. Those little martyrs perishing in a vain endeavor to protect their babies when it would have been so easy to escape, leaving them to our vengeance! We felt like murderers. And yet, what else was possible? Their death was instant, and much less cruel than to let the kits follow their natural instincts to rid us of them. It was the best way; but we have never been able to feel that it was other than cruel and cowardly to take advantage of the parental love of those two noble little mites. Humans have an inherited hatred for all the tribes of rats and mice, and it is quite possible that, given the same circumstances, we would instinctively do exactly the same thing again; but I never recall that deed without a feeling of profound humiliation.

The kits kept on searching for their lawful quarry, and never seemed to understand why those very evident mice did not materialize.

Journeying back and forth, we never failed to remark the wide difference between our two abiding-places. The sweet, refreshing sleep and keen appetite produced by the effect of the pine-breath was noted every time we slept at The Hermitage. After much discussion, we finally decided to move back, and then to arrange to make a home on the water's edge of the West Shore, where we could be in reach of the pine-breath, and yet in touch with the people of the settlement.

It was a perfect day when we again loaded our belongings all into the boat, the cats looking on, then leaping aboard last of all, and paddled home from the boat-house, which had fully satisfied our longing to try a house-boat existence.

There was a blue haze on the face of the waters, and blending the soft greens of the further shores. The islands up and down the Sound, as we looked northward and southward while rowing to the other side, seemed to be suspended in the air—the sky, by some trick of reflection, showing plainly underneath their shore-lines.

The other landing reached, Julius loaded our belongings on a light hand-cart and started off, I following with the two small baskets of breakables. The kits scampered on before us doing all sorts of lively stunts in pure jollity. Now and then they stopped in pretended affright at the flutter of a scrub-oak branch, or the snapping of a twig against our brushing garments, or under the cart-wheels, turning big-eyed and swell-tailed, taking a few stiff-legged jumps like a bucking pony, then relaxing and scampering on again in mad races. When we reached the big half-way pine, we found that the cats had recognized one of the usual resting places and had already thrown themselves down panting in the shade.

Julius stopped and took two camp-stools from the cart for us to sit in comfort for a good rest and cool-off.

As we sat down, I said:

"Julius, we are just like two of these big wood-ants: always frantically dragging things around from one place to another."

Julius laughed, and responded:

"Well, we'll stop it. We'll make just one more move, then take a 'fo'-bar rest.' "

The next morning we awoke to find the wind blowing "half a gale;" the lovely day of our homecoming had proven to be what the sailors call a "weather-breeder."

The water was too rough to venture across to the settlement. We had two boats on the Sound. A skiff, and a small cat-boat which could be propelled by oars when winds refused to blow. Both made boating safe and pleasant in moderate seas; but when waves were rolling shoulder-high we did not feel tempted to venture from shore in such small craft.

These days alone—just we two and the kits—were full of quite enjoyment for us all. We set our attractive rooms in order, making renewed acquaintance with the shelves of books. Then we made some pots of jelly and jars of sweet-pickle of a basket of guavas we had brought from the bushes which shaded the shore windows of our East Side camp. Julius helped to peel the fruit and did stirring, while I measured and seasoned and tested.

When these pleasant tasks were finished, we found that the rain-squalls had ceased; but the winds were still high enough to keep us prisoners on shore; so we gathered up all the linen; built a fire under the big wash-kettle, which stood on bricks in a sheltered spot, and gave our attention to a thorough renovation of everything that needed a bath. We had found it necessary in our pioneering to acquire a working knowledge of the art of laundering. There being no laboring-women to be had on any terms, it was a question of knowing how to do it ourselves, or no fresh garments. Naturally we chose to learn, and found it was really an interesting experience. Julius wore negligee shirts, and crinkled seersucker coats. I had made me a large number of soft unbleached muslin frocks which, washed and shaken out to dry without starch, had the effect of cream wool. So there was neither starching nor ironing to do, only to make things sweet and fresh. Starch, we never used at all, and the only things I ironed were the table-cloths and napkins. For these, I experimented with the irons on some that were ragged, until I learned how to do them. After the proper hotness of the irons had been discovered, it was really fascinating to polish the damask and watch the snow figures shine forth from the back-ground of duller white. To make the coats; shirts; and my frocks dry in shape so they would not need to be pressed, Julius had made a number of wooden shoulder forms of some cut up hoops from a sugar-barrel. These were much better than the usual metal ones, because in a land fanned with salt-breezes everything rusts, so the metal forms would have corroded and left the garments full of brown rust stains.

There is a delightful sense of power that comes with the knowledge of how to do all things which are the foundations of our civilization. People who are brought up with the knowledge unconsciously acquired, by nature of their circumstances, to cook, wash, clean and do all the things usually summed up in the word "drudgery," do not fully realize the blessings of practical knowledge. It is taken for granted by them, and is even sometimes considered a misfortune. But to those who acquire this knowledge after maturity, it comes like a re-birth. The whole world is a different place—a puzzle solved—a riddle to which they have guessed the answer.

In pioneer life, the one who commands the situation, is not the man of means, or the one who has been enervated by a life of luxury; but it is the capable, resourceful man who is looked up to by all who find him rising to meet each emergency and overcome its difficulties. It is only in an artificial life that these things are discounted and ignored. All this was a revelation to me; but to Julius, who had pioneered in his childhood, on Western farms, with his parents, it was all an old story re-told, and he enjoyed it because of my vivid interest in this new, to me, side of nature.

As we worked at our diverting tasks, we always found pleasure in discussing everything, and in comparing our life with the adventures, and described feelings of our favorite child-hood heroes. Julius had, in addition to my own favorites—*Robinson Crusoe, Swiss Family Robinson,* and *The Young Marooners on the Florida Coast,* an old book called *Peter Wilkins. Or The Flying Islanders.* He had kept this treasure, which was long since out-of-print, and we both re-read it at The Hermitage. Often, while busy at some out-door task, we were diverted by seeing immense sand-hill cranes flying from one body of water to another, directly over our heads; and called one another's attention to them, crying:

"There go some of Peter Wilkins' flying Islanders!"

Of course we knew they were big birds; but it added to all the other romance around us to "play" they were winged people, of the sort we had found so fascinating in the old story-book.

After sun and wind had completed the refreshing of our house and body linen, there was still another blowy day to keep us prisoners.

Julius read aloud, while I did all the darning and mending. Then as sunset approached, we and the cats walked down the woods-path to the water's edge to see if the waves were still "A-lashing of their tails."

We found the Sound was not quite so rough as it had been for the past few days; but the waves were still too unruly for comfortable boating.

"The plot thickens," said Julius. "If the wind doesn't go down before long, we will be reduced to eating one another—or the cats!"

With all our camping-things to bring back from our experiment of boat-house living, we had not burdened ourselves with much in the way of groceries. Hominy, rice, beans and coffee, besides sugar, salt, and home-made sweets, had been left in abundance at The Hermitage from our Sunday visits home during all the time of our sojourn across the Sound. In starting back, we remembered there was neither flour nor bacon left there, so had bought a small supply of each, intending to go back the next day for more. The flour had already been consumed, and the bacon was nearly gone. We were using rice and hominy in lieu of bread. Also, the last of the kerosene had gone into the lamps that morning so, after another night, we should find ourselves in darkness.

We laughed about our funny plight, as we strolled back up the hill. Even privation has it charms, when it comes for such romantic reasons—because we were cut off from supplies, and from all mankind by high winds and towering waves!

We enjoyed our frugal evening meal, then sat and talked in the twilight until it was too dark to see across the rooms. It seemed prodigal to use our last lamp-full of oil until we were sure of a fresh supply. It was too early for us to be sleepy; but quoting "Early to bed, and early to rise," we made a virtue of a necessity, and turned in.

The next morning there was a decided change in the weather. The wind was less boisterous, and there was a softness in the air, showing that it was "going around," as the sailors say, when it follows the sun, instead of "backing up."

"The waves will still be high," said Julius, "but 'nothing ventured, nothing have,' and I am going to try to get across."

I don't believe you will find anything at the 'store' if you do," said I; "for most everything was getting low the last time we were there, and it is impossible that a schooner can have entered in this gale; or the mail-boat either."

Chapter Five

WITH THE hope of tidings from the outside world; and, also, a wish for the possible renewing of supplies, Julius set out right after our early breakfast, the next morning. It was a long day - the first time, in months, that the kits and I had kept house at The Hermitage.

About four o'clock I took the gun on my shoulder and called to my little comrades, who scampered joyfully to accept the invitation, and went down the woods-path, from time to time whistling the "Bob White" signal which I knew Julius would answer as soon as he was near enough to hear it. There came no responsive whistle until we approached the Sound; then there was a crystal-clear "Bob White," which told us he was at the landing. The kits recognized the signal and scampered down the bluff. I followed, and found Julius sitting in the boat drying his bare feet with his handkerchief, his socks and shoes on the stern-seat, which he faced from his perch on the gunwale.

"What!" I exclaimed. "Have you been wading?"

"Only about a mile, or two" Julius answered, laughing at my horror-struck tone.

"Why"—I began; and then I noted that the treacherous wind had veered to due north, and big white-caps were chasing each other down the wide expanse of water.

"How in the world did you manage to get back?" I cried.

"Main strength and awkwardness," laughed Julius. "I found I could neither sail nor row against this heavy sea, so I sailed straight across, from the 'store,' and beached the boat. Then I waded and dragged it along shore all the way here. I had just tied up when I heard you whistle."

He should have been "dead tired;" but the feat of overcoming formidable obstacles had produced an exhilaration that more than counterbalanced the effects of supreme exertion.

The first thing he lifted from the boat was a good-sized bag of flour.

"What," I exclaimed, "has our ship really got in?" Julius laughed.

"Well, that depends on how you look at it. A ship certainly brought this; but it was neither the 'Mary' nor the 'Bessie.' There has been another wreck, with more flour and candles. That seems to be a favorite 'blend' in our exports. The beach is strewn with packages of both; so that everybody is over-supplied, and we may have as much more as we can carry home."

"Didn't the flour get soaked in the waves?" I naturally asked, after the first sensations of mixed sympathy for the mariners, and romantic interest in a "sure-enough wreck" had subsided.

"A little," admitted Julius; "but only on the outside. It was packed in immense duck bags; and, as soon as a little water had soaked through the cloth, the flour 'caked,' making a crust all over the outside, so the inside of each bag was dry and fresh. Those who picked up the jetsam had at once dipped out the dry flour from the middle of each bag. They told me they have found from past experience that this is always necessary, or the contents will mold and be no good."

"What else came ashore?" I asked.

"All sorts of things—bales and bales of cotton. They offered me some. You don't want any, do you?"

"No. We've no use for it; and it is too heavy to drag away over here simply because it is to be had 'free-gratis-for-nothing.' "

Julius laughed again.

"I'm glad you're not a bargain-hunter." he said.

"No, it weighs on my mind to have things around for which we have no use. Did you find any kerosene at the store?"

"Not a drop. Everybody is out. Our boats are still unable to get in the Inlet. One was sighted standing off-shore this morning, tacking up and down, waiting for the high rollers to subside. No kerosene has thus far come ashore from the wrecked schooner. The waves are still bringing things ashore, though, and there is no telling what may yet turn up. I would have gone over to the beach, but I knew it would make me so late."

"How about the mail?"

"Oh, that got in yesterday. There are some letters in my pocket, and no end of papers. I have them all tied up together here in the locker to keep them from the spray."

It was getting late, and we hurried to load everything into the hand-cart which Julius had brought down with him in the morning and left in the bushes near the landing. Making all possible speed, it was late twilight when we reached The Hermitage and got our "cargo" unloaded.

We used the last of our kerosene that evening to devour the large bundle of papers and the pocketful of letters that Julius had brought; and, as the kerosene famine still continued over at the two "stores," while we waited for the waves to go down so that our ships could come in, we thankfully availed ourselves of the candles that had come ashore from the wreck, which were of the commonest tallow variety, and returned to "the light of other days." They made a very dim glow; but it was much better than sitting in darkness; and, as there was such a good supply of them many candles could be burned at once, the necessary candlesticks being improvised in all sorts of ingenious ways. We often laughed, during these days of many privations, at our conception of pioneering during our first year or two in Florida. We had then thought we were "roughing it" with a vengeance; but not once during those days had we been more than three days without mail, or more than twelve miles on good, solid, dry land, from every sort of supply, including ice, and a meat-market. Compared with a city life, we had roughed it then; but it was luxury compared with our experiences at The Hermitage. And this severe pioneering was not without its wholesome lesson. It taught appreciation of what we had always taken as a matter of course. Julius and I have never since then turned on a drop-light, for an evening of enchantment with our books, without thinking of the blessing it is, and comparing its comfort with our pioneer makeshifts.

Although there was a degree of pleasure, heretofore unknown in our quiet days at The Hermitage, just our two selves and the lively kits, we never once changed the plan of making another, less-isolated home. We looked up and down the West Shore of the Sound, pricing the various pieces of land which were available, and weighing the advantages and the disadvantages of each.

At last, we came to a decision.

The place chosen was a five-acre tract on the shore, about a mile south of the landing place which was our outlet from The Hermitage. Three acres were already cleared, and two were set with pine-slips. There was a small new house so constructed that additional rooms might easily be added. There was also a wharf long enough to accommodate any boat not drawing more than eighteen inches. The deed to it called for riparian rights, which to us was a great attraction. We were also attracted by the natural beauty of its high front sloping down to the water, and the excellence of the soil, which had been covered, next the water, with a forest-growth of mixed spruce-pine and hard-woods.

Thus we became the happy possessors of The Blessed Isle.

It was not really an island; but, like The Hermitage, it was across the water from everything, and the only way to go anywhere, was by boat. We looked across to the settlement, and, on clear days, could signal to the other side. Out on the wharf we had a fine view up and down the Sound, of points running out from both shores, and of islands of various shapes and sizes, covered with palms and other growth.

As soon as the papers had passed giving us possession, we began to make preparations to transfer our belongings. These were few and simple; but it does not take much to make moving a rather formidable task under the circumstances which then surrounded us.

First, it was necessary to put up a fowl-house and wire-netting fence; for, as soon as we had gone back to The Hermitage we had again conjured around us a flock of hens and a chanticleer both for the eggs which we "couldn't keep house without," and for their sociable cackling, clucking, and crowing. These must be moved with us; for they could not be left alone, even for a single night, to the forest's dangers.

Julius found a man to help him, and went down to The Blessed Isle for a long, busy day, while the kits and I stayed at The Hermitage, sorting and packing things ready for carting. The kits did their best to help. They seemed to divine that some great change was pending, and were, by turns, frolicsome; wistful and coaxing. It was a day filled with strong and varying emotions.

There were many pleasures and many regrets in the proposed change. The Hermitage had been so completely our home—so really our own creation, evolved from wildest nature, that it was harder to give up than was any other we had ever left. We had found it an unbroken forest, tied together with wild vines and undergrowth and we had made it a home blest with a charm of real comfort and beauty.

I took down the white draperies from the windows; and rolled up the crimson rugs with feelings of regret tempered by the hope that events might so shape themselves as to let us return some day. We had already packed the books, Julius and I together, in boxes of convenient size for handling. I took down the pictures, and packed the bits of statuary—souvenirs, brought from our city home. Thinking today, of this dismantling, brings the inviting living-room of The Hermitage vividly to mind. Its fluffy white window-draperies; the artistic bits; touches of crimson; shelves of books and the tall jars of branches and wild grasses.

Big pine-trees, dark and stately, were just out-side the windows and doors, yielding cool shadows, spicy odors and mysterious murmurings. Just beyond the biggest, seen from our North windows, our tents had been pitched. Everything about this forest home reminded of some difficulty met and conquered; and, as it is one of human nature's strongest traits to value things in proportion to what they cost. The Hermitage seemed a part of our very selves.

Julius returned just after dark, with a favorable report of the day's work. They had finished the house for our feathered family, all except shingling the roof, which could be left till we moved, as the roof-strips were close enough together to be some protection from both rain and wild creatures. The wire netting had been set up temporarily around the coop so the fowls would not stray off in their strange surroundings; he had stopped, on his way home, to engage a large roomy sloop to be at our landing place the next afternoon, to take our belongings from the old landing to the new. The books, and a few other things, were too heavy for us to handle alone; so two men had been engaged—one of them was the skipper, and the other was the "crew" of the aforesaid sloop—to come early in the morning and help about the carting. Julius found that I had everything packed except the "livestock." This was to be done at the last minute, in boxes, with slats nailed across the tops to keep them from escaping.

Two big boxes were required to hold the fowls; and a small one for the cats. It was necessary to confine the kits; because they were so unused to the sight of strangers that one glimpse of an unknown form; or the first word of an unfamiliar voice, always sent them scampering away to hide, and no amount of coaxing would bring them back until they had seen, from their hiding-place, the departure of those who had so startled them. This being the case we knew that the only way to be sure of having them go with us, was to shut them up in their traveling-case before our helpers had arrived. This was done the first thing in the morning. Both cats and fowls were nailed up in their crates and set to one side to be out of the bustle, all ready to set on top of the last load. From time to time, I snatched a minute to go and assure them it was all right. At first, all were indignant at the confinement; but the kits soon adapted themselves to circumstances and went to sleep; and the fowls, after eating and drinking the supplies given them, sat on the floors of the crates "talking" in their queer way, as if exchanging views of the probable meaning of it all.

When the last load was completed by the addition of the three crates, Julius insisted that I should be perched up beside them; but I chose to walk behind, carrying the cast of "Meditation" which I had not been willing to trust in any of the packages.

As soon as the cart started down the hill, a concert began. The fowls fluttered and cackled in indignant protest; while the cats yowled plaintively. These discordant sounds, and the many incongruities of the procession, suddenly sent me into one of my absurd fits of laughing. The bewildered expression on Julius' face did not help matters.

The helpers were plodding along, drawing the cart; Julius walked along side, steadying the packages, and watching me over his shoulder; the live-stock protested at every jolt; and I brought up the rear, hugging Meditation in my arms as if she were a big doll, while I struggled with fits of laughter which shook me anew, with each fresh outcry from the "passengers."

Sometimes I think it is great luck to be foolish; for it enables one to find amusement in things which are only annoying from a sensible point of view!

The afternoon was drawing toward twilight when we arrived at the landing. The boat was there waiting, and the loading at once began. I was not needed to help about that; so I sat down among the boxes of livestock to talk to them and help to calm them so they could gather their scattered wits and make ready for their voyage.

I kept one eye on the loading; and was not surprised to see that, after a few of the larger pieces had been carried aboard, the skipper cast off from the landing, and poled out into deeper water to anchor. Then he paddled in with the tender and all the rest of our belongings were lightered out to the sloop. The wind had shifted to due south; and the tide was also ebbing, so the water was going down with a rapidity which made everybody ready to take all precautions against getting stuck for the night on the sandy bottom of the Sound.

It was slow work lightering out boxes and bundles, and the final load, of which cats, fowls and I were the last parcels, were loaded into the tender, with barely light enough to prevent slips. As Julius helped me from skiff to sloop he said:

"We have filled the sloop pretty full, and the cats and fowls must stay in the tender and be towed."

"Must they?" I protested. "I am afraid they will not like that at all. I was counting on having them close to me, so I could talk to them if the waves upset their nerves."

"It can't be helped," said Julius. "It is the only place left for them, and they will soon quiet down."

As soon as the anchor was lifted aboard, the boat began to drift stern-first. The wind held dead ahead, and had freshened with sunset. The sails snapped like pistol-shots. Presently, they filled; the sloop answered her rudder with a stately swing, and we were off on the first tack. It was not what sailors call "a long leg and a short leg" breeze; both "legs" were short. As the East shore loomed up close before our bow, we "came about" with much snapping of sails; cackling of fowls; and protests from terrified kits; then, cut a bright arrow of foam on a merry clip toward the West shore.

Back and forth we tacked, from the sandy points running out from the Western shores, to approach again the rocky banks of the East side. Julius sat beside me in the cock-pit, tired out with the day's struggles against that total depravity of inanimate things, of which one is always convinced anew at moving-time. He seemed to doze a little, and took no notice of our surroundings. My fits of laughing had thoroughly rested me from the effects of the toilsome day, and I sat, still hugging Meditation, with every sense alert. Sympathizing with the cats and fowls each time the boat jounced them by wallowing in the trough of the waves as we turned; and between whiles, enjoying the wild beauty of the waves and sky. The water was full of racing "white-horses," and the Heavens were tumultuous with vast armies of scuds flying up from the Southern horizon, and speeding over our heads to disappear to the Northward.

After a long time of beating back and forth, I became convinced that we were not progressing as we should, and reached over to Julius, saying:

"Julius, there must be something the matter with the boat. We have passed that same light on shore, there, four times."

"We have?" he exclaimed, springing up and scanning the shore-line.

It did not take long for him to grasp the situation. Then he called out to the skipper:

"What's the matter with your boat, Jim" We aren't making any headway!"

"Yes sir. I see," answered the skipper. I jes' been studyin' about it."

"How's your center-board?" asked Julius.

And without waiting for the answer, he went over to investigate for himself.

It was drawn up tight in its well, with its rope cleated to hold it fast.

"Of all the idiots!" muttered Julius. Then to the skipper:

"What's the matter, Jim? Have you forgotten you are running a flat-bottomed boat?"

Jim was profuse in his apologies, and could not explain why he had been so forgetful. He meekly reached for the end of the center-board rope, assuring "Marse Julius" that he wouldn't forget it any more, and that now we should "Begin to hump along shore-nuff."

Having lost so much valuable time, the skipper was desirous to make it up, if possible. He held the boat so close to the wind as we sped away on our Westward tack, that she tipped over until we felt like flies on a wall, as we clung to the rolling waves. It looked as if we and all our helpless cargo would end by being swallowed up in the raging waters which boiled up with roars of protest at our progress.

All at once, we heard a harsh sound of scraping; and, before our skipper could change her headway, the sloop was hard aground—stuck in the sand of a West Shore point. The little boat behind came bang up against us as we stopped in our mad career, and stirred up the crates of fowls and cats to the most frenzied protests. The fowls fluttered and cackled. The cats made the most dismal caterwaulings. The sails snapped, and winds whistled through the rigging. Pandemonium reigned.

Julius sprang to the tiller, shouting to the skipper and his "crew" to take the poles and push as hard as they could to force the boat back into the channel.

Chapter Six

AT LAST the two men succeeded in poling the boat back into water deep enough for us to swing free. Julius kept the tiller until we were far enough out in the channel to let the center board drop again, then the skipper came back to resume his rightful position. Before giving it up Julius asked what in the world was the matter with him to make him bungle things as he had done; and received in response a renewed profusion of apologies and excuses about drowsiness after "sech a hawd day's wuk" and "de way de moonlight gits inter a fellow's eyes." Julius gave him the necessary sympathy for his state of fatigue, then urging him to be more alert, came back to his place beside me. All went well on the Eastward tack. We stood up close to the rocky East shore, gaining more than on any previous tack. When we swung, and started on the Westward tack, all felt encouraged. We were really making progress, and the shore-light we had passed so many times was now some perceptible distance in our wake. The white-capped waves raced to meet us; the West shore rose up close and distinct in the moon-light; then, again came that ominous grating sound, and there we were, repeating the whole program on the next point. In short, every point along the West Shore between the landing we had left and the one we finally reached, received, on its bosom, the impression of our boat's keel. Under ordinary circumstances, that is: with winds, not too high for full sail, and either beam, or following, the voyage from wharf to wharf should have consumed about twenty minutes; or, at most, half an hour; we were from twilight to one o'clock in the morning making this short run.

When we finally reached a place in the racing waves which was directly opposite to the wharf of The Blessed Isle, our skipper declared it would not be possible to land. The continued South winds, and the low tide, had carried out the water, so that, heavy-laden as we were, it would be dangerous to try to reach the wharf. We anchored out in the edge of the channel, then Julius and I crawled meekly over the side of the boat into the dancing little tender among the cat and chicken crates, followed by the "crew" who rowed us to the wharf. We dragged ourselves thankfully up on the good firm boards, which we felt like embracing after our half night on the uncertain deep—and shoals. Then, together, Julius and the "crew" lifted up the boxes of livestock. Past midnight, though it was, each took a box and hastened up the bank to the fowl house to let the poor creatures out into roomier quarters. Left alone with the kits, I looked around for something with which to open their prison. An oar was the first thing I spied, and sticking its handle-end between the slats, I soon pried off one of them.

The cats did not stop long enough to say a "thank-you;" but dashed from the box, raced madly along the wharf, and disappeared among the inky shadows of the moonlit shore. As they were swallowed in shrub-shadows, Julius came back down the bank talking earnestly with the man who had helped him carry up the fowls. As soon as he reached me, sitting on the wharf beside the emptied cat-crate, with Meditation again clasped in my arms, where, except for the few seconds of standing on the wharf while I released the kits, she had been ever since the beginning of the voyage, Julius said:

"Judith, how few of our things can we get along with until daylight?" We can't ask these men to do any more now than is absolutely necessary; so we must leave as much as possible out on the sloop until morning. We ought to get along with only one more row out and back. Everybody is hungry. The men can't get home this time of night for food. What can you give them?"

I thought for a few seconds, then told him we must have the kerosene stove; the oil-can; the basket of cooked food; and a box,

146

containing tinned food; kitchen utensils; coffee, sugar and so forth; which I directed him to recognize. These things, with the skipper and "crew" would make just about a skiff-load, and I had packed the big box with such care to have all the first-needed things together, that nothing more would be necessary. Well-pleased with this, he left me, and I proceeded to open the house and light a small lamp which, luckily, had been left there. Very soon, Julius appeared carrying the tea-kettle in one hand, and the food-basket in the other. He was followed by the men, one with the kerosene stove, and the other with the oil-tank. They set these down on the floor and went back to the wharf for the box of supplies, while I filled and lighted the stove. Julius, meanwhile, was busy at the well, which needed a thorough pumping out before the water came clear enough for use. The kettle soon began to sing. Julius ground and watched the coffee coming to perfection, while I opened tins and concocted a big pot of stew—a mixture of beef, tomatoes and various seasonings, thickened with broken biscuit—known among sailors as "scouse." The main thing was to have something hot and savory; for nobody had eaten since noon, and all were thoroughly chilled and damp from wind and spray. The two good men were as helpful as possible; and, before I took time for a bite, I filled mugs and bowls for them and sent them out on the sheltered porch where they could sit at ease to enjoy their hot coffee, bread and stew. As soon as they had eaten, the men slipped out, and I supposed they had gone to the wharf to smoke; but they came back in a few minutes with the bale of mattresses, pillows and bedding, having made another trip to the sloop in the little boat. We had not intended to ask this. In fact, after being buffeted by wind and wave for half the night, there was no hardship in the idea of sleeping on a good, hard floor, on the dear solid ground. When we thanked the men for being so thoughtful they assured us they "never meant Misis to be leff widout a good bed to res'," and wishing us a "good-night," though it was nearly daylight, they went back to sleep on the boat while Julius and I soon had a comfortable resting place arranged where we passed the remaining hours of darkness in dreams of being dragged by raging winds through stormy seas.

Just as I was losing consciousness, there came a sound of scratching at the door, and a faint "meow." I sprang eagerly to admit the two tired little travelers, who scampered straight to the dishes of food I had saved for them and ate with gratifying enthusiasm. Then, after washing their coats from noses to tails, they curled up together on the edge of my pillow and purred happily to dream-land.

We were awakened at earliest dawn by the hungry fowls. Crocus crowed vociferously, which started an eager clamor among his wives.

Thrusting his feet into the slippers, which I, by this time an experienced mover, had rolled up in the bale of bedding, Julius sallied forth in his night-toga to feed and water the inmates of the fowlery.

He protested, on his return, to find me already up and dressing, that I should go back to sleep, and lie long enough to get well rested; but I assured him there was no rest for me so long as all our household gods were out there pitching around on the boiling waves. The wind was now blowing "half a gale" and I felt especially anxious about our books and pictures. All were still out in the sloop—all our art-treasures, except Meditation, who had come ashore with me, and now stood, with finger on lips, lost in thought among a few incongruous little trinkets I had packed in the food-basket.

I had filled the kettle as soon as I waked, and it was now boiling merrily. Julius ground the coffee, and, by the time he was dressed, I had breakfast spread on the box which had contained the kitchen things.

As Julius 'rose from the table, I asked him to go down and call the men to see if they wanted some breakfast. He soon returned saying the little boat was gone, so we knew they had rowed home for refreshment. It was blowing harder than ever and the waves were high; but, in broad daylight there was no danger, for experienced sailors, in a short row through such a sea.

While waiting for the men to return and begin lightering in our precious freight, we busied ourselves washing dishes and folding up the bedding, of which we made a heap, beginning with the mattresses, in an out of the way corner. The soap, dish towels, and all needful supplies, were in among the kitchen things, and the bale of bedding had contained a package of fresh hand-towels, so we lacked nothing for comfort in beginning a new day.

The kits raced around, exploring every corner, sniffing at Meditation when they encountered her, in making the circuit of the larger room, then giving her a roguish slap, as in greeting to an old friend discovered among such unfamiliar surroundings. They were apparently no worse for their strenuous voyage, and eagerly responded to the invitation to make a hearty breakfast before engaging in a lively game of romps.

Julius reported the fowls to be in equal condition—gaily gobbling up the fat worms and bugs in the wire enclosure, then exploring nest-possibilities.

It is great fun to watch fowls when they are first turned out to "graze" on virgin soil. They have such an enthusiastic way of going for the "small deer" awaiting their pleasure. From the worm and bug point of view it is probably less amusing; but, as our French cousins say: "What would you?" Somebody always has to pay the price of each pleasure in this world; and bugs, worms, and so forth, seem to be provided solely for the enjoyment of feathered creatures.

The men soon re-appeared and announced themselves ready to begin the day's work of unloading. Julius went out with them, and, the tide having risen, they managed to pole the sloop nearer shore; but the wind still blowing from the South kept the water too low for the heavy-laden boat to reach the wharf. It was almost an equal struggle—a tug-of-war between the tide coming in the Inlet, and the due-South wind sweeping the water North-ward out the Inlet—that gate-way from sound to ocean.

The sun shone brightly; and, as fast as our effects were brought ashore, I unpacked and spread them out to get the benefit of sun and wind after their damp voyage.

All went well until the last load started. This consisted of the boxes of books, which, being the heaviest part of our freight, had been loaded first; and, until now, had reposed on the floor of the boat's cabin. From the top of the bank I anxiously watched these heavy boxes being lifted out and lowered into the little boat which was dancing and tipping in all directions, the sport of boiling waves and whistling winds.

Apparently somewhat steadied by the weight of the heavy boxes, the boat made a good start; but, midway between sloop and wharf, a big wave raced up to give the skiff a broadside slap which turned it completely over in a twinkling. My heart seemed to turn with it, as I saw the boxes of books spill into the waves, sink then bob up around the boat. The water was only about eighteen inches to two feet deep, so there was no danger of losing the boxes; but the soaking in salt water was almost worse than a total loss of them would have been. The boxes were loosely put together, with big cracks on all sides—simply crates to hold them bunched for convenience of handling. Julius had not gone out for this last trip, but had remained on the wharf busy with boxes already landed. He called to the men, who were floundering in the waves, to catch the floating cargo and get it out as quickly as possible; for the packages contained "books we wouldn't take a farm for." They hustled them out at once, and carried them dripping and leaking up the bank on the ground directly in front of the house. Julius came running with the hatchet, and all the boxes were quickly opened. Then all hands fell to unpacking them. The soaked volumes were spread out on the dry sand in the sunniest places; and I mounted guard, turning them every few minutes for the rest of the day, only snatching hurried minutes for pressing housekeeping duties. Everything was neglected until the books were made as dry as possible; but they never entirely recovered from this wetting. Their bloated, discolored appearance is still a constant reminder of our difficult and adventurous move to The Blessed Isle.

Now began an entirely new chapter in our pioneering experiences. Although I was often all day alone, except for the kits and fowls, we were in sight of human habitations, and boats were constantly passing. Sometimes they, with head-winds, tacked in, almost grazing our little wharf. Again, they were mere specks in the distance; but always, they gave the welcome knowledge that human beings were near; and there was among all the 'long-shore settlers, the understanding that a white flag displayed on any wharf meant some sort of emergency which the first boat passing must investigate. This gave a feeling of security which was doubly welcome after the isolation of The Hermitage, where nothing was in sight that even remotely suggested anything except wildest nature and a loneliness which sometimes made me wonder—when there alone—what would happen if Julius were in some way prevented from returning home. If I should "dry up and blow away;" or if the eagles, which constantly passed and re-passed overhead, would swoop to carry me off. These morbid imaginings disappeared entirely on The Blessed Isle. When alone, I carried my work to the front of the house, or out under the trees, where I felt the companionship of passing boats; or of specks moving on the opposite shore which I knew to be humans.

Living on the water's edge was also very much easier for Julius, because the long walk from the Sound's edge back to The Hermitage had always been the most laborious part of his home-coming; especially, as there were many burdens to be transported. At The Blessed Isle there was only the trifling exertion of the short distance from the wharf up to the house. I was always on the lookout for his return; and, on very clear days, could see his boat detach itself from the further shore. Then I would go down to the wharf, always followed by the kits, and we three formed a reception committee always on hand to welcome and escort the king of The Blessed Isle to his throne.

The dear home we had left with such reluctance and with so much difficulty, was not long regretted; for we found that as soon as the new rooms were set in order and were decorated with our own belongings, the home-fairies had moved with them.

The kits accepted the change with the adaptability of youth; but they were shy and bashful to a degree. They so invariably scampered to hide under the house at the approach of visitors, that their ideas of the outside world of human-kind were confined to the difference in feet, ankles and voices.

A few weeks after we had made the change of residence, Kitty-Winks came in one day, as I sat sewing by the open door, and climbed up on my lap with the air of having a great secret to impart. She was so insistent, that I soon gave her my whole attention. First, she coaxed with all her "endearing young charms"—purring, and reaching up to thrust her little muzzle against shoulder and cheek. Then she sprang to the floor and made the rounds of the rooms, exploring all the sheltered nooks and corners before coming back to offer more caresses.

Anyone wise in the lore of Cat-dom could not fail to understand these maneuvers. She was announcing the—to me—astonishing fact that she was grown up and was ready to go housekeeping. She was still so kittenish and full of pranks, that it was a complete surprise to find that she realized herself to be no longer a kitten; but a full-grown cat.

I emptied a basket, showing it to her to see if that was really what she was asking for. Yes; that was it. She climbed in, treading and digging at it with her claws until I had lined it to her satisfaction with some soft fragments of worn garments. Then, treading it to shape the nest to her liking, she curled up in its depths and purred herself to sleep.

We had already begun setting our hens. Several had been supplied with as many eggs as they could cover; and others were beginning to cluck and to ruffle up their feathers in the self-important manner of the hen who is ready to perform the ever-wonderful miracle of summoning life from the sealed egg shell. We began to look forward to much joyous young life around us. The various birds of The Blessed Isle had given us so sweet a welcome on our arrival there, that we wondered if they were not our friends of The Hermitage who had moved with us. Redbirds made themselves at home in the yard with the fowls—sharing their drinking-fountain and food just as they had done at The Hermitage. The quails came first in pairs, and then with their broods of spidery youngsters, to fraternize with Crocus and his wives. Wild doves joined them; thrushes and mocking-birds too, and jays, the sauciest, boldest and most irrepressible of birds, quarreled impartially with all the others, including the fowls and the kits. Often an entire meal was taken from the little cats by these robbers; who flapped impudent wings at them, and then snatched morsels and made off before the kits realized what had happened. Following their example, the mocking birds also began to bully the kits in so barefaced a manner, that their little porch was often invaded by several pairs at once, and they coaxed to be fed inside, where these marauders could not follow. There is something positively uncanny about the blue-jays' fearless impudence.

Hunters call them the policemen of the forest, and many a good shot has been spoiled for the pot-hunter by a blue-jay, who gave the alarm in time for the quarry to escape.

One day we heard a workman, who was helping us, violently apostrophizing some enemy, and found he had been robbed as he sat under a tree enjoying the contents of his dinner pail, by a blue-jay that swooped down to snatch a toothsome cake, just as the mouth had opened for a first bite. The robber flew with his booty to a safe distance up in the tree and held it with his foot against the branch while he jeered at the offered abuse, and then proceeded to enjoy the purloined dainty. As we found that any effort to drive away the thievish, quarrelsome jays, made the dear songsters shy, we soon abandoned the effort and decided to get what fun we could out of their rascality and let them stay. In some mysterious fashion, they evidently understood our attitude toward them, and it seemed as if all the jays in the country flocked to nest on The Blessed Isle, and to share the good things provided, a never-failing supply of fresh water, much appreciated in a land where only salt-water was to be found; and all sorts of inviting eatables provided for cats, fowls and any wild creatures that had the audacity to come and eat. There was one mocking bird which was as shameless as the jays. He did not hesitate to watch for the cat-dishes to be filled, then swoop down and hold the poor pussies at bay until he had "sorted out" all the morsels that pleased his taste. When he alighted on the side of their dish, making a harsh scolding sound, the kits always flattened down their ears, shut their eyes, and backed away until the belligerent little snatcher had made his choice and flown. Later this robber, as well as the jays, brought half-grown fledglings to share the stolen feasts so that there was nothing left for the cats, and this was the way the bird-table came to be an institution on The Blessed Isle.

Chapter Seven

AN OAK sapling was sawed off, making a post about five feet high, and a small board was nailed on the top. This was the bird-table; and it did not take long for all the birds far and near to receive a "wireless" inviting them to come and join the happy throngs always to be found there. Each morning a fresh dish of water was filled for them and a pan of grain, usually wheat, was set beside the water-dish. It was diverting to watch the feather guests bathe in the dish and then sit on its edge to drink from their bath-water. Their splashings were often so vigorous, that before the morning was over, complaining chirps usually called me to refill the dish for late comers who found it emptied. Sometimes this happened several times a day and it was dramatic to see the birds grouped around on neighboring boughs waiting for the water and then beginning, as soon as the dish was filled, to squabble over who should have the first baths and drinks. This bird-table has, ever since, been one of the institutions of The Blessed Isle and many generations of birds have happy memories of the Bird-table at The Blessed Isle, where food, drink, baths and good company never failed them.

There were, in those days, not many expert accountants in our remote corner of the world, so Julius soon found himself possessed of two public offices—that of Assessor, by election and that of Collector, by appointment. The work was not difficult to one so at home with figures as he has always been; but there was one great hardship attached. It was necessary for him to go all over the county, personally interviewing the head of each household and inspecting every piece of property. In a spacious county, where there is not one single mile of railroad and no steamboats, this is far from being an easy task and the time consumed made it a real hardship. Julius began to find it necessary to be from home two and three days and nights at a stretch. An unattached spinster of mature age used to come from across the Sound to keep me company on these occasions.

When Julius was at home, between trips, he and I worked together on the tax-books. I have ever belonged to that grand army of women who have to count on their fingers to make change; but it does not take a brilliant mathematician to copy rows of names and figures; nor to manipulate one of those ingenious little contrivances called an "adder." We passed many long days and evenings at this work, sitting until we were benumbed from toes to brain; then dropping pen and pencil to go racing down the bluff and out to the end of the wharf to take what Julius called the "kinks" out of our bones. Then back at it again, as fast as we could work; for there was a limit to the time allowed for making the tax-books, much of which was necessarily consumed in going to interview the tax payers.

It is not possible to give one's best efforts to even the stupidest and most uncongenial task without taking a vivid interest therein; and, as we neared the end of making the set of tax-books, we were both full of eager thrills to see if they would come out even. There was a corresponding degree of satisfaction and many mutual congratulations, when we found that the balance was exact between the totals. As the multitude of tiny sums began with parts of mills, ranging up through fractions of cents, to dollars in imposing array, I had more than ever a great admiration for the mathematical knowledge and skill which Julius displayed in his work—as one always admires the accomplishments one does not possess.

Our pleasure in the completion of this great undertaking—the making of one great book and its two exact copies—was not unalloyed. We knew that as soon as they were done Julius would be obliged to leave home and complete his work by traveling over the county to collect all that vast array of sums, little and big. This series of trips was not without its many hardships, and even dangers. First, there was the long journey to the county seat to have the books approved. Several of our neighbors had, from time to time, had occasion to make this voyage and we knew it meant a twenty or thirty days' absence for Julius, with no opportunity for a single exchange of letters during the separation. All sorts of things might happen to either one of us during this tedious interval, without the other knowing anything about it. We both dreaded it inexpressibly; but we had long since learned that the necessary is always the possible; so we busily engaged in the preparations for his departure. A big coasting-boat was chartered and several tourists who had been awaiting the opportunity to make the voyage were notified that there was room for them on board, at once sharing the expense of the trip and adding to the pleasure. The chartering of the boat and her captain were the only large expenses of the trip, as each member of the party carried his own supply of food and bedding and all were willing, even eager, for the romance of taking turns in every kind of work—from cooking, in the boat's little galley, to steering and handling sails. All seemed to take it for granted that I should be of the party; but I saw no way to leave our Blessed Isle. There were the two kits to make happy, to say nothing of all the faithful hens dreaming on their nests of fluffy little biddies asleep in the eggs under them. There were also birds to feed; plants to be watered; and, more than all the rest, business matters that must be looked after—people coming long distances; or sending their messengers—to question and arrange about paying their all-important taxes. These must be attended to and there was no one who could answer their questions, take their money and give them receipts for it, with Julius gone, unless I stayed to take his place. The feeling that I positively could not be spared from home held me there; and I saw the gay party set sail with a sinking of heart that no one was allowed to guess. For several days, after all preparations had been complete, favorable conditions for sailing had been awaited. To pass out to sea through the Inlet with any degree of comfort and safety, it was necessary to have the combination of a light Westerly wind and an outgoing tide. For half a week grips, food-boxes, rolls of bedding and the big box of precious tax-books, had been in a state of readiness awaiting the Captain's signal. This came, like all long-expected things, at an unexpected time.

The wind suddenly fell and changed one afternoon just as the tide turned. The long, musical notes of the Captain's conch-horn were wafted across the Sound; and, in a twinkling, all was hurry and confusion. We could see the white-winged sharpie gliding along close to the further shore of the Sound, then touching at the wharf long enough to get the other members of the cruising party aboard, before coming, last of all, to take on the piles of "plunder" heaped up on the wharf of The Blessed Isle and complete its passenger list. The spinster who had promised to stay with me during the three or four weeks of Julius's absence was to come across with the cruising party and be dropped as Julius and his baggage were being taken aboard. At the last minute this lady caught the enthusiasm of the cruisers and, instead of having her "big box, little box and band-box" handed out on the wharf of The Blessed Isle, she commanded that they be left in the boat's cabin, where she had decided to stay and join the cruising party. Julius was, to use his own words, "floored" by the disconcerting change in the program, as were all his sailing companions. It would be more of a crowd than anyone wished, with one more added to the list of passengers; then I was left, at the last minute, with no provision for company during the month of loneliness. Julius hurriedly named over several who might be willing and at leisure to come for a change, each one for a week or more of the time of his absence and told me to send, at once, a note by a hired man who was then busy in the pineapple field and would, at sundown, go back to his home across the Sound. I re-assured his uneasiness; but was very careful not to promise anything, for it was late in the day to make new arrangements and I had already resolved in my own mind, to try the experiment of a night or two alone. There were unmistakable drawbacks to being shut up in a small house with a comparative stranger who must be cared for and entertained. And who possibly would be full of contagious panics and tremors at our isolation. All my various families would be company and occupation enough for me; and then, there was some work I had been neglecting while we were so absorbed in the tax-book-making, which I had been longing for leisure to get done. There would be scant time for anything, if I had a visitor to look after and amuse.

When the boat had cast off and swung into the channel on her way northward to the Inlet, a silence that could be felt, swooped down on The Blessed Isle. There had been the hurry, bustle and confusion of embarking—rushing back to the house for some important item that had been overlooked—boxes of matches, a bag of salt, an extra blanket, one more camp-stool. Then the mingled shouts of goodbyes and sailing orders; the snapping of sails as the ropes drew them into position; the rattle of blocks on mast and "traveler"—all these sounds were finally hushed in the swishing of cleft waves and murmuring wake-ripples.

The cats were sitting on the piazza as I went back to the lonely house and came scampering in a race to see who would first reach me at the top of the bluff.

The fowls had gathered at the chicken-park gate and were calling and "singing" for their evening meal.

Jays and song-birds were circling around their table scolding because their dishes needed replenishing. There were all the usual evening sounds; and yet, the thought of the long separation, lying like a stone on my heart, made all these sounds only a part of an infinite silence—a vast emptiness.

Happily, there was plenty to do. First, the fowls and birds claimed attention. A handful or two of grain in the bird-dishes; many handfuls scattered in the enclosure for Crocus and his greedy family; then nests to explore in their house for the new-laid eggs that were numerous enough to heap up the grain-measure which had held their food. When these were carried indoors, there were the rooms to be set in order, where gathering up the necessaries for the departure of Julius had left confusion. The cats had waited patiently for their dishes to be filled and while they were making a dainty meal of bread and "tin milk" I had time to realize that the sun had sunk and the short tropical twilight was giving place to night-shadows. The kits cut short their dinner and followed me out to lock up the fowl-house, then scurried away to stalk a cricket which was creaking dismally as if his works needed oiling. When I had returned indoors, and locked all but one door, I called them for company, and they raced madly in, following me from window to window, as I drew them shut and snapped their fastenings. As soon as I had lighted the reading-lamp and had settled down with an absorbing book, they sprang to cuddle in my lap for a snooze.

One is always surprised to find how much philosophy there is lurking in one's depths to be called up when needed. After reading for some hours, with always a haunting feeling of something to be met and reckoned with, I laid down my book and looked the invisible presence in the face.

There was a possible month of this sort of thing before me. From twenty, to thirty days and nights, with the exception of short calls, in fair weather, from neighbors across the water, I should be left entirely to the society of feathered creatures and the two cats. There would be no real companionship in the calls of my distant neighbors; for they would doubtless pass every minute of the time they were with me in exclaiming and protesting about my lonely life.

I raised a window-shade and looked off across the water. A few friendly lights blinked out along the other shore, showing that there were still people in the world. Then I turned and looked at my little shut-in kingdom. The cats yawned and stretched elaborately, where I had set them on the floor. Kitty-Winks came to hook her claws in my skirts and pull, coaxing to be taken up again. I drew down the window-shade and dropped back into my chair, allowing them to spring again to my knees and thus addressed them:

"My little kits, we are left all alone here and we'll have to take care of each other. Nothing will hurt us; but it will be awfully quiet and the days and nights will seem endless. Do you think we can stand it?"

They seemed to understand that some demand was being made on their loyalty and both, with little throat-sounds they always made when trying to talk, reached up to rest velvet paws on my shoulders, rubbing their little muzzles against my cheeks.

"You are game for it, are you?" I asked. "Well, so am I. And I'll tell you what we'll do. We can't write to Julius, because there is no way to get the letters to him; but we'll keep a diary of everything we do while he's gone, to show him when he comes again. Let's begin it right now."

I set them on the floor and looked around on my writing table for a suitable book for the diary. On top, lay the one in which I kept the record of life in the chicken-park—of the sacks of grain and bran we bought for food; the number of eggs gathered each day; the date of setting each hen, the number of eggs put under each and the number hatched. Also how many "fell by the wayside" before maturity. All these items—expense and results—I had kept, prompted by a discussion Julius and I had had early in our pioneer days, because he maintained that chickens were a luxury, instead of a source of profit. I had proved that they very much more than paid their way and the chicken-book was one of my treasures. On its cover I had printed in big letters, "THE FOWLERY" and every night I entered the daily eggs, hatches and so forth. It was a good-sized book and by turning it upside down and beginning at the other end, there was plenty of room for recording a month's happenings.

I sat down to the table and began at once; consulting the kits about each sentence as I scribbled. They had started a game of mouse with a ball of darning-cotton Catty-Meow had fished out of my work-basket; but they paused and came to mew an answer to each question, pretending—sociable little frauds—to understand it all. They doubtless did know that the questions were for the sake of companionship and, in their own matchless way, they 'rose to the occasion.

After I had made all I possibly could of what kits and I had done in the few hours since we had been left alone, I felt much less solitary and suddenly discovered that I was tired enough to think of going to bed.

The cats asked to be let out of doors, as soon as they saw me begin to prepare for sleep; and I heard them scampering around in the moonlight, the sound of their antics indicating that they had captured the luckless cricket and were having some amusement at its expense.

It is well to say right here, before leaving the subject of the diary, begun that first evening, that it was kept religiously—the last thing each night I set down therein everything that had happened during the twenty-four hours since the last entry—and that I proudly handed it to

Julius on his return, to his great amusement. At first I was rather hurt to see him laughing over it and declaring it was four-fifths "fed the cats and chickens;" then I glanced over it as a whole and it made me laugh too; but I saved the situation by quoting "Happy is the country that has no history" and made him admit he was glad the diary was such tame reading.

The next morning, before kits and I had finished breakfast, we had a caller. There was an old German Professor who had bought a piece of land not far from us. He intended building on it someday. In the meantime, he amused himself playing with it. Every pleasant day he rowed himself across from the little hotel where he lived, bringing a hatchet, a saw, his luncheon and a jug for drinking water. All day he prowled around on his land, botanizing; pruning the wild trees and shrubs; cutting paths through the undergrowth and fraternizing with such bugs, worms, snakes and so forth as he happened to meet. There was, as yet, no well on his land and we had two—one in the kitchen and one outside for the fowls and plants. He had always come through our place to fill his water-jug and Julius had reckoned on his kindness to keep me in touch with the settlement—had asked him to bring and carry our mail for me and to attend to such small errands as cats and I might require during the absence of the man of the house. So the kind old gentleman had called to tell me he would be by the house on the way back to his skiff, which he had tied to our wharf and would carry any letters I might have ready to go across to the post-office. He also assured me he would come across every fine day and if I would have ready each evening a memorandum of what kits and I needed from the other side of the Sound, he would be "most glad" to bring it the next day. He was very small, pale and gentle and had the very un-German characteristics of being a vegetarian, a teetotaler and a tobacco-hater. My sympathy for him had been won, early in our acquaintance, when he had told me in his pathetic broken English that long ago he had lost a wife and an only daughter, who would have been near my age.

The fact that the kits had promptly made friends with the Old Professor, as we always called him, was another point in his favor and his almost daily trips through our place to his land had been among the pleasant events of our life on The Blessed Isle.

Although the mail South, to that Jumping-off-place to which Julius had voyaged, was very uncertain—sometimes once a month and often only twice a year—our northern mail came, barring accidents, or unusually rough weather, twice a week. Every mail brought business letters for Julius which, during his absence, I had to answer, so it was a great advantage to have someone constantly coming and going who could be depended upon to attend to the mail. This needed attention to business was also a great boon to me, making some days quite short with the rush of letters to get ready against the evening when the Old Professor would come by on his way home across the Sound.

Other frequent callers we had during our lonely month were the Indians, who came with venison or wild turkeys to sell. By this time I had lost all fear of our red neighbors. I had discovered their passion for pale-face cooking, for, as soon as they felt well enough acquainted, their greeting was always followed by the prompt hint: "Hot coffee, you got um? Heap hungry." "Hot coffee," meaning any kind of eatables or drinkables, either hot or cold. I always fed them, delighting in the study of their quaint, artless ways. Their mode of eating was to begin with the delicacies—any kind of sweets one happened to give them—next the meats; then vegetables; and last, the bread, hominy or oatmeal. They thought it impolite to leave a crumb; but always, like Jack Spratt and his wife, "licked the platter clean."

I had a curiosity to know the limit of the one who came oftenest and kept increasing the amount offered him each time he came, until finally I knew his measure. We had a large square biscuit-tin which, heaped high, held just enough to satisfy him. When he finished with it, it looked as if the cats had licked it and when he tried to answer my question of how he had enjoyed its contents, his voice was subdued to a husky stage-whisper, showing that he was literally "too full for utterance."

"Heap plenty; heap good; heap thanks!" was the way he summed it up.

Chapter Eight

THE INDIANS' cleverness at understanding and adapting themselves to our customs seemed to us to be really marvelous. One day, during the time we had camped on the East Shore of the Sound, one had come with venison to sell when I was alone in the boat-house. I told him to cut off half a "back-strap." After it was weighed, I opened the purse to pay him and found that Julius had emptied it of change; so I said to the Indian:

"Take it back. No money."

He looked intently at me for some seconds; then, emphasizing each phrase by tapping his fingers on the door-jam, beside which he was standing, said slowly:

"Lady make talk-paper; Indian give talk-paper store-man; store-man give Indian money."

I was truly amazed; having already thought, as soon as the emptied purse was inspected, of giving him an order on the "store," but had dismissed the idea, as soon as conceived, because I thought it would be impossible to make Lo understand and accept the "talk-paper."

While Julius and I were still discussing this and wondering about it, I chanced to meet a young woman who was camping, for the winter months with her husband, over the country "store" near Jupiter Light and in discussing the Indians, she related an experience of her own, which Julius and I found to be interesting to a degree.

She said, one day she was sewing on her machine, when all at once, she looked up from her work and there stood a big Indian in the doorway, intently watching her. He had heard the machine's clatter from below; and, in his artless way, had come noiselessly up the stairway to investigate. As soon as he caught her eye, he asked, in his broken English, to "make go." She felt sure he would smash something about the machine, but was so full of curiosity to see if he could "make go," that she could not resist, so she told him "all right."

Instead of going at once to take the chair she hastened to vacate, the Indian said "Come soon" and disappeared long enough to go downstairs and make some purchases.

He returned shortly with enough gay calico for a shirt and a quarter of a yard each of plain blue, plain red, plain green and plain yellow cotton cloth. He pointed to the scissors, saying: "Me take?" and, when they were handed to him, he squatted on the floor and cut out a shirt, using no pattern, but shaping it skillfully. Then he sat down to the machine and deftly stitched up the seams. Again squatting on the floor, he took bits of plain cotton-cloth and cut them all in narrow strips. These he folded and arranged in strange patterns, holding them and guiding the machine to stitch them on the flowing skirt of the shirt where they made a barbaric trimming, not unlike the patterns to be seen in pictures of the old Aztec walls, potteries and baskets. When the garment was done to his liking, the Indian calmly proceeded to doff the old one he was wearing and putting on the one newly completed, he grunted his thanks and strutted off, as proud as a peacock.

These long, flowing Indian shirts are a complete costume and those I have since remarked—feeling a lively interest in them after I found that they are usually built by the braves who appear in them—all have the strange patterns made of the strips of plain cotton cloth, folded and stitched in the prehistoric designs. In these garments and their ancient decorations, we found food for endless discussion and speculation.

The long, flowing shirt and a turban, complete the usual Seminole toilet. For high days and holidays, a waist-coat is added. For a very glad occasion, two waist-coats and sometimes three.

In cool weather they often wear fringed buckskin leggings, the shirt falling outside, because the leggings are made to come no higher than the top of the legs.

Julius and I were much amused the first time we met a group of Indians in the "store," where they were making purchases. Each article was paid for as soon as selected, the attendant being obliged to make change for each separate purchase. We stayed to watch them and the young man who was waiting on them told us in an aside that it was their unfailing custom to do all their buying in this way—that he had often seen an Indian "trade all day on a dollar." At first the boys in the "store" had found it to be very diverting to serve Lo and his family; but, as soon as the novelty wore off, they found it added so much to the day's tiresome labor, that they learned to dread the sight of a fleet of tippy, dug-out Indian canoes approaching the "store" wharf.

One striking trait of Seminole family life is the rule of the petticoat. The men make no bargain without consulting Madam Indian and what she says is final. This is quite refreshing when one considers the abject position of the Western squaw.

Altogether, the Indian visits were interesting and welcome breaks in the monotony of the long days while Julius was gone, aside from the variety their game gave to our bill of fare.

The kits were always terrified at their approach and disappeared as soon as an Indian voice was heard; but, as Lo vanished from the scene, both cats promptly turned up and began an eager clamor for little snacks of fresh venison.

We had ten days of fine weather after Julius had gone, then the rains began. For three days kits and I were completely cut off from the rest of the world by heavy wind-squalls with pelting rains. Some of the showers were like cloud-bursts and shut us in as with thick walls, so that nothing was visible twenty steps from the windows. The hens had begun hatching just before the rains set in and caring for the young chicks was something of a problem. After I had twice run out to rescue little biddies from drowning and had come back so drenched that every garment had to be wrung out and hung by the kitchen fire to dry, there came an inspiration. I got out my bathing suit and so garbed, with its long woolen stockings and a pair of India-rubber sandals, I was ready for unlimited prowls in the rain. It was like having wings, to be rid of the damp, flapping skirts and I told the kits I could understand just how they felt in their close-fitting fur suits, but every time they tried to follow me out in a shower, they turned to scamper indoors as soon as the first dash wet them; and, on my return from the dampness, they looked up at me with the most disgusted expression as I rallied them for being quitters. I always found them elaborately licking the drops from their coats and their disdainful air as they regarded me rubbing the drops from my head and shoulders with a bath-towel, then dashing out again to look after the little flocks, seemed to say they were persuaded I must be a lunatic to be ready to take so much trouble for foolish biddies that ought to be left to shift for themselves.

One hard shower came so suddenly that, by the time I could get out some of the youngest broods were apparently drowned. They lay around on the ground with closed eyes and half-shut claws. Two even had the rigidly out-stretched legs and toes which seemed to proclaim that they were beyond help. I gathered them all up in the skirt of my bathing-suit and, with a glance around to make sure none had been overlooked, fled indoors to spread them on a bit of carpet under the stove. Then, remembering a northern experience with some young chicks that were frozen in a late spring snow-storm, I put a tea-spoonful of spirits in a half-cupful of warm water and dosed each drowned biddy with a drop or two. Then each was gently squeezed in a towel and the whole lot of them wrapped in an old flannel garment and packed in a basket close to the fire. Two hours later, hearing a great racket in the kitchen, kits and I found all the little chicks, some perched on the edge of the basket and the rest running around on the floor, all making the most ear-piercing demands for their various mothers. Not a single one stayed drowned and when the sun came out, a half-hour later, all were given back to the distracted mothers who had been chasing around in the rain trying to find them. I did not know which was whose, but they soon settled the matter to everybody's satisfaction.

It was Saturday evening when the rains ceased and the sun went down with a promise that the morrow would bring clear skies. The weather was clear and sparkling the next morning, but there was a flawy west wind that told me I should have another long day, unbroken by human companionship. True, there were some boats to be seen on the water, but there were no women aboard them. They were occupied solely by boys, old and young, who were venturesome enough to enjoy risking the chances of a watery grave. It was nerve-racking to watch the boats go skipping over the waves—one moment leaning until the booms tore up the spray and the next, righting so suddenly that they almost went over the other way. It made one's back ache trying involuntarily to straighten them, so I tried to forget about boats and busied myself as long as possible with the fowls, cats and household affairs.

Toward mid-afternoon there came over me such an over-powering hunger for music, that I was driven to the childish device of a comb covered with a bit of thin paper. I went out and sat down on the steps of the front porch to give a concert of one for an audience of two. The cats sat blinking up at me with exactly the bored expression one sees on the faces of drawing-room victims at an amateur performance. Now and then they yawned frankly, exchanging such weary glances, I was forced to interrupt the witching strains long enough to laugh at them. The program was long and varied. All the airs from the various oratorios I could remember and melodies from sonatas and so forth; repeating, several times, Consolation and the Andante from the Pathétique. Then three favorite hymns—*Lead Kindly Light*, *Abide with Me* and *My Faith Looks Up to Thee*. And, last of all, the air to Tennyson's "Sunset and Evening Star," suggested by the approach of star-light time, just as the tide turned and the breakers out on the reef began to roar and thunder.

Then came the cry in the night.

It seemed but an instant since pillow and cheek had met when I was awakened by a piercing wail. I started up, thrilled and terror-struck, reaching for the gun which stood beside my bed.

It came again and I recognized Catty-Meow's voice, at the same moment that his form appeared on the window-sill outside its wire-screen silhouetted against the night-sky.

"What is it, Catty?" I asked.

He answered in an insistent tone that showed he wanted something and was in earnest about it.

I went in to the outer room and opened the door that gave on the porch.

Kitty-Winks, who was there waiting, slipped in as soon as it was unlatched.

I called to Catty-Meow, who answered with a low note of satisfaction, then leaped from the porch and made off in the darkness.

As I went back into the inner room, after locking the outside door and spoke to Kitty-Winks, whose black coat made her invisible in the darkness, I found, from the direction of her voice, that she had gone straight to her basket, which I had pushed, some days ago, to have it out of the way, under my bed. She was in it treading and purring away in happiest content.

I lay down again and all my dreams were full of cats.

As soon as it was light enough to see, I leaned over and drew the basket from under the bed.

Kitty-Winks reached up to kiss the hand on the basket's edge, then drew back her body to show four lovely kits—two jet-black, just like herself, except that they laced the snowy tail-tip; and the other two pocket-editions of Catty-Meow.

As far as the happy little mother was concerned, these were the very first kittens that ever gladdened a grown-up world, for they were the only one she had ever seen since her own and Catty-Meow's forgotten baby-cat days.

I stroked her head, praising the babies, even to her satisfaction, for they really seemed to be the very prettiest kits I had ever seen.

Before I had finished dressing, Catty-Meow's face appeared at the window, putting me in a state of uncertainty and uneasiness. He was the first boy-cat we had ever owned and I had heard shocking stories of his kind—that Mr. Cat is prone to show his appreciation of young kits by devouring them. I could not believe my Catty-Meow would be a cannibal and yet—best to decide the matter at once.

He met me at the door and went straight to the kitten-basket, where he stood on his hind-legs to investigate.

Kitty-Winks lifted her little muzzle to meet his, then proudly drew back to show her treasures.

Catty-Meow regarded them for an instant, with a look of what seemed like blank amazement; then, approached his face in turn to that of each shut-eyed baby-kit, for what looked oddly like a fatherly salute.

The kits made no protest against this attention, so he proceeded to climb into the basket, Kitty-Winks drawing herself to one side to make room for him.

As he settled down, he began purring, so that, with the music Kitty-Winks had never ceased to make, there was a real cat-duet of happiness.

The two kits nearest Catty-Meow drew closer in response to his purring and began rooting their tiny noses in his coat.

Flattening down his ears, with a wild look of terror, he edged away and spat at them. This naturally enraged Kitty-Winks, who boxed his ears, saying in plainest Cat-Latin:

"If you can't behave better than that, get out!"

Catty-Meow tumbled over the edge of the basket and ran, in a panic, for the door, which I opened, much amused to see him speeding away to hide in the bushes and collect his dazed thoughts.

Apparently, it did not take long for him to adjust himself to the new order of things. He soon returned, mewing outside the door to be admitted and went again to look at mother and babes in the basket.

Kitty-Winks received him kindly and they exchanged some remarks, which both evidently found to be satisfactory, for she gave up her place in the basket to Catty-Meow and asked to be let out of doors.

I opened the door and watched her go galloping out to disappear between the long rows of pineapple plants back of the house, then turned to see how Catty-Meow and the baby-kits were getting along together.

He had settled down in the basket and was giving each kit a conscientious bath from nose to tail.

This occupation was so evidently to his liking, that, encouraged by the mother-like attention and his loud purring, the baby-kits again ventured to root in his velvet coat.

Again came the look of mixed terror and disgust, but wise Catty-Meow looked around carefully to make sure that Kitty-Winks was out of sight before showing his resentment.

When convinced that the coast was clear, he spat on the little ones, rebuking them also with gentle taps of his paws. They soon showed an understanding of the situation.

This big cat was not their mother, he was only her substitute, who came to love and cuddle them during her needful outings, for whiffs of fresh air.

They cuddled down under and around him and, when the little mother hurried back to cast anxious glances into her nursery, she found father and babies all sound asleep. There was an eager clamor from the kits, with a gentle sound of protest from Catty-Meow, when Kitty-Winks climbed into the basket and lay down impartially on top of the heap of "cattles." Each began to squirm and twist, until there was room for all. The kits found their dinner and the two cats lay curled around them purring a happy duet.

Henceforth, Catty-Meow showed himself to be a model parent, always taking charge of the nursery when the little mother needed an airing and doing his share to teach the little ones to be good cats—to play, to box, to groom themselves and to have pretty house manners—showing both affection and responsibility in his care of them.

He was, indeed, a model father in all respects—a constant source of surprise and interest to all who saw his attitude toward his little family. The climax of his career came in the maturity of his wonderful son, our big black Satan, but that chronicle must appear later, as it is a story in itself—or, as Kipling used to say: "Another story."

* * *

Early one morning, while I was busy in the kitchen, there came a sound of steps on the front gallery, than a rap at the door.

I breathlessly untied the strings of my kitchen apron and ran to see who might be so early a caller. There stood a youth—son of a neighbor across the Sound—with a letter in his hand.

At a glance, I saw that Julius had addressed the envelope and was so eager to see inside, that I scarcely heard the boy's explanation as to how the letter had come. I grasped only that a "beach-walker," who had arrived in the settlement the night before, had asked him to bring it across to me and he had made the early start to keep the promise extracted from him.

170

As I turned the letter over to open it, noting its swollen, water-stained appearance, with all sorts of inward tremors, I found scribbled in pencil on the back of the envelope:

"This letter was picked up on the beach, washed ashore by the tide." A name was signed to this statement of a man I had never seen, but I had heard of—how he was constantly taking long tramps up and down the ocean beach gathering rare shells, sea-mosses and other treasures tossed up by the waves.

The letter had evidently been thrown overboard from a boat, with something buoyant attached to keep it from sinking and had washed ashore. Strangely enough, its date showed that it reached me only a week after it was written! It related a most successful voyage down to the Jumping-Off-Place; a pleasant stay there; then, an attempt to return. In fact, the boat had come close enough to our Inlet to see the flashes of far-away Jupiter Light; but was driven back, by high seas and head winds, to take shelter in a safe harbor half way back down the coast where it was now waiting for favorable winds and seas smooth enough to venture on another start. The letter seemed almost like a message from another world and was read and re-read almost to bits. The cats were called to hear it after the first eager devouring of its contents and seemed to respond to the delight I felt in assuring them that Julius was on the way home and would soon be walking in to surprise us.

But, although the harbor where the cruising-party took shelter is now—in these days of rail-road, rock-road and canal—only an hour or two, in any weather, from The Blessed Isle, it was nearly another half-month before the little coasting-boat could venture out into the big ocean and enter our Inlet to bring Julius home.

Julius was the only one of the party who was impatient to be back. To the others all the delays, with their endless adventures, only added to the romance of the trip. Even the fact that they came near to being shipwrecked, and, that in the darkness and storm, the little boat's captain became so confused that he lost his bearings and, fearing that the boat was about to be driven ashore among the big, cruel breakers, tried to anchor away out in the fathomless Gulf stream, was, to them a thrilling adventure to be treasured in memory for the dear delight of relating it to envious inland friends.

* * *

One afternoon, when fair women and brave men were gathered together in that exquisite music-room of Fairyland, across the Sound from The Blessed Isle, listening to a program of perfect music—voice alternating with harmonies of wood, string and reed—while the eye was feasted with everything which the ingenuity of inspired man has produced to charm the soul—art, splendor and luxury; profusions of rare blooms and Heaven's crowning beauty, lovely women—and then, at the end of the program, there was the music of soft voices and rustling of rich raiment, as all adjourned to that enchanting Inner Court, where the fountain's ripple made obligato for chat and laughter, while the enraptured guests partook of refreshments—not prosaic eating and drinking, but more of Fairyland's enchantment—where flowers offered magic ambrosia and nectar. In these blissful surroundings, all at once, by some trick of memory, there came to mind the scene, in the little kitchen at The Hermitage, of that night when the long delayed mail came and we had no kerosene; so had to scorch the backs of our heads trying to decipher our letters by the fitful light of pine-knots in the fire-place of the cooking-stove.

I looked around, studying the faces of the happy guests, with a clear-eyed comprehension of their usual environment. It was easy to see that they had no experience of anything like hardship—that their ideas of life in the country were formed entirely from experiences in summer house-parties, where country luxuries gave variety from their accustomed city homes of up-to-date comfort and charm.

It was with a feeling of real compassion that I realized this fact—that to all present these exquisite delights of Fairyland were only extreme degrees of their usual luxury. Only Julius and I, of all present, with souls receptive and attuned to beauty and charm; and with memories of life's real hardships endured and conquered in our pioneering, could enjoy to the full these golden moments in a Fairyland which was a dream come true.

In our isolation so remote and wild—so denuded of all the

172

luxuries of life's centers—the world had come to us, just as we had dreamed it would, bringing everything we lacked and completing what Nature had so perfectly begun.

The coming of the King and Queen of Fairyland and all that their coming meant, had completed the enchantment of our far-away tropical paradise, where the opaline wavelets of its inland sea swing ever to and fro between the palm-fringed shores of Fairyland and The Blessed Isle.

The End

THE SPILMAN FAMILY. The Spilman family with five of their six children appear in this composite photograph. Seen are parents Eliza Sarah Taylor and Jonathan Edwards Spilman, children (from left to right) Julia Bird Spilman, Charles Edwards Spilman, Anna Louise Spilman, Clara Lee Spilman and William Magill Spilman. Not pictured is Lewis Hopkins Spilman. *Courtesy Janis Lydic Hebert.*

BRUNO AND REBECCA. In the only known photograph of the Dewey's beloved pets, Bruno the dog and Rebecca the cat are seen in Salem, Illinois. *Private collection.*

BEN TROVATO TEA PARTY. This iconic image from 1893 shows the Deweys at the far right hosting an afternoon tea party for the new minister. The emerging Palm Beach society is seen in all their Victorian finery. *Courtesy Historical Society of Palm Beach County.*

BEN TROVATO. The Dewey's home named Ben Trovato on the shores of Lake Worth. The name means "well invented" in Italian. Today a 19 story condominium resides on the property. *Courtesy Historical Society of Palm Beach County*

BYRD SPILMAN DEWEY. Mrs. Dewey and four of the Blessed Isle cats at Ben Trovato in 1900. In the background Lake Worth can be seen with Dewey's Wharf. *Courtesy Historical Society of Palm Beach County*

THE DEWEYS IN JACKSONVILLE. Byrd Spilman Dewey and husband Fred S. Dewey pose with dog Van in a 1907 portrait. *Private collection.*

BYRD SPILMAN DEWEY. Mrs. Dewey posing with cat Billie, Palm Beach, 1918. *Private collection.*

BYRD SPILMAN DEWEY. Mrs. Dewey with dog Fritz in Palm Beach at the Frederick Guest estate in the early 1920s. *Courtesy Janis Lydic Hebert.*

FOOZLE. The Dewey's dog Foozle figures prominently in Byrd Spilman Dewey's book *The Blessed Isle and its Happy Families*. *Private Collection.*

BEN TROVATO. Seen here in the 1950s, the house was expanded with a north wing. It was demolished in 1970 to make way for the Rapallo Condominium complex. *Courtesy Mary Baldwin Woodland.*

The Blessed Isle and its Happy Families

Forward to
The Blessed Isle and its Happy Families

Byrd Spilman Dewey's sequel to *Bruno*, *The Blessed Isle and its Happy Families* did not enjoy the same commercial success as *Bruno*. Published in 1907 by the Press of the Record Company in St. Augustine, she had tried to get other companies to publish the work, including her friend Richard Watson Gilder, the well-known poet and editor with the Century Company. In a letter, he responded that such a work where cats played the major roles would not find a large audience.

In 1901 *Vogue* magazine commissioned Mrs. Dewey to write short stories about her cats. The stories were widely syndicated in newspapers and well received. Mrs. Dewey decided to expand the cat story line of life at The Blessed Isle, the Dewey's lakeside estate where their home Ben Trovato stood. The cats took center stage, along with a few dogs—Foozle, the irreverent bull-pointer, and Van, the refined collie from the Biltmore estate. The vignettes and tales offer a glimpse into the cottage life in West Palm Beach in the early 1900s.

The book is divided into two parts; the first tells the detailed cat stories; the second tells of leaving their beloved home Ben Trovato and The Blessed Isle, as Mr. Dewey's health was in decline. He needed medical care that could only be provided in Jacksonville at that time as West Palm Beach had no hospital until 1914. The book ends with perhaps the most beautiful piece of writing Mrs. Dewey ever did—a tribute to her dog Van, called realities. It causes one to think about what is really important in life.

Chapter First.
The Adopted Kitten.

MRS. HELEN had promised me a daughter of her old Tabby, and when I received a note from her saying that Madam had ascended the kitten-tree, I was delighted.

The kitten-tree was a large Banyan, or rubber-tree, back of Mrs. Helen's house in which Tabby had discovered a natural cat-nursery. A hollow had formed high up in the trunk, sheltered overhead by a branch, and screened all about by the large thick leaves which rubber trees always produce in such profusion. Crumbled bark, dry leaves and other debris had accumulated in the bottom of the hollow, forming an ideal cat-boudoir. To this delightful retreat madam Tabby always retired at the crises in her domestic affairs. Here she welcomed the visits of the stork; remaining in the upper chamber, except for brief trips below in search of food and drink, until her kits were so mature that they could scramble down with her.

It does not require many weeks for kittens to grow large enough to leave their mother, so I was soon gladdened by a sight of the mail-sloop tacking up to land at the wharf of our Blessed Isle with a promising-looking box stowed in the shelter of the boom against the mast. When its slatted top was lifted, I found that Mrs. Helen had been even more generous than her promise. She had sent a pair of kittens—perfect little beauties. The male jet-black, with a glossy coat like silk plush; and the other, black with white markings.

The black kit was at once christened Satan, in memory of another black Satan-cat, the chronicle of whose happy days here on The Blessed Isle must make another story.

The little girl-kit nestled up to me with a wide-eyed, comprehensive glance of affection which brought a response from the same heart-string that had vibrated for Catsie, the kitten beloved of Bruno, so we named her Catsie the Second.

Anyone who has grown cat-hungry, through long months of catlessness, will understand how our joys were more than doubled by the charms of those two lively little creatures scampering about. They would frolic around me as I sat busy with sewing or books, springing on and over me in their games of tag; stopping to investigate my book, or to study with lively interest the mysterious movements of pen or needle; toying with the little curls they dragged from confining hair-pins with their mischievous claws, and sent into an ecstasy of delight if they could succeed in dislodging all the pins and bring down an avalanche of locks in my lap or on the work-table—claw, with delightful abandon until chaos was the result; then perform a war-dance around me when I remonstrated, and deposited them on the floor that I might rise to repair damages.

But kittens will not remain kittens. The first thing you know they have become cats. One day Catsie came to ask me for a larger bed. She climbed soberly into my lap, purring, and making little inarticulate sounds in her throat, treading with her feet like a soldier "marking time." Then she jumped down and searched all the snug corners of the room, investigating the paper-basket and easy chairs, then returned to climb again into my lap. When I rose, saying—

"Yes, Catsie, Judith understands. She knows what you want," she sprang to the floor and followed me to the store-room, where I chose a box deep and roomy, putting a layer of excelsior in the bottom, and then folded over it a piece that had been cut from the end of a too-long ironing-blanket. When all was arranged she climbed in, purring and treading it down into a cozy nest, then curled herself up in it for a trial-snooze.

That night I propped the door of the store-room slightly ajar, before we ascended to our own bower, and continued to leave it so for the succeeding nights; in the meantime, watching to see that Catsie was perfectly satisfied with her bed. I found that she visited it several times a day, treading it each time, and remaining therein afterwards for little naps.

At last, one morning we found Catsie in her nest, surrounded by four minute kits; but something had gone wrong. The stork has been careless—perhaps had dropped them in its flight.

They were all stone dead.

Catsie was just beginning to discover that something was amiss with them. As there were no other cats on our Blessed Isle, she had never seen any young kits, so she had not known just what to expect. She had washed and dressed them as instinct told her it should be done, and was trying to make them understand that breakfast was ready.

She mewed, and reached up an appealing little paw to me, saying as plainly as possible: -

"What's the matter? Can't you help me to wake them?"

Evidently the kits had arrived hours ago; probably quite early in the night. When she heard our words of compassion, and saw that we made no effort to waken the kits, she seemed to give up hope. Her head fell again to it resting-place, her eyes closed, and her lips parted in little gasps of anguish.

"It's the milk," said I; "it makes her feverish, and she will be ill."

"This won't do at all!" cried Julius; "do you suppose, if we could find another kitten anywhere, that she would take it?"

"Of course she would!" said I. "It's the very thing!"

He hurried for his hat, and a few seconds later I heard him down at the wharf hoisting the sails of the little sharpie. I left Catsie long enough to fly down and call to him to refuse nothing in the shape of a kitten; but to get the youngest one possible; then I returned to the store-room. Between times, while I comforted Catsie, I sought a suitable box, which I proceeded to line with the glossy leaves of the bay-tree, to have it ready to bury the poor little dead kits when the time should come to remove them to make room for the little stranger.

In an incredibly short time I heard the snapping of sails at the wharf and hurried out to see if Julius had been successful in his kitten-hunt. As soon as I appeared he held up a small parcel, crying: -

"Such luck! The mercantile-store-cat has a family of kittens born last night! They said that all were promised except the ones they had picked out to raise for themselves; but, when I told them about poor Catsie, they felt so sorry for her that they gave me the most promising one that they had selected to keep."

I found the parcel to be a little card-board box, which a legend on the outside showed had been baby-shoes. Twin holes had been punched in the top to admit air; and, when Julius removed the cover, I saw that a handful of soft paper had been crushed into the bottom on which sprawled a tiny squirming kit.

We hurried to Catsie with the treasure. She raised her head with languid interest at our approach, which quickened when she saw me removing the little hopeless mites; then she bristled up and spat viciously at the first glimpse of the squirming little stranger.

"What's the matter?" cried Julius in dismay.

"It's all right," said I, laughing. "This is the first live kit she ever saw, and she doesn't understand it yet."

I took Catsie's face in my hands, covering her eyes, while the kit began to explore vigorously. As soon as he had found his breakfast I felt Catsie's little form thrill and become rigid. I kept my hands over her eyes until her muscles relaxed, and she began to purr; then I looked to see the mother-light dawn in her eyes.

She raised her head to look at the kit, curving her arm around him and reaching over to give his toilet some finishing touches with her tongue, the while purring loudly. Then she looked from me to Julius with a light of mother-rapture on her face that was almost human.

I am not ashamed to tell that, so far as Julius and I were concerned, there was not a dry eye present.

Chapter Second.
Roi.

THERE ARE some women who, as soon as they realize that they are mothers, cease to be anything else. Every thought, instinct and faculty is merged into a passion of motherhood. Catsie was in Cat-dom what these women are in Woman-dom. From the minute she realized that she held, in her clasp a real kitten, alive and responding to her tenderness by accepting from her all the comforts and joys that appertain to kitten life, she was blind and deaf to everything except her little treasure and the things that concerned him. Her attitude toward her baby reminded us of the poem "Philip, My King," which suggested "Roi" as a suitable name for the kit.

Though we always wrote it "Roi," it was soon corrupted, in pronouncing, to "Roy"; for Roi is a word that the English-speaking tongue finds a little difficult. It requires thought and a particular twist to get it just right. "Rex" would have given the same idea without the difficulty of pronunciation; and, had we lived inland, "Rex" would doubtless have been the name chosen. But here on the salt water one sometimes sees this name painted across the stern of a boat that is built for speed, so there seems a certain incongruity in giving it to a kitten.

It was at once amusing and touching to see Catsie's devouring anxiety as to the safety of the baby Roi. She dared not lose sight of him for one instant. It was almost impossible to coax her out of doors during the weeks that he was too small to follow her. She would stay with him until I am sure she must have ached in every bone of her small body for a good scamper over the lawn; then she began to try to make up her mind to leave him alone for a little while. She looked him over carefully to make sure he was all right; then, climbing reluctantly out of the box, was resolute enough to get as far as the door. After one glance outside, back she came to spring into the box and reassure herself that her treasure was still safe. This was repeated until she was almost frantic with indecision. Then I would say:

"Oh, do go along, Catsie; nothing will happen to your baby; Judith will sit right by his bed, and will watch him every minute while you are gone."

Then she would hook her claws in my skirts, lifting herself up to look in my face with the most imploring expression while I assured her that I meant it, and that she could go for a run with an easy mind. Then away into the garden she galloped, finding relief from long hours of inaction in all sorts of antics, pausing suddenly in the midst of wild scurrying to come dashing back in a panic, mad with fear lest, after all, something bad had happened to the beloved kit.

Poor Satan found himself to be utterly neglected. After soundly boxing his ears the first time he ventured to approach his nose inquiringly toward the little stranger, Catsie took no further notice of him. Julius and I tried to console him with extra petting and the daintiest fair; but he was distinctly bored and began to go on long prowls in the woods back of the house. One evening he failed to return, and, though we searched carefully, we never saw him again. We concluded he must have been caught by some of the wild creatures which roamed there, harmless toward humans but always on the lookout for cats, fowls and "such small deer," or else that he had been shot by an inexperienced hunter, who had mistaken him for a wild creature. We grieved for him; but Catsie never seemed to miss him at all. She was too much occupied with her little treasure to give a thought to her former play-fellow.

Urged constantly to eat, and having no fellow-kits to share the food which nature had provided for a family of four, Roi grew so rapidly it seemed almost as if we could see him increase in size from day-to-day. He was soon large enough to follow Catsie everywhere, and they ceased to occupy their box except at night. She brought him to share our society, and it was very diverting to see her attending to his education; teaching him to box, to wrestle, and to wash himself; pausing, from time to time, to hug him in an ecstasy of delight at his cleverness.

One day Julius chanced to remark in her hearing: -

"I declare Catsie makes a perfect idiot of herself about that kitten!"

The little mother, who, at the moment, was engaged in "the pleasures of the chase" after an imaginary flea under Roi's fluffy chin, paused and turned to look at Julius, the little pink tongue still showing between her lips, as if frozen there with horror that anyone could speak so disrespectfully of her darling. There was something so absurd about her air of horrified amazement, that Julius and I burst out laughing; whereupon Catsie picked up her kitten and stalked from the room with the air of a tragedy queen.

When I saw that we had really hurt her feelings, my amusement vanished, and I hurried after her to apologize. She refused to notice me at first; but I picked up Roi, petting him until he began to purr his content, then Catsie climbed into my lap to join him, and I felt that all was forgiven.

I used to think that cats understand little or nothing of what is said to them, responding only to the tones of the voice; but long ago I learned that when they are much petted and talked to they really do comprehend what is said.

I once knew a cat, belonging to a French family, who would not pay the slightest attention to words spoken in "United States," no matter how endearing the tones of voice; but when addressed in French she was all alert, showing every sign of delighted response.

Catsie could never makeup her mind to wean Roi. She continued to nurse him until he was much larger than his foster-mother. It was most amusing to see them. They made a capital "T" as they lay purring together. Little Catsie happy in giving him his dinner, and big Roi equally happy in absorbing it.

As he learned to like solid food, Roi gradually weaned himself; and he kept on growing until he was almost twice as large as Catsie.

When they both realized that he was no longer a kitten their devotion continued; but with a difference.

Although Catsie had been a mother to him, there was no real tie of blood between them, and Roi did what so many little boys have declared their meant to do—he grew up and married his mother!

The stork came again to happy Catsie, and this time one of the kits it brought her was alive.

It is still a puzzle why Catsie should have been so unfortunate in this respect.

Nearly always the stork is exceptionally kind to cats; bringing them unlimited kittens, all very much alive; but "Deedie" is the only live kitten the stork every did bring to Catsie.

Deedie received her name in memory of a cat I had when I was a very small child, the name being an infant corruption of Phoebe.

Roi was such a good father that Deedie had practically two mothers. The three slept happily together, Deedie in the middle; and they took turns staying with her during the day.

Catsie used to go off on long excursions, leaving the baby-kit in Roi's care. He played with her, taught her, and kept her coat in order with frequent lickings; so that the only difference she noticed was that one parent fed her and the other did not. Once or twice, just at first, she had tried experimental explorings in Roi's coat. He resented this, gently; but so unmistakably, that she learned to understand the situation, and to accept it as it was.

Like her father, Deedie grew rapidly, and became an unusually large cat. It was a beautiful sight to see the unspeakable devotion of these two splendid big creatures for the little mother who had concentrated all the love which most cats divide among numberless offspring upon these two—the kitten she had adopted, and his baby.

Chapter Third.
Deedie and the Robber Cat.

NO ONLY child belonging to a devoted human couple was ever more indulged—more "spoiled"—than was Deedie, the only kitten of Catsie and Roi.

When they were fed, the two parent-cats habitually stood back until they were sure that there was more than Deedie could eat; and, in every-way, she was made to understand that they consider nothing to be too good for her.

As this state of things is very apt to make human children willful and selfish it had, to a certain degree, this effect on Deedie. As far as affection for her parents went, she was a model daughter—unhappy if either parent were long absent; basking in the affection of her big father, and uniting with him in bestowing a matchless devotion on the little mother. But when food was give them, if it happened to be something that needed to be divided into morsels, Deedie had a naughty habit of gathering them into a heap so she could crouch over the bits, drawing them singly from under her body to devour, while Catsie and Roi sat looking on, happy in her enjoyment. This used to put me in such rages with the little beast that I once caught her up meaning to give her a good shaking; but she disarmed my wrath by beginning to purr as soon as she felt my grasp. It is not possible to punish a creature who shows such confidence in one's affection; I preferred to sit down beside them at their meals and feed them with morsels cut small and tucked in turn into the three eager little mouths. As often as possible I gave them dishes of "spoon-food," which they

190

could be trusted to eat unattended without danger of Deedie having more than she needed and her parents less.

Roi often went a little way into the woods and came back bringing some choice tidbit for Deedie—sometimes a katydid, or a big grasshopper; more often a chameleon—a kind of small lizard which in Cat-dom seems to rank as the daintiest of morsels.

One never-to-be-forgotten day after he had gone on a little hunting excursion we heard firing in the woods, which was not an unusual occurrence. When I went out later to feed my cat-family, I found Catsie and Deedie in apparent agitation which increased when I began to call Roi. They paid no attention to the food I offered them; but stood looking anxiously up the path in the direction he always came when returning from the woods. As I paused after calling, they looked up mewing and then towards the woods-path and again at me, evidently trying to say: -

"Call him again; don't stop!"

I continued calling for a long time, my uneasiness growing as I realized theirs; but Roi did not answer, nor did we see his large, graceful form come gliding and leaping along the path as always heretofore.

I knew instinctively what had happened—as evidently the cats were thinking and fearing—he had fallen, alone in some leafy nook, a victim to the same fate that has overtaken poor little Satan. But Catsie and Deedie utterly refused to submit to his loss; and, day after day for many weeks, each time I went out to feed them, they continued to say to me in their own way:

"Call Roi again; don't stop!"

I always called just to satisfy them, while they stood beside me looking off up the path, craning their necks and waving meditative tails as they listened intently for the longed-for response.

They follow us with evident understanding of our quest in the search we made on the chance of finding him lying wounded somewhere unable to return home; but no trace of him was ever found.

If he was shot, as we have always believed, the hunter realized his error and concealed all traces of the tragedy.

Thus left, the fatherless daughter of an over-indulgent mother, it is not without precedent that when the time came for Deedie to choose for herself she should have formed an undesirable attachment.

In my nursery days I delighted in a tragic rhyme-story called "The Robber Kitten" beginning: -

"A kitten once to his mother said:

I'll never more be good.

I'll go and be a robber fierce,

And live in the dreary wood!

Wood-wood-wood, and live in the dreary wood!"

This "poem" with its lurid pictures and the dismal echoes which were the refrain of each "verse" came back to me from the limbo of forgotten nursery delights when I found what sort of admirer Deedie had picked up and brought in for our approval.

Naturally, I investigated his past and was rather aghast to learn that he was a genuine Robber Cat. But, unlike the Robber Kitten of nursery lore, he was not so from a determination that he should "never more be good;" he had been forced to become a bandit by circumstances.

Inquiry developed these facts as to his kitten-hood.

His mother, a respectable Tabby belonging to the family of a man who had not long since been placed in charge of the pineapple fields just back of us, had become disgusted by the adoption into the same family of an indiscreet young dog, and had carried her kits off to the woods to rear them in concealment. So many dangers had there been encountered that Deedie's friend was the sole survivor of this cat-family.

He was not a beauty; but he had a wicked eye and a rakish swagger calculated to ensnare the fancy of the illogical young person.

Catsie repudiated him with the utmost scorn; and gave me to understand that she wished him refused the privileges of the screened porch, with its little swinging door, which we call the cat-room.

So I reasoned with Deedie until I saw that if he were driven away she would go with him; then I succumbed to the inevitable, and concluded it would be a better plan to reconcile Catsie to his presence, and to try to reform the poor Robber Cat, whom we knew to be the victim of an unfortunate early environment.

To begin this plan of adoption we formally christened him "Johnny Bull."

I preferred not to tell why this name was chosen for him, lest the reader should be led to imagine that I am averse to the typical Briton. I should regret to convey such an impression.

By going back only a very few generations I find myself wandering over ancestral acres under English skies; so my attitude toward any unpleasant characteristics that are admittedly typical of the Mother-country, is that of the affectionate toleration one feels for the short-comings one sees in the members of one's own family circle.

Johnny Bull accepted and recognized his name with an encouraging intelligence, and soon learned to adapt himself to the cooked food which he had at first found to be so puzzling.

Catsie's scorn for him went to the extreme of refusing to recognize Deedie when he was with her.

I found it was necessary to feed her separately, as she would not touch even the most tempting dish if she found that Johnny Bull was to share it.

He hung around with a guilty air, watching his chance to make friendly overtures to me when Catsie's back was turned; and soon showed he understood that my good-will to him depended on his keeping to the rule we made that he was to kill no more birds. This is always the first thing our cats are taught, and they are fed with such unfailing regularity that temptation is reduced to a minimum.

So matters stood when Deedie's four kits appeared on the scene.

"Now," said I, "is the time for a grand reconciliation!"

But, instead of welcoming the little grand-baby-kits, Catsie's bristles all turned the wrong way and she spat at them in a manner that left not a shadow of doubt as to her feelings on the subject.

It was necessary to serve her meals on another porch.

Deedie was very happy with her young family. The only fly in the ointment was her mother's disapproval. I often reasoned with Catsie about it, and she showed that she felt herself to be in the wrong.

She tried to overcome her dislike for the little creatures, going tentatively to look at them from time to time; but, as soon as they began to squirm, or to stretch open their little mouths, her distaste for them conquered; then, spitting at them in disgust, and shaking a disdainful paw, away she would fly!

I knew she was surprised and distressed to find herself to be in this state of mind. One often hears masculine statements regarding the puzzles of the feminine heart. The simple truth is that the reason no man can understand woman is because she does not understand herself. She is constantly surprising unexplored corners in her own nature which cause her to stand aghast—exclaiming, with the old woman in Mother Goose's Melodies: -

"Lawk 'a massy on my soul, this is none of I!"

Poor Catsie was passing through one of these spiritual crises, and she showed, in many ways that she knew I understood and sympathized with the difficulties of her position.

Deedie's happiness in the possession of her little family was of short duration. Three of her kits fell asleep and refused to be awakened. The fourth was found, on examination, to be reduced from his original roly-poly shape to a mere skeleton. I divined that there was something wrong with the food furnished by nature, and took the little fellow in hand. He soon showed that my diagnosis of his case had been correct, and responded to an unlimited diet of cow's milk by resuming his round shape.

In the meantime Johnny Bull, neglected by Deedie, and utterly scorned by Catsie, had found that he was so unmistakably in the way that he had effaced himself; and his absence, together with Deedie's bereavements, brought about the longed-for reconciliation.

One morning I came down stairs earlier than usual; and, on going out to the cat-room, there was Catsie sleeping in the nursery-box with Deedie, and the grand-baby-kit was cuddled up between them, all three purring happily together just as we used to find Catsie, Roi and Deedie in the happy days gone by!

Chapter Fourth.
The Twins and Peterkin.

DEEDIE'S KITTEN was soon large enough to leave the nursery-box and join his mother and his grand-mother at the general dish. We found it difficult to agree on a name for him, so we usually spoke of him as "The Grand-baby."

Just as he was beginning to scamper around and make the place merry with is pranks, the time came for us to go away for our usual summer change.

Our hired help, for whom we have a little house screened from view by a grove of trees back of the pineapple field, always take care of the pets when we are away from home. When the time came for us to start they were given even more than the usual number of directions, with much stress laid on the care and diet of The Grand-baby. I promised Jincy an extra present over and above what she had come to consider as her just due for looking after them. This present was to depend on our finding, when we returned, the birds, cats and flowers in as good condition as we were leaving them.

Then I gave Jackson a number of stamped and addressed envelopes that he might send us weekly reports of "the cattle."

The first letter, and the second, gave good news from The Blessed Isle; the third was as follows:

Mr. Julius sir I takes my pen in hand to noterfy you that the plaise is lukin well an us an the birds an the cats is duin fine skusin of the maddams Kiten which I foun hit layin daid by the Back Steps when I cum in yistiddy jincy sais she seed that Bobb tale pupp hangin roun a wensdy an he shore dun hit my respeks to the Maddam an I hope she wont blame me about the kitten case I wuddent of had it Happened fur no Munnay Sir i hopes you has yore Helth Yore respeckful amos jackson.

Thus perished the Grand-baby-kit, victim to the "Bobb tale pupp," a wicked little fox-terrier, from whose cruel jaws Deedie, herself, had been rescued, just in the nick of time, when she was a small kitten.

We grieved sincerely for the little fellow, and I constantly regretted not being at home to console Catsie and Deedie. I knew they were both longing for us. They do not find our hired help very congenial and never deign to notice them except during our absence, when it is necessary for them to accept their attentions.

On our return, some six weeks later, I knew at once that they were still grieving for the little grand-baby.

Catsie and Deedie both climbed into my lap; purring, and making those little throat-sounds which in Cat-dom are a substitute for speech. They were evidently trying to tell me all about it.

Whenever Julius and I return home after any absence the cats go through with the same program. For several mornings they come to the door with the idea that our return was only a dream, and that we are still far away. When I go out to greet them they make just as much fuss over me as If they had not dared to hope that the door would open. They keep this up sometimes for a week or longer before they realize that we really are at home again; and then they settle down to their usual quiet happiness.

About two weeks after our return from the Mountains we were surprised one morning by the appearance of Johnny Bull, who came leisurely walking in. As soon as they saw him coming Catsie and Deedie began to growl, and, when he was close enough, they both flew at him like little furies. They clawed him until it was necessary for me to interfere, which I did—soothing his wounded feelings and bringing out a dish of nice bits to make amends for their lack of cordiality. He ate hurriedly, with one eye over his shoulder on the lookout for fresh onslaughts from the two growling little beasts; then, after a grateful glance at me, he trotted off toward the woods, commenting audibly to himself as he went on the uncertainties of feminine favor.

I was sorry to see him go.

He had taken very kindly to civilization, and had shown himself to be possessed of an unusual amount of natural chivalry—never crowding or snatching at meals; and, though big enough to avenge all his wrongs, never retaliating when unhandsomely treated by the other cats.

Left alone, Catsie and Deedie seemed more devoted than they had ever been. They had learned what it meant to be at odds with one another; and both had suffered. They began to appear quite elderly. Catsie especially gave herself up to dowager-like airs. She liked dishes of catnip tea, made by pouring a cupful of boiling water over a pinch of dried catnip leaves, then cooled delicately with cream. Over a bowl of this delectable mixture she often sat, taking now and then a sip, with exactly the same expression of countenance that I remember seeing on my Grand-mother's face when she used to come sometimes to sit by the nursery fire, when we were little children, and dream over her afternoon cup of tea.

A year went by, and one day Julius asked: -

"Aren't we ever to have any more kittens on the place?"

"It seems not," said I. "It begins to look as if Catsie and Deedie are on the retired list, so far as kittens are concerned."

"Well, let's get a fresh start. We can't keep house without kittens."

A day of two later I went, one morning, across to the Village to make some purchases. In one of the groceries there was a big black cat which sprang up on the counter and began to make advances to me. I love black cats; and, remembering Julius's wish for "a fresh start," I was inspired to ask the man who was waiting on me if this beauty had any kittens. He answered smilingly:

"No'm; he's never had any so far's I know."

An old man who was standing near the door then spoke to the grocery-man saying:

"If the lady wants a black kitten I can get her one, I think; and, maybe, two."

I thanked him, then he added to the grocery-man:

"I'll bring them in here for her, if I find that I can get them."

"If they come here," said the grocery-man to me, "I'll send them right over in the delivery-boat."

The very next day the boat came, bringing a box, which contained the twins—two jet-black, bashful little creatures who hid in the darkest corner of the room as soon as the box was opened, and had to be coaxed out. It was some hours before they began to feel at ease with us and their new surroundings. One of them was entirely black, all over. She was christened "Velvet." The other was all black, except a little white dot under her chin like a collar-button. We called her "Plush."

As soon as Catsie and Deedie came in, I knew there was to be trouble. They promptly spat at the strangers and backed away growling. Deedie was angry; but Catsie was hurt. Deedie refused to eat with them and had a separate dish given her; but Catsie would not eat at all. She gave me one reproachful glance, then walked away, down the steps, across the grass to a large mango-tree, and sat down close to the trunk, with her back toward the house.

I went after her, calling as coaxingly as possible. She did not look around; but got up when she heard me coming and started across the garden. I followed, and she walked on, keeping just out of reach, until she came to the edge of the woods. Without a backward glance she entered, and it was a distinct pang that I saw her disappear in the undergrowth.

I hurried back to the house with the account of her obduracy, but Julius laughed, saying:

"Don't you worry about Catsie; she'll come around all right after she has sulked awhile!"

After dinner, when the cats were given their evening meal, I called Catsie; but there was no response. And with dismal forebodings I sat down to my books.

Toward bedtime the screen-door opening on the front gallery was gently shaken and a plaintive mew was heard. When the door was opened Catsie sprang to my clasp and reached up to rub her head against my cheek. She had ever been an affectionate little beast, but this time she surpassed herself in endearments. As soon as she had fully expressed her repentance I took her out to the kitchen where I gave her the bowl of soup I had put by on the chance of her coming back before bed-time. She devoured it with great relish while I sat beside her and talked about the two little new-comers; assuring her that she would find them to be charming play-fellows as soon as she had made their acquaintance.

She seemed to be in such a melting mood that I took her out on the porch and called the twins to see if she would make friends with them. They came up purring and offering to rub their heads against hers; but as soon as Velvet's little nose touched her face Catsie bristled up, spitting in disgust, then dashed off and vanished through the little cat-door, disappearing in outer darkness. This was discouraging. Still, I had the consolation of knowing that the sore little heart was less heavy; and that my dear Catsie was no longer wandering unfed amid the dangers of the forest.

Catsie, Deedie and the twins, with always a possibility of Johnny Bull's return, gave us a large enough cat-family; but Fate loves to play pranks.

The third morning after the arrival of the twins Jincy, who was sweeping the back gallery, called suddenly to me, through the window:

"Laws, Miss Judy, look a-yonder! Yonder comes the scrawniest, measliest lookin' little kitten I ever seed. Hit looks like 'taint never had nothin' to eat since 'twas bawn!"

I looked out, and Jincy had not exaggerated. It was truly a sorry little tramp that came meandering down the path from the direction of the woods. It was so thin it looked as if it had been "pressed" in a book like a flower; and, when I had picked up the little creature, I found that its spine felt like the edge of a coarse-toothed saw. It attacked the offered dish of food as if it were half-famished; then, leaving it, began to make friendly advances to the other cats, who were looking on from various points of vantage. Catsie would have nothing to say to it; but Deedie examined the little stranger with much interest. It was just the size of the unforgotten Grand-baby-kit—more bony, and not very clean; still, it might be—but, after sniffing it all over carefully, she concluded it was not hers—it was an imposter, who had come to wring her heart by re-opening a wound which Time had almost healed. This point decided, Deedie bristled up and gave the tramp a blow with her paw that almost upset the frail little fellow; and, shaking her foot with a look of utter repudiation, she made off.

The tramp-kitten then approached the twins. They stood back, close to one another, eyeing the stranger, just as one has seen two dainty children of prosperity look at a dirty little street-waif. They were not actively unkind; but they did not yearn for such an uninviting play-fellow.

The stray kit was no whit embarrassed.

If nobody wished to play with him, there was still the dish of bread-and-milk to be enjoyed; and he devoted himself anew to giving some shape to his flat little body.

His utterly forlorn appearance reminded us so forcibly of "Peter the Tramp," whose history is chronicled elsewhere, that this name was chosen for him, and he was forthwith claimed by Julius as his own especial pet. In fact, it was a mutual affair between Julius and Peter; for, from the very first day of his appearance on the scene, Peter kept a close watch on all the movements of Julius, tagging after him from one end to the other of our Blessed Isle. This seemed the more remarkable because our cats are supposed to be my especial property; they almost invariably show a preference for me, just as all dogs do for Julius. Some people will argue, perhaps, that this fact shows Julius to be of a nature larger and nobler than that of his Judith. Well, we need not quarrel about that, for it is just what I think!

Little Peter filled up rapidly and soon his back-bone, and his ribs, were well cushioned. Then he began to show an interest in his personal appearance. At the end of the first week he was so respectable-looking that the twins admitted him to a share of their dish, and invited him to join their endless games of "tag." Then, one day I surprised Velvet giving him some instructions about his toilet; - attending, herself, to the top of his head and the back of his neck—places that even mature cats find to be a little difficult.

Now that these three young catkins found themselves to be quite at home together it was very diverting to see their attitude toward each other. The twins were always more gentle and high-bred than was the little tramp who had come from nobody knew where; but they sweetly overlooked his lack of politeness; and condoned his manner of crowding and snatching at meal-time in a way that was truly edifying. When he unceremoniously snatched a choice bit from Velvet or Plush the one who had been despoiled looked in gentle amazement, for a few seconds, at the greedy little beast, then came to tell me about it; and to ask in prettiest "cat-Latin" for another bit. They never seemed to feel the least ill-will toward Peter for his rudeness; but accepted it with quiet resignation as part of the daily program.

Regarding them in their hours of relaxation, I learned much about the details of Cat-etiquette. Also I found that it is considered a delicate attention in Cat-dom to chase each other's fleas; and their superiority to the human family was shown in the fact that they could submit to the trying poses necessary to "the pleasures of the chase" with no loss of dignity, nor even of grace!

Just after Peter had been accepted by the twins, Johnny Bull came walking in at early lunch-time one day, and seemed not at all surprised to find the new arrivals. My own theory is that the news of these three new members being added to our family was carried to Johnny Bull, as he wandered in the forest, by a saucy old jay-bird who had ever been one of his dear enemies—stealing choice bits of food from him in the most bare-faced manner; obviously presuming on the well-known fact that all the cats dwelling on The Blessed Isle are forbidden to interfere, in any way, with the bird-families.

Peter and Johnny Bull made friends with one another on sight; and the gentle twins soon lost their first shyness. Then Johnny Bull seemed to forget that his kitten-days were past, and renewed his youth in gambols with these three young cats just as one sometimes sees an elderly bachelor "spruce up" and begin to act as if he were having an Indian summer of youth.

Deedie and Catsie no longer fought him. In fact, Deedie acted as if she repented of her former cruelty; and even Catsie would sometimes let him share her dish. She hated Peter with such supreme loathing that it swallowed up all smaller dislikes.

Peter was the only creature that ever caused Catsie to lose her dignity. Soon after his arrival in our family he made up his mind to be friends with Catsie, in spite of her evident distaste for him; so he began to persecute her with his attentions.

One day he approached her; and Catsie, tired of squabbling with him, turned to walk away out of his reach. He followed; she walked faster, and still faster, until she began to run. Peter accepted this as an invitation for a frolic, and galloped after. Catsie ran at full speed, and Peter sped at her heels until both disappeared in the undergrowth; leaving us shouting with laughter at the ridiculous sight of a mature cat fleeing from a little mite not much larger than a golf-ball.

Peter's greedy, saucy, independent ways had, from the first, made us quite sure, without asking him any questions, that "Peter" was a suitable name for him; but later he gave us reason for believing we had made a mistake.

We could not make a complete change, though, for she had accepted the name, and all the other cats had learned that she was Peter; so we added a syllable to make it sound more feminine, and called her "Peterkin."

Chapter Fifth.
Four Mothers and a Half.

CATSIE AND Deedie held the original cat-room against the new-comers, never allowing them to show therein so much as the tips of their little noses. Therefore, a separate room had to be provided for their accommodation.

On the side of the kitchen opposite to the door that gives on the little cat-room is another back porch screened in with wire-netting. It is larger than the other; so commodious, in fact, that it is utilized as a laundry. The set-tubs, supplied with running-water by the wind-mill, are at one end, filling its width the narrow way across. In the outside screen-door of this porch, Julius made a tiny cat-door, hanging in it a small square of sail-cloth, so the kittens could push under it; but all flying creatures would be excluded. This was the way the cat-door had always been in the room of the other tribe, to their evident comprehension and satisfaction.

Plush and Velvet saw at once how the new door and its little curtain were meant to operate; but Peterkin found it to be an unsolvable puzzle. She was almost always to be found sitting on one side or the other of it, waiting for someone to come and open the door. Over and over again I showed her the way it worked; pushing her gently through, first one way, then the other; but it was labor lost.

I often sat with my work-basket where I could observe what was going on in their room, and it was no uncommon sight to see Peterkin sitting tireless beside the little door waiting for it to open. In the meantime she regarded, with puzzled looks, the other kits as they skipped nimbly through and through the little doorway, its canvas curtain dragging along their backs and flapping shut behind them.

We never had owned such a stupid cat. I often tried to explain, in some satisfactory way, why she should be so dense. Whether she was, like the girl in the old-song:

"Bawn dat way";

or whether her early hardships had blunted a natural and usual amount of "cat-sense."

This latter hypothesis seemed to be the more reasonable of the two and accounted for much of the patience I showed in wrestling with her education. She responded slowly; but surely, to the care she received. In appearance she was completely changed and she kept herself sleek and spotless, except for the inky markings with which Nature, in sportive mood, had decorated her coat.

The wild frolics of the two glossy black kits and snowy Peterkin were most diverting. They occupied their rooms during the day only when it was showery outside, or when I brought my sewing to sit and enjoy their company. The rest of the time they were on little prowls outside on the lawn, or racing and scampering through grove and garden.

The twins were apparently, very near Peterkin's age; but, never having known hardship, they matured more rapidly, so were larger and in all ways finer-looking. Still, I was taken by surprise when one day they both came to tell me that they need a larger bed.

And before we had fully accepted the fact that these two young kits were really cats one morning we found Peterkin in her smaller box, which stood near the larger one contain Plush, Velvet and their twin kits, surrounded by five spotted, squirming mites! This was too big a family for her to attempt to rear; so I watched for her to go for an airing, then called Jackson to slip out all but one of the kits; and Peterkin, although she looked rather surprised on her return, never seemed to resent the shrinkage in her family.

Of course I selected the prettiest one for her to rear. It was all snow-white except a spot on the back encircling the root of the tail. This spot and the tail itself were jet-black, which gave the kit a strong resemblance to a cotton-ball. Its white body was the fluffy cotton; and the spot and tail of black made the calyx and the stem. And that was the way she got her name—she could not have been called anything except "Cotton."

The three young mothers soon proved that their own kitten days were by no means past. As soon as their babies began to "take notice" the fluffy little creatures were daily wound up for simultaneous slumbers while their three mothers engaged in the wildest larks— running races, playing tag, chasing and scampering around in a perfect abandon of foolish jollity.

Knowing that they must continue their own development, as well as give sustenance for their babies, I kept the mush-and-milk bowl always replenished in their room; but, in spite of the most generous diet, they were more lean and lank in appearance than I like my kitties to be. Jackson took the cast-net down to the wharf twice every day to catch minnows for them; often bringing up more than they could possibly manage to eat; so that the surplus was added to next day's chowder.

All the cattles understood about the net; and as soon as Jackson took hold of it the sound of its leads dragging on the floor gave warning and gathered both tribes. The one that reached him first always followed at his heals; and the other tribe left an interval of space between, and followed at a little distance in the rear of the other—two distinct and separate groups. It was diverting to watch the absorbed interest each individual cat took in every throw of the net and the excitement all along the line when it was drawn up bunched, and throbbing with the struggles of its silvery captives.

We named the two black kits "Jack and Jill," and they grew so rapidly that they soon tumbled out of the nursery-box to join the three mothers at the family dish. Then they went exploring and discovered the little white play-fellow in Peterkin's box. So there were two sets of frolicking kittens—the three mothers and their three lively babies.

Meanwhile Catsie and Deedie, who had never become reconciled to our "fresh start" of cats, seemed to have consulted together, trying to see if their united wisdom could not originate some scheme for the confusion of the interlopers.

This resulted in a genuine surprise for us.

Deedie, who during nearly two years had given us grounds for the belief that she was on the retired list so far as "multiplying and replenishing the earth" with cats was concerned, suddenly appeared with four kits which she and Catsie proudly placed in a heap on the floor of the little cat-room, then crouched around them, nose to nose, making a circle of their own bodies to enclose the young family.

As soon as I appeared at their door Catsie sprang up; leaping, as was her pretty way, to hook her claws in my frock so she could rub her face against my cheek. She kept this up, purring loudly and "talking" in such a coaxing manner, that I knew she was imploring me to send away the new cat-families and let these babies take their place.

As Deedie was fully grown and matured—a fine, big cat, in perfect condition—we had no hesitation in letting her rear all four of her catlets. She and Catsie took such equal pride and interest in them that one not in the confidence of the family would have felt at a loss to determine which cat really was their mother. But the kits knew that Catsie's mothering was only make-believe. They recognized Deedie as the one to whom they must look for the real necessities of kitten-life.

When our friends hear of the startling developments in the domestic affairs of the cat tribes of The Blessed Isle they were vastly interested and diverted. They came by twos, threes, and half-dozens to see the new arrivals and to congratulate the proud mothers.

Peterkin, Velvet and Plush were happy enough in displaying their treasures. In fact, they and I used to give a performance of our own while the three babies were being handed around and admired. I sat down in the smallest rocking-chair, giving them the sign to leap to my lap. Then I began to rock as far forward and back as the chair would swing, while the cats held on by hooking their claws in my skirts, and purred and swung their heads in rhythm with the rocking. Peterkin always squeezed around next to my hand so I could spank her in time to the swinging, and humped up her back to meet each slap. The children called this "Old Peter's cake-walk," and they and I had a way of laughing ourselves into a state of breathless delight that brought an end to the show.

The two mothers of the other cat-tribe were filled with terror and dismay every time their nursery was invaded by visitors. Catsie had always been extremely timid; more, it seemed, of strange voices than of the people themselves. Often she did not move on the approach of a stranger; but scampered off, utterly demoralized, as soon as he or she spoke. Deedie was not so bashful; but she seemed to think that each new-comer had designs on her precious babies—those darlings whose joyful arrival had renewed her youth.

It was about this time that our friends were reading, as they appeared in VOGUE, the stories about Catsie, Roi, Deedie, Johnny Bull and the Grand-baby, so each visitor wished to have a talk with the cats in whom they were kind enough to show a vivid interest.

The result, on Catsie and Deedie, of this plunge in the mad whirl of Society with a big S, was to fill them with tormenting apprehensions. One night after a day of thrills, caused by numerous callers, they carried off their family, secreting the kits under a broad leaf close to the root of a scrub-palmetto in the edge of the woods.

At first we had no idea where they had taken the kittens, and I was afraid something would happen to them; so I watched the two mothers and soon trailed them to their snug retreat.

And there I found only one kitten left!

Evidently some marauding animal—probably a 'possum—had succeeded, despite the prowess of the two brave mothers, in getting away with the other three. It seemed more than likely that the thief would come back for the fourth, so I carried him back to the little cat-room, giving his mothers a lecture for their foolishness.

After that I conducted no more visitors to their room; but when anyone asked to see Deedie's baby I carried him inside the house where Catsie and Deedie could not see it being handled by strangers; so they believed that it was taken to our part of the house simply because we wished to have it for a little visit to Julius and me.

This last kit spared to Deedie was, by good fortune, the prettiest she had ever owned. He had a coat of glossiest black, with white shoes, stockings and trousers, which made him resemble the babies of Velvet and Plush, which were all black except their white shoes. He was christened "Tommy Traddles" and, as "Tommy" can scarcely be called a distinctive name for a cat, we dropped it, and he was simply "Traddles." The good care and attention he received made him grow with most amazing rapidity; and he showed an unusual amount, even for a kitten, of vitality and joy in all lively pranks.

As Plush, Velvet and Peterkin reached mature cathood they developed stronger individual traits and characteristics.

Velvet had, in some ways, a disposition like Catsie, to who she was in no way related, so far as we knew. Like her, she would never begin to eat anything offered until she had thanked me for the food with loud purring; meanwhile rubbing her head, in most caressing fashion, against my knee; or shoulder; or cheek; whichever she could reach. She never leaped, like Catsie, to spring to my shoulder; but gentler even, and more patient, waited for me to stoop.

Yet this patient, gentle loving little Velvet had the strongest will I have ever seen exhibited in any animal. Often at bedtime when I went to put her out of the kitchen, after she had been allowed to come in for a little visit while I was getting ready to lock up for the night, she, not wishing to be so soon dismissed, ran to hook her front feet around the leg of the table, holding with such a desperate clutch that I sometimes found it impossible to detach her without help. For as soon as one foot was uncurled from its anchorage she took a firmer grip with the other set of claws. When Julius was within call he was often summoned to hold one foot while I detached the other. When I was alone, and had to wrestle unaided with her determination not to leave me, I could never conquer without some sort of strategy; and then I had to square myself with her by a few minutes of heart-to-heart talk before telling her good-night.

There were other battles we fought to a finish because this same willful little Velvet was the one cat, of all The Blessed Isle aggregation, that gave me trouble about the birds. Not that she offered to molest our own especial pets—the redbirds, jays, mockers, thrushes, cat-birds, blackbirds, or any of the daily visitors at the bird-table—these were all accepted by her, as members of the family; but she went, from time to time for a prowl in the garden returning with a poor little wren in her mouth.

Even when I did not see her as she entered the cat-room, where the others were sleeping or frolicking, I always knew when she had caught some unfortunate little creature by a certain triumphant throat-sound which she did not seem to be conscious of making.

Hurrying out, I found, sometimes, that it was only a katy-did or a grass-hopper—creatures we were glad to have destroyed because they ate the bloom-buds as well as the tender growth from our trees and plants.

When this was the nature of her catch it was very droll to see Velvet's look of reproach as I tipped up her head to make sure that it was not a bird in the cruel little mouth. But, when it did proved to be a bird, then the fight began.

Finding that the more I tried to loosen the tight-shut jaws the more desperately she held on, an inspiration came to give her a wetting which, like all cats, she detested beyond anything.

Many a time Peterkin and Plush sat looking on, with solemn disapproval, at our struggles; Plush, in extreme cases, even attempting to remonstrate with her rebellious sister.

The last resort, which was to hold the offender under the tap in one of the set-tubs, invariably freed her prisoner. As Velvet was generally careful to grasp her prey in such a way that it could not be hurt, wishing it to serve as means of sport and as an object lesson in educating the kits, the wren was ready to be carried back to the garden, where it was given a drink from the spray that kept the ferns damp, and left to calm its quivering nerves and smooth its feathers.

Once in a great while, naughty Velvet, as soon as she saw me running to snatch her, took a firmer grasp on the poor little bird, and bit it fatally. For this crime she got a scolding, a shaking and a ducking; then I buried the limp, lifeless atom where she could not get at it to dig it up.

Next to Catsie, Velvet was the most loving cat we have ever owned; and yet, her strong will made her the most troublesome pet, of any kind, we have yet tried to train. Plush was neither so affectionate nor so intelligent as her sister, but she was much more docile.

These black twin-cats began to give me real thrills of horror, when I discovered the delight it gave them to torture butterflies. It was not that we objected to having the graceful creatures destroyed. As lovers of grove and garden, we recognized them all as the parents of our enemies; and felt the necessity of waging an unceasing warfare against them notwithstanding their beauty and the romantic touch they give to a garden when they drift dreamily or flit airily from bloom to bloom.

No; it was the idea of the thing.

The sight of this, the accepted emblem of the soul, being tortured by demons, typified in the two black cats. It was not that the little hunters wished to devour the butterflies; for, as soon as a victim was broken, and had ceased to struggle, it was dropped, and its tormentor sped after another. Often, in these mad chasings, the two cats leaped so high in the air it almost seemed as if they too had wings. And they became so expert in snatching wind-sailors from their airy voyages, that the ground was strewed with bright fragments of soul-emblems - broken—ragged-winged—dead!

I scolded the little fiends so severely for this suggestive series of tragedies that they finally understood and knew that they were disobeying orders whenever they engaged in a butterfly-hunt. So they went farther a-field and tried to conceal the fact that they were still enjoying the wicked sport.

Often they came scampering in to leap on my knees, as I sat with sewing or book, to caress me and to demand responsive caresses, their air of exaggerated innocence contrasting oddly with the fact that the little black muzzles were all powdered with shining dust from the wings of freshly-torn victims.

When I began at once to scold them, they regarded one another with gentle amazement as if to ask:

"How did she know! Who has been telling on us?"

Meanwhile the kits of the two tribes were approaching cat-hood, and a housekeeper in the Village sent an urgent petition to The Blessed Isle, telling such a pathetic tale of a cat-less and mouse-haunted home, that our nurseries were reviewed to see who could best be spared.

Peterkin had already weaned Cotton. Then, as ever since, she has shown herself to be very prompt and business-like in this matter. She weans her kittens as soon as they learn to lap, and then she seems to lose all interest in them. Plush and Velvet were still nursing their babies, though they were older than Peterkin's Cotton. And Deedie showed not the slightest inclination to wean Traddles, nor did she ever, for he weaned himself by following his mother and Catsie to the family dish, where he found food that suited his taste better than the thinner diet furnished by Nature's boarding-house.

So Peterkin's baby was the first one listed to be given away. For a mate we selected little Jack, for Plush and Velvet fed and mother their two babies with a hazy impartiality as to which was whose, and we knew they would not feel bereaved so long as one of them was left to be cuddled.

Jack was a well-grown kitty, perfectly able to look out for himself, and to be a well-bred charming house-mate for anyone who might be so fortunate as to win his regard; so he and Cotton packed their trunks, made their adieus, and departed for fresh hearts to conquer, and it was not long before a message came to The Blessed Isle telling us that they had become a source of perpetual joy to the erst-while cat-less household.

Chapter Sixth.
White Slippers.

WHEN JACK and Cotton were sent to carry joy to another family-circle, we changed Cotton's name to Jill as more appropriate. There was harmony in "Jack and Jill," while "Jack and Cotton" was, so to speak, a discord.

Therefore the kitten left to console Velvet and Plush needed a name to replace the one borrowed from her. It happened several times that, when I went out in the twilight, to see to the dishes in the cat-rooms, I found the lone kit that was amusing herself in the big cat-room to be so effaced by shadows which swallowed up her black coat that only the little white shoes were to be seen—the ghostly feet of an invisible cat! So it was not surprising that she began to be known as "White Slippers."

She was the quaintest little creature. Her body was so short that Julius said she looked as if she had been sawed off. To make up for this shortage, she was what the children call "chunky." All her ways were individual and original—not like any other kitten we had ever known. One of her oddest tricks was the craze she had for sleeping in a dish. After her two mothers and Peterkin had eaten from the bowl which was regularly filled for them, it was the usual thing for White Slippers to go to work conscientiously to remove every crumb and drop from it with her pink-petal tongue. As soon as this was done to her satisfaction she stepped into it, curled herself up so that her body filled it to the brim, and there snoozed happily until she was disturbed by one of the mothers coming in to call her.

212

White Slippers had one serious fault. She was a biter. All young creatures have the natural instinct to bite while they are teething. Most kittens or puppies will chew anything and everything while their teeth are finding the way through their gums, just as human babies do; but with White Slippers it was real biting. From the very first she was never taken up by anyone without managing to give the hand that grasped her a severe pinch with her needle-like teeth. Even ankles were often seized and held with her claws hooked in the stockings while she set her teeth in the flesh. There seemed to be no malice in this. It was evidently her way of expressing affection. Of course such a naughty trick could not be ignored, and I began at once to discourage it. She was an extremely affectionate little creature, loving above all things to be with us, scampering over us in playful pranks, or dozing in some warm nook of drapery. So we made a cast-iron rule that she should stay with us as long as she did no biting; but as soon as her teeth were tried on either of us out she must go.

Such a clever kitty was not long in comprehending this rule, and it was really touching to see her struggles to keep it. Often she started to bite one of us, then drew back with an obvious effort and turned her head and bit her own little shoulder or paw. When the temptation was too strong for her, and she had bitten one of us, she often sprang away as soon as she realized what had happened, and took refuge under some piece of furniture whence she looked out imploringly, well knowing that she was to be banished as soon as caught. In these crises I did not scruple to use strategy—to call coaxingly as if I wished her with me; then, as soon as she could no longer resist, and came to be caught, I carried her out to her own quarters where (after telling her that she could not come back to stay with us until she was ready to be a good kitty) I left her outside, and tried to harden my heart against her as she sat gazing mournfully through the screen-door toward the sound of our voices—a pitiful little Peri at the gate of her Paradise.

It was perfectly evident that White Slippers understood the gravity of her one fault, and that she tried to overcome it. She was really as loving as Velvet, and was so superlatively happy in our society that she reminded us of the little girl who begged her mother to come and spank her, rather than to leave her alone unspanked. Our naughty little kit would really prefer being punished and kept with us, to be banished unpunished to the society of the other cats. And this caused me to make a mistake about her. I thought it was simply a taste for human companionship, instead of personal affection for us. Just after we had begun to believe that she was cured of her biting mania, the two little black mothers had another visit from the stork.

White Slippers, who had been for so long a time the only baby in the big cat-room, rather objected to having her nose put out of joint; and, as we were too busy just then to give her much of our attention, it seemed very opportune that Kathryn's mother should call to see if we had a kitten to spare for her little girl. I told her all about White Slippers, who received her advances with evident pleasure, so it seemed to be an ideal arrangement.

White Slippers was so devoted to me that she was always ready to follow me in my wanderings about the place; and, as Kathryn's mother was a near neighbor, I thought it best to let the kitten be personally conducted to her new owners. So I put on my sun-bonnet, and gave the usual "cattle-cry."

"Come, cats and kits."

All promptly showed up at the front steps; some creeping from under the house; others running from the direction of grove or garden; while Peterkin sprang down from her perch on one of the lawn-settees, where she had been watching the maneuvers of a fish-hawk that was sailing over the wharf and diving for fish with much shaking and splashing.

As soon as Catsie saw Peterkin she gave her usual disgusted spit toward the dear enemy, and ran back under the house followed by Deedie. The others all gathered around me, and looked up inquiringly. With a call of invitation to them, I entered the shady path along the shore that leads to the home of little Kathryn.

Plush, Velvet, Peterkin and White Slippers all straggled after; but first one then another paused. As soon as it was discovered that our grounds were being left behind, Peterkin turned and scampered back home, while Plush and Velvet sat down in the path to await developments. White Slippers ran along close to my feet—now in front, and now pausing at my heels to listen to some fancied sound among the ferns which bordered the path.

When we arrived at the home where I was leading my unsuspecting little follower she hesitated about ascending the steps; but came to me as soon as I reached the front door and turned to call her. I lifted her in my arms, and could feel her little form begin to tremble as soon as the door was opened in response to my rap, and she saw that we were surrounded by strange people with unfamiliar voices. In the midst of enthusiastic greetings I divined that it was all a mistake; and, if the little girl had not begun to weep as soon as White Slippers ran to the door, trying to escape her advances, I should certainly have taken her at once back to her happy home; but the memory of my own promises, and the sight of Little Kathryn's tears, gave courage to persevere in the attempt to make her stay. Kathryn's mother understood when I told her that the child's enthusiasm was rather overpowering, and took the trembling little cat in her lap while I knelt near petting and coaxing until the wild eyes softened and a faint purring began. Then I slipped out and hurried home.

Velvet and plush met me half way, where they had been waiting. They ran to meet me, then craned inquiring necks around my skirts to look back along the path for White Slippers.

When we three entered our own grounds Peterkin sprang from behind a bush where she had been hiding—waiting with patience for our return that she might have the pleasure of jumping at us and giving us a scare.

All three of us pretended to be terrified, which so delighted her that she galloped three times around us, then dashed off at a tangent and disappeared under the house.

We missed our absent kitty more than was reasonable, with so many others in the family. I was haunted by the look that had been in her eyes when she had first realized her strange surroundings. Over and over I told myself that it was not fair to give away a half-grown kitten—that the change should have been made as soon as she was weaned, if at all. Still, I knew how good her new owners would be to her, and what a big share of love and petting the affectionate little creature could now enjoy, so I hoped all would be well.

The next afternoon I went down the shore-path, led by the sound of childish voices, and found, just as I expected, all the children of the neighborhood playing at the water's edge in front of Kathryn's home. As soon as within hearing, I called:

"Is the kitty all right, Kathryn?"

"I don't know," was the answer, "she runned away."

"Runned away!" repeated I, horrified, "When?"

"Last night; just before dark. The first time we opened the door."

My heart went down into my shoes. All night, and all day. That timid, gentle little creature alone in the forest! What happened to her? At the best, she would be hungry, thirsty and frightened out of her little wits. She who had never been alone in her life.

Poor little terrified mite!

I hurried home and called Julius. He was equally disturbed. Together we set out at once to search the woods. We looked and called until dusk, then went home for a lantern and began again. There was no trace of White Slippers.

It was nearly midnight when we gave it up.

Several times during the night I waked, thinking I heard her voice; then concluded it was only dreaming.

The next morning I was up at dawn, and went down in dressing-gown and slippers to ask the two little black mothers if they had found trace of our lost kitty.

As soon as the door into the big cat-room had been opened, there was a confused rush and flurry of black cats. As I stooped Velvet, Plush and White Slippers all sprang at once to my clasp and were hugged together—heads, tails—any way they happened to come, while I laughed and they purred in the joy of reunion.

Chapter Seventh.
Pickaninny.

LITTLE KATHRYN did not give up White Slippers without protest.

As soon as it was known that the little wanderer had returned to us her new owner came to take possession. I raised no objection, as I do not wish the children to call me an "Indian giver."

Kathryn was told to take her kitty back and give her another trial. This, as I well know, was easier said than done. In Kathryn's grasp White Slippers was like the proverbial "greased pig." After trying many times to carry the squirming mite, Kathryn gave it up in disgust and implored assistance.

I went readily enough with her to her home, White Slippers following at our heels. We coaxed her into the house; then, after the door was shut, I hastened home. Of course I knew that this clever kitty had now learned the way, and I was not at all surprised to see her out in the cat-room with the others a half hour later.

This program was several times repeated, and then little Kathryn, who is a child of very decided opinions, announced that White Slippers was a "bad kitty," and that I might have her back again. I accepted the gift with all due gratitude, and promised, in return, that Kathryn should have one of the little new kits as soon as their mothers were willing to wean them. Plush and Velvet each had twins, and all four of the youngsters were coming on finely.

Kathryn thought she ought to receive two baby-kits in exchange for a big kitty like White Slippers, and I told her she could have two of them if her mother did not object.

The argument on this subject was later reported by Kathryn's mother, who said that at a crisis in the debate Kathryn exclaimed tearfully:

"I wish I had a nice mother like Mrs. Judith; then I'd have plenty of kitties!"

This so scandalized my old-fashioned ideas of the way children should submit themselves to the wisdom and judgment of their parents that I availed myself of the first opportunity to tell Kathryn that I should not wish so many kitties either, if I had all her mother's sweet children to love. And this scene ended with little Kathryn's arms around my neck, while she was declaring that she would be—

"Half mother's little girl, and half yours."

Anyway, she gained her point, and the two kitties were hers; another went to Minnie, which left us again with only one from the two families of Plush and Velvet.

And this was our adorable little Pickaninny. She was as black as ink all over—not a single white hair.

Julius said that, except during the time when she was a very small kit, he could never distinguish her from Velvet or Plush; but they did not look at all alike to me. True, they had the same grace and daintiness of shape, and, of course, their coats were the same color, except that Plush wore the little white button in her invisible collar—all the rest of her fur being like that of the other two, jet black. Julius said they looked alike, and our friends often asked me if I really could tell them apart, and how.

I always answered truthfully that these three black cats looked no more like each other, in my eyes, than they—our friends—resembled their neighbors.

The difference was in face and expression.

Pickaninny had a wide face, unusually large, clear eyes, with a candid innocence of expression seldom seen in the eyes of any but the

218

youngest kittens. In her, this expression of youth and innocence did not pass with kitten-hood; nor has it ever left her, though she is now the mother of grown cats.

From the first I felt that this kitty, like some humans, had been endowed at birth with the spirit of eternal youth. Most cats put off all their kitten looks and ways with the arrival of their first nest full of kits. From that time they are sober, demure tabbies, caring only for peace, quiet and comfort. In this they are like their human prototypes.

Other cats, like other humans, are always young. Nature has bestowed on them a superfluity of buoyancy and joyance that nothing can destroy.

Pickaninny has always been an ideal cat in every way, quick and clever, docile and loving; handsome, friendly with strangers, and frolicsome. She never cries for what she wants, but coaxes prettily with winning caresses and wistful looks, and with all these charms she keeps her eternal kitten-hood.

Peterkin has her share of the youthful spirit; no amount of sickness or trouble—and she has had both—can dim her enjoyment of life, or put an end to her pranks and frolics. But with Peterkin, it seems to be more a sort of compensation—a making up for lost time—as one sometimes sees an orchard whose spring blooms the frost has nipped in the bud, blossoming giddily the first warm day of Indian Summer. Peterkin's earliest youth—before a kind fate led her to our door—had evidently been devoid of joy—even of reasonable comfort; she had nothing but dire misery. So, ever since her arrival among the scenes of The Blessed Isle, she has been making up for this early lack which gave her, from the very beginning, a certain air of having been born old in worldly knowledge.

White Slippers and Pickaninny, being the only children in the big cat-room, began to play together when little Pickaninny was yet so small that she was like a doll-baby-kit in the clasp of White Slippers. The two mothers and Peterkin sometimes joined in their gambols; but more often the three giddy young matrons were off afield on some excursion of their own, leaving the two youngsters to amuse one another.

Pickaninny was more lively and adventurous in her nature than was the older White Slippers, and she soon found a way to do something which we should have declared to be impossible.

The heir-apparent of the other tribe of cats—young Traddles—son of Deedie and grand-son of Catsie, lived on the other side of the house in the original cat-room. He had been entirely dependent on grown cats for society ever since the tragic end of the three little ones who had been snatched from beside him during his earliest infancy.

His mother and grand-mother, with daily calls from Johnny Bull, were the only cats he ever saw, except at a distance—as Velvet, Plush and Peterkin passed by, giving the other tribe and their quarters a wide berth.

Pickaninny in some way learned about the long hours this lonely little fellow passed in solitude while the adults of his family were afield, and began to go from time to time to peep in at him; scampering bashfully away, in a real or pretended panic as soon as he moved, or cast startled glances in her direction.

It was perfectly evident that his mothers had warned Traddles against the cats of the other tribe as dangerous creatures, and had forbidden him to notice them. It took tireless perseverance to overcome his shyness and his ideas of filial duty.

From day to day I watched developments, always trying to encourage the friendship which I felt should obtain among the three charming youngsters.

Bolder and bolder grew Pickaninny, and one day I found that she had coaxed White Slippers to the door of the other cat-room and was evidently daring her to enter.

Catsie and Deedie had gone off on some excursion together and the coast was clear.

First one kitten, than the other, peeped in through the cat-door. Traddles who, as usual, when they threatened to approach him, seemed terrified and crouched in the furthest corner—now hiding his face, and now casting frightened glances over his shoulder toward his visitors. Finally, with some sudden access of courage or of interest, he relaxed his rigid crouching and turned around facing them. Then White

Slippers and Pickaninny, making soft little throat-sounds, and, from time to time, touching noses, as if consulting together, slipped through the door, one after the other, then turned and scampered out again. This coquetting continued for some minutes. Traddles gradually edging toward them, until finally Pickaninny made a dash for him and kissed him squarely on the lips, or, I suppose in cat-Latin it would be, they touched noses. That broke the spell. And soon the three were playing happily together.

The next day Johnny Bull came in from the woods to breakfast with the cattle, taking a snack, as was now his custom, in first one room and then the other, glorying in the fact that he was the only cat who was at ease with both tribes and little knowing that this distinction was soon to be shared with his under-study. Finding on this particular morning that there was a feast on—in fact, the tri-weekly kettle of fish-chowder, made purposely for the cats—he, after taking the edge from his own appetite, disappeared and shortly returned with two such disreputable old tramp-cats that they were promptly recognized and greeted as "Dusty" and "Weary."

After the poor creatures had eaten as if they had been starving, they and Johnny Bull disappeared together, going in the direction of the grove, and soon the other cats put their babies to sleep and also vanished.

White Slippers and Pickaninny did not sleep long. With one accord they scuttled out through their little door and hurried around the house to waken lazy Traddles.

The next thing we knew the three kittens had taken possession of the big cat-room and were having a grand game of ground and lofty tumbling to the tune of:

When the cats are away
The kittens will play!

It was delightful to see how Traddles enjoyed it.

Picture a dull little boy who all his life has played alone, or has shared the more or less perfunctory gambols of his elders—who has never realized the meaning of youthful companionship—of real response—then, all at once freed—in new surroundings, with two young companions who awaken and respond to all his natural jollity—who set free his bottled-up vitality and prankishness in a wild scramble of reckless rough-and-tumble, and it's no wonder it goes to his head, making him, for the time, drunk with the joy of being alive—and young!

Chapter Eighth.
Catsie.

JULIUS HAS a horror of what he calls a "yeowly cat." That is, a cat which is always mewing or caterwauling. And that is the kind we never, or almost never, have.

Peterkin generally mews for whatever she thinks she wants, and her kittens often resemble her in this respect; but Plush, Velvet, White Slippers, Traddles, Pickaninny, Catsie, Deedie and all of their children have ever seemed to realize that they are sure to be cared for; and that if there is any delay about attending to their wants it is because I am busy, and that I am hurrying to attend to them as soon as possible.

Often I have looked out into the two cat-rooms while something of which they were very fond was sending out delicious odors from where it was simmering on the kitchen fire, and it seemed to me that nobody ever had such reasonable, patient kitties as ours.

On these occasions they were all to be seen sitting facing the doors nearest the kitchen with an air of being at once patient and on the alert.

If I started in their direction, all rose eagerly to receive me; but if I turned before reaching the door, then all sat down again and resumed their waiting, the younger ones alone showing impatience by walking to and fro near the door, pausing from time to time to rub their cheeks coaxingly against it, purring loudly, and peeping in to see how things were progressing toward the coming feast.

In the smaller cat-room Catsie reigned as absolute monarch. She was in every way deferred to by her two descendants. Deedie was much larger than her mother; and Traddles also soon out-grew her, but both were conspicuously deferential toward their little autocrat.

Catsie never came into our part of the house to stay with me, except when she knew that I was all alone.

Julius had begun making another place in a settlement about thirteen miles away; and in seeing to the men who did the heavy labor, he was often from home for two days and nights at a time.

On these occasions Catsie, who never failed to know in some subtle way exactly what was going on in our part of the house, always climbed up on the roof of the one-story addition, then sprang to the window-sill of the room where she knew me to be busy at desk or work-basket, and scratched on the sash to be let in. When I opened the window she came eagerly in, making in her throat a little characteristic sound that denoted satisfaction—a mingled greeting and expression of self-congratulation—then came to curl herself up in my lap where she purred happily until bed-time, passing the rest of the night snoozing behind my pillow.

One night when we had just begun to enjoy our evening together, she suddenly sprang up from my lap to the desk where she stood tense and growling. I listened, and far away, I heard the baying of a dog. The next instant Deedie's face appeared at the window. She called to her mother, and Catsie asked to be let out. When the window was opened the two cats conferred briefly together, then disappeared.

Curious to see what they would do, I went down stairs and looked out into their room.

They were crouched together near the outside door where they could look toward the woods whence still came the sound of a dog which was evidently baying some unfortunate creature it had managed to tree. From time to time they turned toward one another with anxious glances, uniting in keeping Traddles behind them and in snubbing him when he showed a masculine desire to assert himself.

Catsie and Deedie had the gravest reasons for a terror of dogs. The only one they had ever known was the "Bobb tale pupp" which had tried to kill Deedie, and that had killed the lamented Grand-baby.

To them the baying of a dog was as sinister and blood-curdling as to us would be the roar of a lion or the snarl of a tiger that was camping hungrily on our trail. The two mothers were evidently on guard against what they felt was a possible and terrible fate.

I saw no more of Catsie that night. I called to her experimentally before going back upstairs; but she threw me a glance of significant finality, and turned at once to keep her eyes glued to the one spot in the outer darkness whence came that sound which to her was so awful.

Blissfully happy as she always was with me, still my little Catsie was ready to sacrifice all those hours of delightful companionship and perfect security when she felt that duty called her elsewhere. She knew that Deedie could not be coaxed to sleep indoors, for this big kitty had from the first conceived a distaste for any but her cat-room at night, and so the true little mother gave herself up to what she believed was the protection of her offspring or to a share of their fate if the worst happened.

I always made it a rule to see in person to the feeding of the various cattle. No one knows them so well as their Judith, and whenever this pleasant duty has been delegated to anyone else I have always found that some member of our little families had not received a fair share of attention, while some other has perhaps had too much. I know just about what each one needs, making always due allowance for those that are still growing, for those who have little ones to supply, and for all the various circumstances that influence their health and their appetite.

For a long time Catsie, Deedie and Traddles ate what was given them, appearing to be therewith perfectly satisfied. Every morning the water-bowl in their room, as in the other cat-room also, was filled with fresh water; and three times a day their clean-licked platter was taken away and replaced by one which was full of the sort of food our kits are taught to affect.

One day just after they had been fed I heard the screen-door, which opens from their room into the house, gently shaken. This was a trick of Catsie's which she had long since adopted whenever she wished to attract my attention. She never called unless it was something which she considered to be very important. When I went out to her she was still standing on her hind-feet with her claws hooked in the wire. She gave the door another little shake when she saw me coming, then, after purring and rubbing her head against my skirts, she looked from me to the food-platter and back again. It had been completely emptied and she was unmistakable saying:

"We haven't had enough."

I filled the dish again; and as soon as she had thanked me, she fell to and cleared it alone.

This was very surprising, as Catsie had always been a small, dainty eater; but it was only the beginning.

From that time their dish had to be refilled so often—always in response to requests from Catsie—that, to save trouble, larger dishes were provided for this family of three than were needed by the five cats—three of whom were still growing—of the other tribe!

And Catsie was the only one who was consuming all the additional food which was being provided. She was evidently eating twice as much as was even the still-growing Traddles.

For some time I had noticed that she was becoming stout, but that is not an uncommon thing with either cat or human dowagers, so I thought nothing of it until all at once I remarked that she was growing one-sided—that a lump was curving out under her body toward the left.

One of our friends, years ago, lost a dear old kitty from the effects of a tumor, so we knew at once what it was.

Catsie did not seem to suffer at all. She was comfortable; but oh, so hungry. From day to day her appetite increased until we really wondered what she did with all she ate. The heaps of food disappearing down her ravenous little throat often seemed to be more bulky than her own body. I used to ask her how she managed to dispose of such quantities of food; but her only answer was to beg for more. She was fed all she asked for, and every remedy was tried for her growing disorder, but all to no purpose.

Many times a day her own little bowl was filled with catnip-tea; and her water-bowl and plate replenished.

This went on for nearly a year. Then all at once, she refused to eat; but sat moaning and looking imploring at me, as if she felt sure that I could take away her pain.

By this time she was large and shapeless. As her malady had augmented we prepared our minds for this end. Knowing the full experience of the old kitty of the before-mentioned friend, and fearing that our Catsie might also suffer at the last, Julius had bought me a small vial of chloroform.

Now was the time to use it.

The store-room opens from the smaller cat-room, and in this room, the stage-setting of her greatest happiness, I prepared another bed for poor little Catsie.

She came happily with me; almost forgetting the pain when she found that she was to have the exclusive society of her beloved Judith.

A comfortable bed was arranged—Catsie looking on and purring her satisfaction—then, at a word, she climbed in and curled up still purring, with her head in my hand.

I sat on the floor beside her and waited to see is she would sleep, or if the pain was coming again.

All too soon she began to cringe and moan, so I knew we could put it off no longer.

Then I called Julius, who had not gone out of hearing. He came and gave me a bit of cotton-wool which he had wet with the chloroform.

At the first whiff Catsie turned her head to evade the odor, protesting that it was sickening. Then she began to purr again, and I drew the cover up over the box; hiding my tears in the sleeve of the other arm, while dear little Catsie, conscious only of my touch, fell happily asleep—all of her pains ended forever.

Chapter Ninth.
Deedie and Traddles.

WHEN I went out to tell Deedie and Traddles that the little mother had found rest from pain in dreamless sleep, they had disappeared from their room; and, when I looked outside, there they were running at full speed toward the woods where they were shortly swallowed up by the undergrowth. When night fell they had not returned; and, the next morning we found that the dish containing their evening meal was still left untouched in their room. When I called them there was no response. They were evidently out of hearing; and the black cat tribe made it a point of honor never to respond when the names of the other tribe were called.

Johnny Bull came in after a while and took a share of what he found in the little cat-room; but, all day long, there was no sign of Deedie or Traddles.

Toward night I went out to where I had seen them disappear, and after calling for some time, at last saw their heads cautiously poked from the shelter of a scrub-palmetto.

They regarded me with a furtive air, and as I approached, turned and scrambled through the bushes out of sight.

This was a truly astonishing state of things.

Were they thus demoralized because they had perceived with their finer senses, the approach and passing of the Unseen Visitor who comes on the Wings of Silence to quench the vital spark?

Or had they breathed, from outside in their porch-room, a faint echo-breath of the chloroform, and so had misconceived the whole affair?

Who can tell!

I pondered it all as I went back to the house to bring food and drink which I placed under the palmetto where I could see that the two hungry little beasts had improvised a bed.

The Summer was now well advanced and Julius and I were busy preparing to go up to the Mountains for a short stay. It was hard for us to go away and leave things in this shape. From time to time I went out to call the two dear cats, and to try to persuade them to come home.

They always looked out at me; then, as at first, scampered off.

From a distance I had the satisfaction of seeing them creep cautiously from concealment to devour the refreshments I had brought and left there for them. And when the time came for our departure, a week after the death of Catsie, Jincy and Jackson were directed to place food and drink there daily until they relented and returned to their own room.

We were gone about eight weeks; and, the first thing I asked on our return was about Deedie. In the letters we had received from The Blessed Isle during our absence, the questions about her had been answered only by the vague and usual.

"Us an the cats an the birds an plais is all duin fine," so during our absence I had felt a ceaseless anxiety about Deedie and Traddles, fearing that my questions were evaded because of a kind wish on the part of the couple not to spoil our holiday.

We reached home during the night and the next morning Jackson came in to give his report. He said that all the cats except Peterkin and Deedie had come regularly to the big cat-room for their meals, but that no one had come to the little room except now and then Johnny Bull.

Peterkin had moved out to camp with Jincy and Jackson.

Deedie had never been seen except at a distance. Food had been placed out in the woods-edge for her, and the dishes were regularly emptied; but whether she had eaten there, or whether some other cat or strolling animal had found it, they could not tell. This was disquieting; and I felt still more distressed about poor Deedie when I heard that she was even deserted by Traddles, who had taken up with the other tribe.

Was Deedie dead? Or was she wandering sad and lonely in the forest—deserted even by her baby—the only tie now left to her?

Without waiting to unpack, or to attend to the countless matters awaiting attention indoors, I went out to the woods and made a circuit of its borders where, on all sides, it touched our grounds; calling at frequent intervals to Deedie.

At first all the other cats tagged after me, Traddles among them; but, thinking finally that I heard a faint response I sent them all back "scat" -ting, and telling them to go and wait for me at the house.

When they had obeyed, I went a little further in to the woods whence I had imagined came the sound, and called again.

Presently there was another cry, than a crackling of dry leaves and twigs. And creeping along through and under the grass and bushes —

Could that be my big, handsome Deedie!

A gaunt skeleton loosely draped with a coat of rough, unkempt gray fur—a creature wild and hungry-eyed—a typical Ishmael among cats!

And what gave me the sharpest pain was the knowledge that Deedie, a strong, sensible, capable hunter—a cat who was self-sufficient and ever equal to the occasion—could easily have found the woods to be a land of plenty, where all sorts of "small deer" could have been found and trapped to supply her needs—has simply lost courage. When bereft at one blow of mother, home and her faith in human nature, Life had become a burden which she made no effort to carry. She lived only because she was not yet dead.

My poor, poor Deedie!

I had brought a cup of milk with me and as she approached, then crouched as if afraid and on the point of turning to run, I sat down on the ground, placing the cup toward her, and kept on calling.

She came a little closer, then retreated. I pushed the cup a bit further from me and finally she made a sudden dash for the milk. As soon as she began to drink, she seemed to be oblivious to all surroundings; so I crept near enough to stroke her.

Tears fell while noting the prominence of every bone and the looseness of the big coat which once fitted so snugly.

When she had emptied the cup, I went back to the house and filled a bowl with crumbled bread, drowning it with cream, and carried it to where I had left her looking wistfully after me, as if she thought it might be for another long parting.

I found her sitting near where I had left her, and now she was making a feeble effort to arrange the ruffled plumage of her coat. She came to meet me, and soon emptied the bowl, then climbed to my lap as I sat on the ground, and purred while she made efforts to talk, as of old, which kept a queer tightness in my own throat.

Then I tried to coax her back to the house with me; but the very idea seemed to put her in a panic. She gave me a terrified glance, sprang away and disappeared among the under-growth.

The next day I found her waiting where we had met for this interview; and, for three weeks I carried out all of her food to her, she awaiting me always in the same place. And as she grew daily stronger, more plump and smoother of coat, her welcome to me grew always more enthusiastic.

Peterkin often tried to interfere with the daily trysts between Deedie and her Judith. If she could manage to slip along behind me unnoticed until Deedie was reached, it was her wicked fashion to spring out suddenly and fly at her throat in a way that put Deedie to flight; her pursuer following to such a distance in the woods that she was seen no more for that day. This made it necessary to take the precaution of shutting up Peterkin each time before going out to feed Deedie.

We had a week of rains during this experience, and so I had to keep appointments with Deedie carrying the dish in one hand and the umbrella in the other. Then Deedie's welcome was so warm, it seemed as if she were trying to say that she had expected to be left unfed until the skies cleared. At these times she came under the umbrella to eat; and stayed by me as long as I could remain with her, drying her coat with conscientious lickings and telling me in ways easy enough to comprehend, that I was bringing back Hope, and giving her a new lease on life.

Julius often called to me, making dire prophecies as to the consequences of so much pottering around in the wet; but it never seemed to hurt me at all. If one dresses the part—short water-proof skirts and India-rubber sandals—there is a real pleasure about being out in the rain. I used to tell Deedie that we were having a little menagerie of our own under the umbrella-tent, the rain gently tapping on it over our heads as we sat discussing her feast, and she paused in eating or in her coat-lickings to look in mild wonder at me as I laughed at my own whimsical thoughts.

During these rainy days I made renewed efforts to coax Deedie to come back to the house; but this proved to be a lingering and tedious affair.

Day by day I let her come a little further from the woods and nearer to the house to meet me, until, at last, she was but a stone's throw from it. Then one day when, after clearing her dish, she had climbed into my lap, I held her close, with her eyes hidden against my shoulder, and carried her in.

As soon as she was put down on the floor of her own room, she cast terrified glances around and dashed out the little door, fleeing back to the woods as if pursued by demons. But the next day I did the same thing, and the next, and the next, until finally her terror of the house was overcome, and then I ceased to take her food outside; but called to her to come in for it; and, at last, one day, without waiting to be called, she came in, and was there waiting for me; and that night she slept in her box where she and Catsie and Traddles used to sleep, and her son, hearing his mother in there, went into to sleep with her in their old nursery-box.

Chapter Tenth.
The Curly-Dog.

THE FACT that Traddles had deserted his mother had been made even more galling by the very enthusiastic friendship which had sprung up between him and Peterkin.

This had cut Deedie to the heart, for Peterkin was her bitter enemy, and never missed an opportunity to show ill-will, scorn and hatred. It seemed to be with the idea of making things as unendurable as possible for his mother that she encouraged the affections of the unsuspecting Traddles. As soon as this youngster returned to his still-devoted mother she evidently gave him a lecture about the designing Peterkin, for we noticed at once that there was a decided coolness between them. When Peterkin went around to call Traddles to give an account of himself, mother and son both set upon her, and some of poor Deedie's wrongs were then and there avenged.

As before stated, Peterkin had moved out of her own accord, to live with the other family during our Summer absence from The Blessed Isle. On our return Jincy told me with the greatest glee:

"Peter's our cat, now, Mis' Judy, she belongs to we-all."

Great was her disgust when Peterkin promptly returned to the big house, taking up her old quarters in the room with the black-cat tribe, and almost refusing to speak to the hired help who had been so good to her during the long weeks of our absence.

When I called her "an ungrateful little beast" she seemed to take it as a good joke, kicking up her heels and scampering off in high glee.

233

She seemed to delight in humbugging people. One of her tricks was to exact attentions from busy humans. After much drilling she had finally learned how to pass through the little door of the black-cat-room; but if anyone were at hand she always pretended that she did not understand it and insisted that the door be opened for her. It was only by watching when she had no thought of being observed that we discovered how, if there happened to be no one by that she could interrupt and bother with her demands, she slipped through the little door as cleverly as any of the cats. She seemed to be full to the brim of "manners and tricks." Being the one of our cats that is the readiest to meet advances from strangers, she had always enjoyed more than her fair share of popularity. The children all love "Peter-She," as they call her, because she seems to be so gentle and friendly. Of them all Little Prudence is her favorite.

The first time this little lady came to see us after she was large enough to ride alone in a chair, instead of sitting in the lap of her mother or the nurse, Peterkin determined to go home with her, so she stationed herself in the chair, remaining until after it had started, making it necessary that she should be forcibly removed. Then she followed behind until the chair-pusher speeded up and left her sitting in the path with such a dazed expression that Jincy said she looked as if she had been "conjured." Since that visit Peterkin always welcomes Little Prudence with a warmth she shows to no one else. She has a wonderful memory. There was a young boy who all one Winter brought us oysters twice a week. Then he went away, and three years after he came on a very different errand, smelling strongly of kerosene, which all animals detest; but as soon as Peterkin heard him at the back door she went dashing out and sprang up begging him for an oyster. He recognized her at once, and said: -

"Well this cat certainly has got a long memory."

Among the black people Peterkin has always been a prime favorite, for the surprising reason that she is "so white." It is a strange fact that black people dislike, to the point of extreme fear, all-black or even partly-black cats. They think that Peterkin is a beauty, but they are constantly declaring that they cannot understand why we will have "dem ugly ole black cats."

We once had a black cook who would never eat a bite of the flesh of a black chicken. There is something very curious about this aversion to black among the black people!

Jackson's Uncle Tobe had come to make a visit to him and Jincy and, being an industrious old man, who likes making opportunities to pick up odd dimes, he asked Jincy to tell me that he wished to do a little work for us during his stay. I sent word back that there was plenty to keep him busy; and that same evening as I was up in the garden inspecting some young rose-trees which had just been planted, the old man saw me there and came down from the cabin (which is just across the pineapple field from the grove beyond the garden) to ask for directions about going to work the next morning.

We had been noticing the barking of a dog out in the direction of the cabin, and now the riddle was solved. At old Tobe's heels was a soft-eyed, long-haired, little brown fellow, evidently having some spaniel in his make-up. When I stooped to caress him he was introduced as "Curly." Tobe apologized for his presence with a shame-faced:

"Hit cries atter me; en won't stay wid nobuddy else."

I assured him that Curly was quire welcome on the place if he was sure that the cats would not suffer from his attentions. Tobe laughed delightedly at this, assuring me that:

"Curly been licked wunst by a tom-cat, en he shore do run now fum ebery cat he see. He shore do."

All the time I was directing Tobe about next day's work, I kept stroking Curly's silky ears, which were brown, long and wavy-haired, awakening memories of Bruno.

When I started back to the house Velvet was the first cat to meet me. I stooped to take her up, but she drew back as if startled, and sniffed at my hand. Then her tail swelled, her coat bristled up all along her spine, and turning from me, away she sped!

In an instant I understood. It was because I had been stroking the dog.

Next came Plush, who went through with the same program; then in turn, White Slippers, Peterkin, Pickaninny, Traddles and Deedie, all through the list. It was so funny to see each cat come to be caressed, then give her startled sniff - fluff up her tail and coat—then turn to flee—each one doing exactly the same thing, in the same way, one after the other, that I couldn't help laughing. Julius heard me, and came out of the library where he had been reading, book in hand, to ask: -

"What's going on out here?"

He was just in time to see the last three cats swell up and scamper off, and his look of amazement as he asked what ailed them made me laugh so much harder that I could not answer him.

When he finally understood what it was, it struck him as being so funny, that I called the cats to come back and have the whole show over again for his benefit. They came obediently, one after the other, each kissing my fingers, and blossoming out into balls of fluff, then scampering off in a panic, while we laughed.

Chapter Eleventh.
Almost a Tragedy.

THE PRESENCE of the Curly-Dog, who soon learned to come to the back door every morning for some little bit I had put aside for him, had varied effects on the different cats.

Deedie and Peterkin seemed to be the first ones to discover his terror of cats. On their different sides of the house these two matrons watched for his approach, and sallied forth, as soon as he appeared, for the delicious excitement of putting him to flight.

White Slippers showed no disposition to be so aggressive; but as soon as he came near enough, she began to utter dismal howls and growls, evidently saying things that no gentleman could reconcile with his self-respect. The Curly-Dog always slunk away with most dejected mien as soon as she began her remarks.

After repeated lectures on the subject this little scold at last learned to be quiet on his approach, except at those times when she believed that we were not within hearing distance.

Velvet, Plush and Pickaninny were so gentle and lady-like, that they simply effaced themselves when warned of the approach of The Curly-Dog. As soon as they learned to expect him to come to the house at least once every day, for his little snacks, they vacated their room and found a bed for themselves out-of-doors. This was in a wind-break which had been built by piling up palmetto logs, for the purpose of protecting the garden from the salt-breezes sent across the

237

Sound by the ocean. The three cats established themselves out in this retreat, coming to the house only for food, and choosing the hours for their meals when they knew The Curly-Dog to be out at the cabin with his master.

The snug nest, where I trailed them and found they were safely sheltered by over-frowning log-ends and screening ferns, was by no means a bad place for them; and, knowing that The Curly-Dog would soon depart, leaving them again in peaceful possession of their cat-room in the big house, I made no effort to coax them back to their own beds.

And here, in this out-door nursery, were born Velvet's twins. When they were about ten days old their little mother came one day to see me, evidently trying to tell something which distressed her. On going with her to the nest, both her little kits were found to be lifeless. Evidently they had been for some time dead, and Jackson was at once called to bury them under a rose-tree in the garden, where their untimely death might be atoned for by a return to The Blessed Isle in the form of rose-blooms.

Then I remarked that Velvet seemed to be very thin, even for a mother-cat, who is always naturally inclined to a lean and lank condition and, taking her back to the house, I prepared a platter of food, calling all her tribe for an extra lunch.

Velvet looked eager while I was preparing the food, and made a dash for it as soon as it was set down among the clamoring little group. But when the others began the feast she put her mouth to the dish and then turned away. Thinking she was disappointed to find there only bread and milk, and was wishing for something special, I took her into the kitchen and offered her various bits from the safe and the refrigerator, to which, one after the other, she put her nose, then turned away. As a last resort, I broke a fresh egg for her, which I knew to be, from her point of view, the very greatest treat; but this, too, after the first eager approach, was turned from in the same manner.

Just then I was called to the drawing-room, and Velvet was, for the moment forgotten.

After that, whenever Velvet saw me at leisure to attend her, she came coaxingly, always seeming to wish for something; but never satisfied with anything that was offered. Daily I noted that she was becoming thinner and weaker.

Thinking it was grief for the mysterious death of the twins that cause her strange symptoms, I tried in every way to console and cheer her; but she never seemed to find what she was craving to eat, and daily she moped and shrunk.

At last, she was only a skeleton, almost too weak to stand, staggering around in a manner that was too pitiful to be endurable; she began to moan and complain and was never for an instant out of my sight if she could help it. I told Julius I was sure she had some serious illness, and as we could not get her to swallow any remedy—catnip, or any of the various things one coaxes animals to take when one is sure something is needed without knowing just what—it seemed that the only recourse left was a painless putting to sleep with chloroform.

Julius agreed with me and went for the bottle while I held the little sufferer who had never yet (patient little martyr!) failed to purr all the time that she felt the comforting touch of her Judith. Then he got a box and brought it out to where I was sitting by the cat-table—a recent institution, placed out-of-doors for their fish-feasts. There was a dish on the table where the other cats of Velvet's tribe had been refreshing themselves, and where I had just been trying again, for the hundredth time, to coax her to eat.

While Julius was preparing everything I held the poor little skeleton, stroking and petting her, as I believed, for the last time.

Pondering on her happy kitten-hood and the fulfillment of all that early promise of intelligence, grace and beauty, half absently I slipped my hand around her throat noting how slender it was. Thumb and finger-tip almost met. There was a lump in front. Was it a cat's Adam's apple? I pinched it gently, then rubbed it between finger and thumb. Velvet looked up quickly, and stirred her neck, with an eager movement, in my clasp.

Again I squeezed the "Adam's apple," impelled to do so by something indefinable in her manner.

All at once she sprang from me, and leaping to the table with more strength than would have seemed possible from the weakness she had been showing, she reached in a bound the half-emptied dish and eagerly began eating. As she ate, from either corner of her mouth came a fine trickle of little drops of blood. Some sort of foreign growth had been in her throat so that she could not swallow. She had been starving to death, as her kits had starved for lack of the food she did not have for them, and that opportune, accidental pinching of the throat had come just in the nick of time to save her. I realized then, when I remembered the length of time she had been without either food or drink, how true is the saying that cats have nine lives.

From that moment Velvet ate to make up for lost time, and soon was again her plump, glossy self; delighting us with her beauty and grace, as well as with her more-than-ever fervent expressions of adoring affection.

Chapter Twelfth.
Poor Little Plush.

OUR FRIENDS have always shown an interest in all the live-stock of The Blessed Isle. Indeed, one of the dearest among the Winter Cottagers across the Sound, offered to present me with a pair of Angoras, saying it was a pity to give so much time and trouble to the care of "just common mongrel cats." He was so surprised when this generous and charming offer was declined, that an explanation was in order.

I told him that cats are to us dear for their own sakes. The little creatures are so responsive to good care—so patient under neglect and suffering, it is a joy to prove that, if only they have a fair show, they are all interesting and full of charming possibilities.

Should we abandon our pets for a pair of the aristocrats of Cat-dom, the only good accomplished would be our own pleasure. People could well say:

"Oh, it's easy to make something of fine cats like Mrs. Judith's; but everybody cannot afford to have Angoras!"

Now, anyone in the world can have common cats, and it is a benefit to all Cat-dom to prove that these often despised and neglected creatures are so full of delightful possibilities.

Those who have not investigated the matter are prone to think that all cats are alike; but there is as much difference in them as there is in humankind. Of all the cats and kittens we have owned there have never been two that were exactly alike in either intelligence, disposition or affection. Just as with humans, some are more interesting than others; but not one is unworthy the opportunity to be its best self.

Just after the recovery of Velvet from that mysterious illness which was responsible for the death of her twin-babies, and came so near to making an end to her own happy life, The Curly-Dog departed, he and his master going back to their distant home at the termination of the visit with Jincy and Jackson.

The cats all knew as soon as he was gone, and the black-cat tribe signified their relief by an immediate return to their own sleeping-room. All were in perfect condition, showing that the change had been beneficial rather than otherwise.

Plush, for the first time in their history, asked for a nursery-box without Velvet needing one at the same time. She had never before looked so well. Her eyes were bright and clear; her coat soft and sleek; and in all ways she seemed to be everything that goes to make a fine, healthy, well-grown cat.

I prepared her bed according to the directions she gave for it; and, there being just then no young kittens in either tribe, looked forward with pleasure to the arrival of her little family, knowing that all the cats in the big cat-room would unite in welcoming the kittens.

Peterkin had just recovered from an attack of staggers which she had contracted in an attempt to live a double life. A family passing the Winter near us had taken a fancy to this friendly cat, and, as they were great fishers and fish-eaters, Peterkin formed the habit of slipping over to take a seven-o'clock fish breakfast, turning up innocently at our own morning meal which occurred an hour later. At this repast she pretended to have a hunger dating from the night before, and eagerly demanded her share of the dish prepared for the rest of her tribe.

Two breakfasts a day make a severe demand on the digestion of any creature, and the first we knew of her little scheme was a message which came from the fish-eating neighbors to the effect that Peterkin was lying in their grounds unable to stand.

Jackson intercepted the messenger, and went at once to bring the sufferer home. During this illness her temper was in such an uncertain state that, by the time she had recovered, all the cats were disgusted with her, especially Traddles, who had again begun an intimacy with his prankish old playmate.

Deedie was again very gentle and tender with her returned prodigal, and amused us by washing and dressing him after each repast, just as if he were again a tiny baby-kit.

Traddles has never since deserted the little cat-room where his infancy was passed. He is now on good terms with all the members of the other tribe; but they meet on neutral ground and he invariably returns to his own quarters to eat and to sleep.

Johnny Bull still came daily for a short visit to each cat-room, sampling the food which he found in both and making a good meal before he went back to the woods.

Sometimes Dusty and Weary came with him and ate with ravenous appetites; prompting some of the cattle to come and ask me to replenish their platters.

So matters stood when Plush announced that she and her expected family were about to occupy the center of the stage in Cat-dom.

One morning I found her lying in the bed which had for some days been ready. One black kit lay beside her. Velvet sat close to the box, and seemed to be strangely uneasy. I stroked the little mother's head, and complimented the new arrival; then asked if that was the only one the stork could spare her for this time.

There was a look of suffering in her eyes, and I hastened to bring a refreshing cup of catnip tea.

She took only a swallow or two, then rubbed her cheek caressingly against the hand that held the cup, purring faintly.

That was an unusually busy day. The Season, with a big S, had just closed, leaving, as it always does, mountains of accumulated matters to be attended to. There were numberless small distractions to fill every minute, so that it was several hours before it became possible to go again to see about the cats. And when the nursery-box was reached, instead of finding, as I expected, a happy little mother nursing a healthy pair of kittens, there was poor little Plush quite dead, with a little dead kit lying against her body.

We never knew what went wrong.

The dead mother-cat had wide open eyes and half open mouth as if she had died in a spasm. We supposed that the kit must have tried to nurse after the mother's death, and that the milk was not good for it.

Anyway, they were both cold.

Velvet and Pickaninny lay outside the box on the floor fast asleep in one another's clasp, as if they had been grieving together like two humans.

Thus ended the happy life of poor little Plush.

We buried her at sundown, with the little dead kit on her arm, in a grave lined with ferns, bay-leaves and the blossoms of the white star jasmine.

That night I dreamed I saw her entering the Cat-Heaven carrying her kitten, mother-cat fashion, in her mouth. All the waiting Tabbies in the Cat-Paradise came forward to welcome her, and to lead the way to a soft, cool nest they had made ready among the catnip bowers; where she and her baby-kit lay down to rest without fearing that their retreat might be shared by that pitiless intruder, which on earth we call PAIN.

Chapter Thirteenth.
Peter Junior.

ONE DAY I was writing in the study when, all at once, I heard that thrilling sound which once striking the ear is never forgotten—the whirring of a rattle snake. It seemed to be close by, and, going out on the front gallery, there was Peterkin crouched under the Calabash-tree, watching with eyes narrowed to green slits, an immense coiled rattler.

Julius had just gone up in the grove; but Jackson was at work near the house, planting a hedge of white periwinkles and red hibiscus along the front fence of the poultry-yard, where the palmetto-log wind-break had been before the palm-grove had grown large enough to act as a protection.

I called to him, and he came promptly, recognizing, as soon as close enough, the whizzing of the rattle-snake. At once he turned that ashy color which with the Negro race is a substitute for pallor, and cried:

"I shore can't go clost enough to hit him wid a stick; please ma'am jes watch him, and lemme run home and git my gun."

"Here's my revolver," said I, having instinctively caught it from the desk where it always lay.

"Oh, no'm; I wouldn't resk dat. Dis yer is shore a time fur de shot-gun!"

He sped away, and when he returned with the gun Julius was following, having asked:

"What's the excitement?" as he saw Jackson dashing frantically across the grove on the way to his cabin.

Noting how Jackson trembled, Julius said:

"Here, give me the gun. I'll settle him."

Jackson, glad to get out of the scrape, readily handed it over and backed off.

Meanwhile Peterkin sat just beyond reach of the snake's fangs, watching it with an absorbed air of fascination, and his snakeship dared not move with such an enemy there ready to spring on him.

Julius unobserved by either snake or cat, who were deaf and blind to everything except one another's movements, crept around to where he could aim at the monster without danger of hitting the unsuspecting Peterkin.

Finally a good position was secured, and "BANG" went the gun.

The rattle-snake began to struggle in death-throes—the terrified cat bounded high in the air, and dashed off utterly demoralized.

Several days later I understood what she believed had happened. Always she had shown a perfect craze for catching the little green or black snakes, which we like to have around, as they are a benefit. They catch and eat various detrimental creatures in the garden, and never do the least harm. I saw her look at one of these little snakes as it was gliding along, and instead of, as always heretofore, giving chase, she backed cautiously away, and sped terror-struck in the opposite direction. Then I knew she believed that the rattle-snake had blown up while she was watching it, and that some new freak of Mother Nature had inspired her to load all snakes for the undoing of unwary cats. She has feared them ever since. She always gives them the right of way, and shows every sign of terror if she has a glimpse of even the tail of a little lizard slipping through the grass.

To return to the rattle-snake.

We had Jackson bury the head which was shot entirely off (the full load having torn through its neck) for fear that one of the cats might in some way get a taste of the venom and be injured thereby. Then Jackson cut off the rattles for me, and I watched him dig a deep-trench where he buried the still-squirming body.

After dark that evening two men who were at work on a

neighboring clearing, and had happened to hear that a rattle-snake had been killed on our place, came, lantern in hand, to ask if they might have the body for its skin.

They were told that it had been deeply buried; but if they wished to dig it up they were welcome to do so. Jackson was called to show them where to dig for it; and, when they reached the place, great was the superstitious terror of the three negroes to find the headless and tailless body of the snake lying on the surface of the ground, where it had evidently dug itself up by those contortions which the black people say never end in a killed snake until sundown, and which they regard as conclusive evidence of their kinship with the Evil One, and therefore as a sign of the possession of supernatural power.

Two weeks after Peterkin's experience with the explosive rattle-snake, she asked to have her bed in the large cat-room relined and made comfortable for a present which the stork had sent word he was about to bring her.

While the black cats never had more than triplets at one time—often only twins, and sometimes a single kitten—Peterkin and Deedie usually had four or five.

On this occasion four was the number left in Peterkin's box, and, instead of all having the usual spotted white and black coat of their mother, one was tiger-striped with a white breast.

The three spotted ones were less robust than Peterkin's kittens had always been, and soon succumbed to infant ailments; but the little tiger-cat was vigorous enough to have absorbed the vitality of the whole family. He waxed fat and round; and, at an age when most kittens hardly begin to take notice, he climbed out of bed and joined his mother and the rest of her tribe at the family dish.

Noting that he invariably responded when Peterkin was called, tumbling and rolling along at her heels, we promptly named him "Peter Junior."

In fact, he may be said to have named himself.

Never was there such an original and enterprising cat.

He made the rounds of the place, undaunted by anything, even making friends with Deedie, and going from time to time to pass a few hours in the little cat-room with her and Traddles, serenely unconscious of, and indifferent to, the lordly airs of the son Deedie was so fond of treating like a prince in Cat-dom.

Peter Junior followed his mother out to make a condescending call on Jincy and Jackson, thereby greatly delighting these two ardent admirers, then went with her to see the neighbors who still availed themselves of every opportunity to give surreptitious bits to Peterkin so as to encourage her interested affection.

His next venture was to learn to open the screen-door into the back hall and to slip upstairs, making a nest, first on my bed, then going for a snooze with Julius. And one morning we came down to the dining-room to find him curled up in a dish on the breakfast table, which had been set over night to save time, as Jincy had some extra work on hand for that day.

When I tried to frighten him with ferocious "scats" he looked carelessly around at me and then yawned with such an elaborate appearance of indifference, so utterly at his ease and so debonair, that we both burst out laughing, and Julius said:

"It's no use to scold such a cheeky little beast; you might as well let him do as he likes."

But cats cannot be allowed to sleep on dining-tables; every housekeeper knows that, so I gave the little scamp a good shaking and carried him out of doors, telling him that if he could not be a good kitty he must expect to have things happen.

Julius laughingly called after me:

"Oh, let him alone. He's all right; let him follow his own ideas, and see what he'll do next!"

But I know that it is not kindness to let kits be naughty, any more than it is to wink at the amusing faults of young children. Both are sure to suffer for it later—when the charm of youth is gone, and when to be bad is simply to be uncouth and troublesome.

So little Peter Junior had what Julius calls a "rocky time" until he was completely broken of the habit of making a bed of the table.

Just as he had made up his mind that it paid better to be a good boy, the mother of Dorothea and Frankie came over to ask for a kitty to come and stay with them the two remaining months of the sojourn in their cottage across the Sound to scare away the mice which were becoming troublesome, and also to give joy to the children who are never quite happy without a kitten to share their nursery meals and games.

Peter Junior, as our most charming kitty, and also as the one who could best be spared by his mother, was selected to take this journey.

It is a curious fact that Peterkin, who is a model mother so long as her babies are dependent on her, is the only one of our cats that seems to lose all interest in them as soon as they are weaned.

Deedie was Catsie's baby to the very end, and Catsie showed equal affection for her grandbabies.

It is so of all our black cats, too; but Peterkin is never a mother except while her kits are absolutely dependent on her for existence. After they are weaned anybody may have them without asking her permission. She has been known to punish a newly-weaned kit which approached her with the natural wish to be mothered, until the terrified little creature rolled over on its back and lay there a quivering heap, with its heels in the air, not daring to move.

We missed jolly Peter Junior, Julius often asking when he would be home again, and on his return we welcomed him warmly. He received our blandishments with his usual debonair manner as being all in a day's work, and took up his old ways; frequenting his former haunts in a manner that showed he had forgotten nothing about the place, so that it was difficult for us to realize that the little mite had been gone for so long a time—for months to a kitten should really seem longer than years to a human child, reckoning by the comparative rapidity of development.

Little Peter had, like Pickaninny, that look of eternal youth, with an added something, a sort of concealed wisdom of expression as if he could tell us a few things—if he liked—which was very fascinating. There is something alluring and mysterious about that expression of eternal youth with which some creatures are endowed. When young children have it we say they will not live to mature—that it is a sign of premature death; but that is not always the case. Often they live to old age, keeping to the end young hearts and that youthfulness of expression which has such irresistible charm when seen where one naturally expects to find traces of weariness and of approaching dissolution.

White Slippers had, from the very first, taken a mysterious dislike to Peter Junior, and, after having teased her to his complete satisfaction, he assumed the air of not knowing that there was such a cat in the world—passing her without taking the least notice of her growls and looking her direction with the abstracted air of seeing only empty space where she stood.

Just after his return home White Slippers asked me to give her a nursery-box for her first present from the stork, and seeming to have, in some unaccountable way, an intimation that her present was not to be very munificent, she first went and took possession of a lone kit belonging to Velvet.

This helpless little mite, carried off during its mother's temporary absence, was carefully deposited in the bed which had been given to White Slippers.

Then, as if feeling that this was not quite enough of a start, she ranged restlessly around for a little while, and made a sudden dash for Peter Junior.

He was entirely unprepared for this abrupt change of heart, and mistook it for battle, murder and sudden death.

His wails of terror and protest were most tragic.

At first such an original and ridiculous performance had seemed to be only amusing; but when we realized how serious the matter was to the little victim, I took a hand in the game and persuaded White Slippers to leave Peter Junior to his own family ties. Disdain, and even enmity were more agreeable than such violent demonstrations of sudden and unaccountable affection.

After peace and confidence had been restored Peter escaped and went off with Traddles, who had conceived quite an enthusiasm for him since his travels, and White Slippers returned to her nest where she was left bestowing the most bewildering attentions on Velvet's purloined kit.

The next morning we found that her present from the stork was limited to a single baby, and that gentle Velvet, rather than make a disturbance, had consented to share her kitten with the queer little mother, and that all four—Velvet, White Slippers and the two kits— were occupying together the nest to which had been carried the kidnapped kitten, while Peter Junior stood on his hind legs, his elbows resting on top edge of the box which contained their bed, regarding this queerly mixed family with his usual inscrutable and debonair expression.

Chapter Fourteenth.
Foozle, the Bull-Pointer.

ALL OF our friends, and more especially after the publication of the history of Bruno, were constantly asking why we did not have a dog.

We did not find it easy to explain this in a way that would convey a clear idea of just how we felt on the subject. The pain of the loss of Bruno lasted so long, and there was such a strong feeling that no other dog could ever fill his place in our home-life, that we felt an overwhelming reluctance to make the attempt to replace him.

Still, we really needed a dog.

Since Julius had begun making the other place he was often from home for a day or two at a time. And, though I felt no fear, there was always a certain feeling, even in my sleep, of being on the alert.

The presence of a watch-dog removes this nervous strain, because he always hears every sound, and as long as he is quiet one can be sure that all is well. When he gives the alarm one has the satisfaction of knowing that whatever or whoever is approaching will, if bent on mischief, be frightened away.

One day I received a note from a friend who has a winter home on the other side of the Sound inviting me to come over to see a family of newly-arrived puppies.

Their mother was an English bull-dog belonging to a man who had charge of our friend's grounds, and the mother's mate was a thoroughbred pointer belonging to a neighbor.

Of course I hurried over to see the little charmers, and my heart at once warmed to them.

Julius was much interested in the account I brought home, and went himself the very next day to see them. He knows much more than I do about such things, and he said that these puppies were "a fine cross," the pointer being so gentle and teachable and the bull such a faithful guardian. Then he added that dogs born here would be adapted to the climate and would have a better chance for health and vigor than would an imported dog. On his return from the inspection of this interesting little family he told me he had left an order for the puppy which had most pleased his fancy, and that if it were accepted there would soon be a new pet to add to our menagerie.

The next day, just after lunch, feeling tired on account of a gay dinner the evening before, I went up-stairs for what Julius calls a "four-bar rest."

Just as I had begun to feel the approach of slumber, the door-bell rang. I listened, dismayed at the sound of footsteps on the stairs, fearing that my nap was to be given up, or at least postponed.

When the door opened I saw Julius, who was all smiles, with his eyes lighted up the way they always are when he is sure of pleasing me.

He came over to the couch and stooped to lay a puppy in my arms, then stood off looking at us both and laughing.

The little fellow was as cold as a ball of snow. A Norther was blowing on the Sound, and the crossing, with only his short-haired coat as protection against chilly breezes, had taken away all his natural warmth. Now, being in out of the wind, the first effect was to make him drowsy. He looked sleepily at me, with drooping eyelids, then, with a contented little sound, he nestled down in the curve of my arm and went fast to sleep.

Julius stooped to caress his fat side, then exchanging with me glances of amused satisfaction, left us. I slept too, until the puppy began to wriggle and we both waked to make a beginning of our acquaintance.

The little fellow opened the conversation by asking unmistakably for something to eat.

I carried him down stairs and took him into the big cat-room where the tribe had just gathered for the sunset repast.

Their dish was filled and the puppy did not wait for an invitation to share its contents. He fell to at once without stopping to greet his new play-fellows.

Velvet and Pickaninny looked at him in gentle amazement. Peterkin and White Slippers were openly displeased—even disgusted, while Peter Junior regarded the whole affair as a most tremendous joke.

He walked around the puppy who was so absorbed in his repast that he was oblivious to all surroundings, sniffing him over with evident amusement, then galloped about performing all sorts of ridiculous antics.

The new arrival soon cleared the dish without any assistance from any of the cats, and began afresh as soon as I had refilled it.

Evidently he was a creature of tremendous appetite and corresponding capacity.

Peterkin and White Slippers had reached the limit of their patience. They had for some minutes been glaring at the puppy with narrowing eyes, and they now attacked him both at once from different sides.

He yelped, and shut his tail in tighter; but kept right on eating.

Then they realized that the only way to keep up with this greedy little monster was to try also to get away with the food.

They began to eat, one on either side of him, and the dish was soon cleared.

Still Velvet and Pickaninny had done nothing but look on with gentle amazement and meek disapproval. So I led them indoors and gave them a saucer to themselves that they might not be obliged to go hungry.

That night a bed was made for the new-comer in one corner of the big cat-room, and he slept until awakened by the cats next morning, beginning, as soon as his eyes were open, to make the most enthusiastic demands for breakfast.

The first effect on the cattle of this change in their happy home was an increased attention to, and interest in, their food. They had all become extremely fastidious, often refusing to eat unless the dishes were very tempting. Now the puppy showed such an enthusiastic appetite, it made them realize that the only way to get their share of what was going was to manifest an equal amount of enthusiasm. And so, instead of a languid approach to the platter and a deliberate, dainty tasting of its contents as had for some time been the custom in Cat-dom, all formed the habit of a simultaneous dash for the dish as soon as it appeared and never was seen a busier family than they with a platter full of heads all racing to see who could absorb the fastest, and with the puppy several laps ahead, frantic for fear that Peterkin or Peter Junior would manage to defraud him of the last morsel.

Our new pet named himself by his clumsiness.

There never was such a creature for stumbling around and falling over himself. And so we called him "Foozle."

No weed ever grew more rapidly than this greedy little puppy. He really seemed to swell while we looked at him—like blowing up a toy balloon.

As soon as his legs grew strong enough he followed us all over the place.

Of course he loved Julius better than he loved me; but I attended to all his wants and taught him the things necessary for a well-bred dog to know. And, when Julius was gone, the only time he was not at my heels, or asleep on the edge of my skirts, was during those blissful minutes when he was busy absorbing food and more food. At such times he was oblivious to everything—deaf—blind.

As soon as his manners were sufficiently polished, Foozle was allowed to come up-stairs every night to sleep on a mat at the foot of my bed.

It was pleasant to have his companionship; but the idea of his being a protection was only a pleasing fiction. During all the time that he was still growing, his slumbers from dark till dawn were so profound that one could drag him all over the floor without any result except a sleepy grunt.

The cats were all utterly disgusted when they found that such an unwelcome creature must now always make a third in the hours that each one passed with me.

For a little while they waited, not asking to be let in, hoping that this puppy, like The Curly-Dog, was to be only an episode. When they finally accepted the fact that he had come to stay, they began coming again, making Foozle keep his distance—openly triumphing over him that he must sit on the floor while they were luxuriating in my lap or on the desk beside the ink-stand. White Slippers scolded him unceasingly. When I reproved her she often dropped her voice reviling him in whispered growls until I assured her that they were overheard, and that unless she mended her ways she was to be banished from our society without delay. This had its effect, and she contented herself with looking him out of countenance, which was easily done, as the little fellow found her to be a most terrifying creature.

One of her naughty tricks was to find him sweetly sleeping when she believed us to be out of hearing and to begin at the extreme tip of his tail to sniff, holding, meanwhile, her mouth half open, with a most disgusted expression. She kept this up, moving her nose with each sniff until his body was reached, then, all at once, she set up such terrific howls that the unsuspecting sleeper leaped up, bounced away and turned to look at her with such an expression of horrified amazement that we could hardly scold her—for laughing at the absurdity of the whole affair.

Foozle soon showed that he possessed a roguish, jolly nature, delighting in all sorts of pranks and jokes. As a puppy he used to put his feet in the dishes, disgusting the dainty cats with his table manners, then go out in the sand and get himself in such a state that he seemed to need more than a reasonable number of baths.

I scrubbed him conscientiously, and he never failed to wink at me when I stood him on his hind legs to wash his chin and stomach.

When he was still quite a youth he came in from the garden one day with such a knowing look I saw at once that he thought he had a joke on somebody.

He followed me around, winking every time I looked at him, and finally I noticed that something was sideways in his mouth, holding his lip from his side-teeth. I caught his head in my hands, opening his mouth, while he made a roguish pretense of resisting, and found that he had between his teeth a shell-hairpin that had dropped from my hair the last time I had been in the garden.

He winked again as I took it from him, and when I laughed he dashed off in a gale of fun, barking and almost wriggling himself in two.

He carried away and tore up so many shoes that everybody on the place was warned to keep such things out of his reach.

Jincy was deeply mortified when he found a pair of her stockings where she had laid them on the grass to dry, instead of on the over-full clothes line, and carried and spread them out on the front lawn where they lay in full view of our first callers the next morning.

Then he found the bunch of keys that she had laid on the steps "for a minute," and carried them under the house. I knew at once that he had taken them when I heard her wondering when she missed them "how they could have walked off."

When I scolded him about it he winked knowingly at me, and galloped away pretending he was looking for them.

For three days Jincy went keyless, shut out from her trunk and unable to lock the cabin when she and Jackson must leave it at the same time. Then the rogue went under the house and got the string of keys. He came prancing around me with them, leaping and shaking his head to make them jingle together.

I never could help laughing at his funny pranks which seemed to delight him beyond anything.

His crimes were never very black, the worst being to tear up a new and expensive hat for Julius.

The wind came in and blew it to the floor when no one happened to be about, and Foozle could not resist such a temptation. When discovered, the largest piece left of the unfortunate hat was the leather band from the inside and Foozle was just trying his best to mince that.

Everybody on the place was glad when he found a plaything which was just to his taste. In nosing around, exploring the palm-grove which borders the Sound he found an old dry cocoanut with the fiber of the hull partly frayed out like a head with disheveled hair. This was fine, because he could grasp the hair in his teeth and threw it from him, then run to pick it up and throw it again. For days this was the most absorbing of games. Then one morning he thought it had begun to retaliate. Happening to catch the hair by the extreme end, he ran, shaking his head in an abandon of sportiveness, and the nut banged against his ears, on first one side of his head and then on the other. It was dropped with the utmost suddenness. He stood looking wonderingly at it for some seconds—poked at it with his nose, turned it over with his foot, then shook his head and walked thoughtfully away. He never could be induced to touch another cocoanut.

They were dangerous.

After a certain amount of teasing they were apt to take a hand in the game on their own account.

Never was there such a ubiquitous creature as our Foozle. He seemed to be everywhere at once. No matter where one went about the grounds there was Foozle waiting, a committee of one, to do the honors.

One day when I was going over the place with a caller and Foozle met us, first in the rose garden, then the fern house, the poultry yard, the palm grove, out under the mulberry tree, and then received us on the front gallery, the visitor innocently asked:

"How many dogs have you, Mrs. Judith?"

When I answered, she exclaimed:

"What! Is this all the same puppy that is meeting us everywhere?" And she was so amazed that it was several seconds before she accepted the fact and joined me in peals of laughing.

The boy taught Foozle to sit in his chair. As soon as he had learned this comfort he refused to sleep anywhere else. It was brought out doors for him to sit for his portrait and placed before the big Calabash tree where Peterkin had her adventure with the loaded rattle-snake.

Children are always interested in the Calabash tree because it is like the one that furnished cups to the Swiss Family Robinson on their wonderful island. It bears a little gourd just the size and shape of two tea cups set together at the open ends. Sawed across, it makes a pair of cups, and I always tell the children that Mr. Robinson sent us the seed from the inside of the first cups he made and we planted them, growing the tree in that way. They accept this story not as a fib; but as a bit of romance which gives a flavor of vivid reality to one of their favorite books.

The boy taught many other tricks to Foozle during the summer he passed with us on The Blessed Isle when Foozle was a youth. Among them, to beg, to speak for everything, from opening a door for him to having help about scratching a certain spot he cannot reach—about midway his spine—to retrieve, and to leap up in his or Julius' lap to be rocked to sleep. This last is rather inconvenient since Foozle has grown to be such a big dog.

When he first came to us our puppy could slip through the little cat-door as easily as could any of the kittens. It did not take him many minutes to learn how it operated and he was no larger than the smallest of our mature cats.

As he increased in size the door began to be a tight fit and whenever he got stuck it was his funny way to draw back and bark at the frame of the door as if he thought it had caught and pinched him for a trick.

With his incredibly rapid growth he soon became too big to manage this exit and then we promoted him from the cat-room to the back-hall where he had a platter all to himself.

Chapter Fifteenth.
Van, the Collie.

I AM sometimes tempted to believe that Fate takes especial delight in pranks at our expense.

Then again, I know that we are not alone the victims of her sense of humor, for has it not become a proverb:

"It never rains but it pours," or as the Crackers say, "Them as has, gits."

Nearly two years before Foozle was added to our family, during a summer in the Land of the Sky, we drove out one afternoon to visit the Biltmore kennels. There we saw a family of young collie puppies almost old enough to leave their mother. They were so perfectly adorable that after finding they were all engaged we left an order for one of the next arriving family.

After our return home we had a letter saying that the mother-dog had died, and that all orders were, for the present, cancelled. So we had given up the idea of a collie, and that was one reason why Julius had been so glad to secure the little bull-pointer.

Then, to our very great surprise, the matter having been entirely given up—almost forgotten—just as Foozle was beginning to outgrow his puppy ways, a letter came from Biltmore saying that a new mother-dog had been added some months before to their kennels and that our order could now be filled.

This offer brought back so vividly the memory of the puppies that had been so bright and responsive to our advances that far-away delightful afternoon that we found it impossible to refuse to receive the little stranger whose trunk was all packed for Florida.

A letter was sent to say we were ready for the collie puppy, and then we amused ourselves trying to imagine what Foozle would say when it arrived, and how he would like to see an intruder appear on the scene just as he had bounced into the midst of the happy family of kitties.

It took two days for our letter to go to Biltmore, and a day and a night for the puppy to come by express to us. We calculated it all to the fraction of a minute, and Jackson was waiting at the express office for the arrival of the crate so that the little traveler might be set at ease as soon as possible.

At the first glimpse and sniff of the cage containing this miniature bear, it seemed as if Foozle would go entirely distracted.

He barked, he howled, he yelped, he whined—then he began over again. And all the time he was trying his best to get at the strange creature, evidently determined to tear it to bits.

Nothing could be done until Foozle had been shut up in the poultry yard, where he remained in durance vile, constantly keeping up his ear-splitting barks, howls, yelps and whines.

When the cover was taken off of the crate and the inmate released he showed at once that he was sure he had found his friends.

His name was waiting for him. We promptly addressed him as "Van" and he responded as if he had known it from the beginning of Time.

There was a tin basin fastened to the bottom of his crate, and a bottle was tied to the slats which had evidently contained milk.

This had doubtless been poured into the pan for the little voyager to drink, and it was easy to see that as much of it as had remained after his soft paws had drowned themselves in the basin, the jolting of the train had splashed on to his coat.

After responding with enthusiasm to our greetings, he told us he was nearly famished.

I got a bowl of milk and when he eagerly began to drink I went to the safe for samples of various kinds of food.

He paused in drinking long enough to sniff daintily at these morsels, but declined them all and returned to the milk.

As soon as he was satisfied I took him for a thorough bath.

His long silky coat has first been soaked with the milk which was supposed to serve another purpose during his journey, then the dust of travel had sifted in and powdered him from nose to tail-tip.

After a good soaping it was necessary to rinse, rinse and rinse again before the bath-water cleared. Then I took him in my lap on a bath-towel for a thorough rubbing.

When dry and fluffy he was a most beautiful and adorable little baby-dog.

He asked for another bowl of milk, then he went for a roll on the grass outside.

The cats all came to investigate, and evidently found him very difficult to classify.

White Slippers said she thought he must be some sort of kitten, and being just then in a very melting frame of mind, on account of the recent arrival of a baby-kit, she made an attempt to smooth his coat with a tentative tongue, and was much displeased that her advances were misunderstood and received with a timid, protesting whimper.

All this time Foozle was howling and yelping through the meshes of the wire fence, declaring:

"Just let me out of here, and I'll make an end of that thing in short order!"

Our new pet seemed to be very tired and sleepy as soon as twilight fell. I wrapped him up and placed him in a basket in the big cat-room near the nursery-box occupied by White Slippers and her last baby.

He shook off the wrappings, curled himself up comfortably on them and began at once to snore.

He was still asleep the next morning when I hurried down to see about him. Julius said he probably had not been able to sleep at all on the cars, and so he was making up for lost time.

After breakfast Foozle was allowed to see his new play-fellow and was made to understand that we held him responsible for keeping the peace.

I held Van while Foozle sniffed him thoroughly and made up his mind that it was a dog and that he was to be accepted as a member of the family, instead of being, as he had evidently thought in the beginning, some wild creature for him to worry and destroy.

Van was very timid in receiving his first advances and retreated whimpering to the shelter of my skirts.

This seemed to impress Foozle favorably. He looked up at me and winked knowingly, as if to say:

"He'll do!

And a little later we were glad to see that he was gently playing with the soft baby-dog—rolling him over and over, pretending to bite him and squeezing him up against his own neck.

Van accepted these attentions and responded, making graceful bounces at Foozle's head to the accompaniment of little yaps—the baby-talk of doglets.

All seemed to be going so well that Julius and I congratulated one another on having Foozle to care for the new baby, saying that he would give us no trouble at all.

That night Van said he was not a bit sleepy, so he and Foozle bore us company all the evening—playing together on the floor as we sat reading.

It was not until we were ready to go up-stairs at bed-time that the little fellow was tucked in his basket. Then we went, followed by Foozle, to our own slumbers.

All the time that I was busied with preparations for the night, it seemed to me that there was some sort of racket going on down in the cattle-quarters; but I was not particularly disturbed, for Peterkin often brought in a rabbit as large as herself during the night, which resulted in the most tremendous commotion in Cat-dom without anyone being the worse for it, except, perhaps, the unfortunate bunnie.

These meek little creatures did much harm in our garden and among the young trees, so it was permitted for the cats to destroy them, the only stipulation being that they must be quickly killed.

The cats had learned to understand this and had made it a first rule in Cat-dom to kill and then afterwards to bang around, toss and catch.

I went on with my preparations, never doubting that something of this sort was now going forward among the cattle and that Van would soon understand that the excitement had nothing personal in it.

But just as I extinguished the light there came a new sound, frantic cries and yelps.

I went out in the hall and leaned, listening, over the banisters.

Julius heard me and called from his room:

"It's Van. Don't mind him; he'll soon quiet down and go to sleep."

But as I listened, I heard real anguish and terror in his voice, and calling to Julius to go to sleep and that I would see to the baby, I slipped on slippers and dressing gown and went down to investigate.

As soon as the kitchen door opened Van, who stood against it pawing and bumping his silky head against its obduracy, sprang forward and catching my sleeve between his teeth, clung to me trembling and sobbing like a frightened child.

Vainly I tried to quiet him. He was in a perfect agony of terror and home-sickness.

Then I realized that he had been too weary the night before to be conscious of anything except the need for rest, and that now, for the first time, he felt himself to be confronted with the terror of darkness away from the comforting touch of kindred.

Holding him close against me I carried him up-stairs to the bath-room where I washed his feet—he all the time clinging to me with a morsel of my sleeve between his teeth, as if fearing that he was to be again left somewhere alone. Then I wrapped him in a towel and carried him to a nest on the foot of my bed.

As soon as I loosed him he raised himself up to see what I meant to do. It was only to go for the night lamp which I had lighted in the bathroom, to turn it down and bring it to place behind a screen at the foot of the bed.

As soon as I had slipped between covers and Van saw that he was not to be left alone he lay back, snuggling his head against the bump my feet made near him under the covers and with soft little whispered grunts of perfect content fell into sound slumbers.

Foozle, who had waked when I brought the lamp in and had come to look with sleepy wonder at Van on the bed, now winked humorously at me and wound himself up for a fresh beginning at his night's rest, settling down close beside the bed.

It was now so late that it was almost early, and I lay watching the dim radiance of the lamp's reflection on the ceiling, wondering if this was to prove the beginning of a series of nursery experiences.

As daylight approached Van became restless, rooting along until he had slipped his nose under the elbow of the arm lying outside the covers and then, doubtless dreaming happily of his far-away mother, he gave more of the contented whispered grunts and snoozed blissfully.

The first sound nap that came to me was disturbed by the touch of a cold nose against my cheek and when I sat up Van scrambled over the billowing covers to stand on the edge of the bed, where he looked down whimpering at the idea of taking the frightful leap to the far-away floor.

It was broad daylight, so I again put on slippers and dressing gown and, followed by Foozle, carried my little bed-fellow down stairs and put him out the back door on the grass where he and Foozle started contentedly for a run together.

At breakfast Julius asked how I had quieted Van the night before, and was rather dismayed when he heard all about it, saying:

"You have spoiled the little beggar and now there will be no peace until he is grown. It would have been better to let him fight it out alone. He wouldn't have cried much longer."

But I assured him that he had not realized how serious it was with the poor little home-sick baby, adding:

"It really would have been cruelty to animals to leave him alone after he had become so terrified."

Julius was still sure I had made a serious mistake and that it would result in making a great deal of trouble for me.

I do not yet feel that it was a mistake; but I am very sure that it was the beginning of even more trouble than Julius predicted.

For the next three months this little rogue insisted every night on being taken up-stairs to share my bed and it was necessary to have a light constantly burning through all the hours of darkness.

Some nights his food disagreed with him and he must be carried down stairs for a nibble of fresh grass at intervals until morning, and each time I must wait for him and take him up-stairs, again washing his feet to make him fit to go back to bed.

Sound sleep became as much of a stranger as if I were "raising" a delicate child.

Julius often heard me flying down stairs at unearthly hours and had no patience with my little tyrant; but I told him it could not last always—that dog baby-hood is even shorter than human infancy and that Van would soon find himself able to look after his own comfort.

That autumn there was an unusual number of chilly evenings and I had my desk moved in by the dining-room fire, sitting there at my work when Julius was away.

Van always grew sleepy early; but would never go up-stairs until I was ready to go and stay with him. It was very funny to see him begin soon after eight every night to try to coax me to go to bed.

He sat watching me eagerly, and every time I looked toward him he got up to make short runs to the stairway, sometimes going up a few steps, then looking back at me and wagging his tail.

If I seemed to be so absorbed that he imagined the lateness of the hour had escaped notice he came and slipped his nose under my elbow joggling it until I looked at him, asking plainly if I meant to work all night.

Finally, when pen or book was laid down with an air that convinced him it would not be taken up again, he danced around in delight, following eagerly while the rounds of the lower rooms were made, to fasten windows and to make sure doors were locked. From time to time he made false starts up the stair-steps, running back to try his best to hurry me.

Up-stairs he came willingly to the bath-room to have his feet washed; but would not go to bed until my own bath was finished and I was ready to go, too, so a little nest must be made for his temporary snoozes in the bath-room while he waited for me.

The little tyrant was as much company as a child; and if more troublesome, his winsomeness and all his affectionate clinging ways did take a most compelling hold on the heart-strings.

As the little fellow grew larger he shed his silky coat which was replaced by hair that was coarser and more dog-like. His character developed with each succeeding outward change, and we were diverted to find how utterly unlike in temperament were our two dogs. Foozle made such a joke of everything and Van was so intense in all his emotions that it was not inappropriate to call them "Comedy and Tragedy."

Van showed a jealousy that was almost mania. It seemed to cause him real anguish to see the least sign of affection from us to Foozle or any of the cats. He even objected to our affection for one another and invariable got between us when Julius came to tell me "good-bye" or "good night." At first we laughed at this; but we found it was too serious a matter, from his point of view, to be treated lightly.

Foozle was greedy about food; but Van was greedy only about love and attention, and no nervous child could show a more sensitive nature.

If Julius spoke sharply to him he fled to me and caught between his teeth any portion of my drapery which came first—then clung there, trembling, with face hidden.

Foozle was such a joker that we liked to humor his pranks. Often he came nosing around my work-basket in search of diversion, delighted if I tied a scrap of cloth on his tail. He danced around making the scrap flutter by vigorous tail-waggings until the morsel of cloth finally flew off. Then it was his mischievous trick to chew it to a soft ball and watch for an opportunity to hide it in my work-basket.

On one of these occasions, after decorating Foozle's tail, I tied another scrap just like his, to Van's tail. Van gave me a strange look and went out of the room, disappearing through the porch, where I heard the big dog-door swing shut after him.

I thought nothing of it until time for his evening meal. Usually he was ready and waiting; but this time there was no sign of him.

After calling several times, I went to see what was the matter.

He lay outside near the steps, and at first I thought he was ill or had hurt himself.

I picked him up and carried him indoors. As soon as I set him on the floor he looked reproachfully at me and went right back out of doors, lying down again in the place where I had found him.

No amount of coaxing would move him, so I went in and left him there.

At bedtime he had not moved and when I was ready to go upstairs he gently resisted my attempts to take him in—reaching out to lick my hand; but refusing to get up.

I came down again when I was ready for bed; but he still refused to come in. I left the light burning, as had now become the invariable custom, and just after midnight I heard the dog-door swing open and shut, then Van's claws scratching open the back-hall door, and tapping up the stairway.

He slipped into my room and lay down beside the bed.

I spoke to him, and he reached up to lick my hand before he slept. For several days there was a difference in his manner, and all the time we were wondering what could be the matter—divided between the thought that he might have some slight ailment, or that, in some way, his feelings had been wounded.

Then one day when I was again sitting at my sewing-table and Foozle came coaxingly to me I looked in my basket for the asked-for scrap to tie on his tail, and as I was tying it Van, who had been dozing at my feet, looked up, rose, and immediately went out, turning at the door to look reproachfully at me. I called to him; but he only hurried the more, and going after him, there I found him lying in the place where he had passed half the day and night after he had been decorated, as Foozle had just been, with a tail-pennant.

Then I understood.

He had mistaken this joke for some sort of mysterious indignity and his pride had been wounded.

Evidently he was without the sense of humor of which Foozle had such a superabundant share.

From the night that Van had slept out so late, while he was struggling with his wounded affection and outraged pride, he was never again my baby-dog.

Never again did he ask to sleep on my bed, though he often passed part of the night on the floor beside it.

It seemed as if the mental struggle of that experience had marked a crisis in his development. He was grown up.

It was no longer necessary to keep a night-light for his comfort. He joined Foozle in following Julius all over the place, and in a sort of rough-and-tumble frolic each night in his room while Julius was getting ready for bed; Foozle, and sometimes Van, coming in later to sleep on the floor of my room.

Foozle had often whimpered in his sleep, showing that his dreams were troubled, and Van formed the habit of going to waken him as soon as his cries began. These dreams seemed to leave no impression on Foozle's mind. But Van now began to dream as human children do, and to remember his dreams after waking with the belief that they had been realities.

One night he dreamed that Julius punished him.

Just before bed-time he and Julius had been playing together, and they parted for the night on the most cordial—even affectionate—terms.

During the night I heard Van whimpering and protesting in his sleep. The next morning he refused to have anything to say to Julius—hiding from him, and running to dash himself in my arms every time Julius made any advance to him. He kept this up all day. Julius wondered at it, and finally accepted my explanation, in default of any other.

He tried in every way to regain Van's confidence; but it was several days before the effect of this dream was entirely dissipated.

Then one night, he dreamed that I was dead.

I heard him cry out in his sleep; first mournfully, then in such anguish that even Foozle was aroused and went to root at him with an inquiring nose.

As soon as Van was broad awake he sprang up and made a dash for my bed.

I was not asleep; but lay motionless looking at him in the dazzling radiance of the Tropic moon which was making its stately way through the night-sky.

As soon as Van found that there was no hand put out to him, he made a frantic leap, pulling at the covers and trying to reach my face. Then I sat up and spoke to him.

This was enough. He began to dance around in a frenzy of delight—barking—and running from the bed to touch noses with Foozle, evidently telling him all about it. Then back to me, leaping up to try to lick my cheeks.

The greatest change that Van's advent made in our cat circles was the banishment of Peter Junior. All the cats took much more kindly to Van's gentle, dainty ways than they had to the rough jollity of Foozle. A real friendship formed between him and Peter Junior and they began to have great games together. One day Peter found a cork on the kitchen floor and took it into the dining room where Van lay dozing. As soon as the cork, slapped along the floor by Peter Junior's paw, bounced against Van's nose, he waked and caught it in his mouth. This was just what he had been needing to help a tardy tooth which was swelling the gum on its way through. He began to chew it, and he kept on chewing it until there was nothing left but small crumbs; Peter Junior meanwhile looking on with astonished displeasure. After the complete wreck of this fascinating plaything, Peter Junior bounced at Van, and they had a rough-and-tumble performance which we thought was only one of their usual games, though we noticed that hard words were being exchanged. Then Mr. Peter packed his grip and shook the dust of The Blessed Isle from his heels forever.

After we had missed him for several days, without any idea that his departure was voluntary and final, I went on a hunt for him, which was unsuccessful until I happened to meet Minnie who said he had moved over to their house and was living there as if he had always been their cat—that he slept on her bed, and claimed a share of everything good that was going. She and her family were charmed to have him, and we were too well acquainted with the character of Peter Junior to try to change any of his decisions. So he ceased to be our cat.

The Summer of Foozle's youth, just before Van came, Julius had engaged the owner of one of the boat-yards on the Sound to build us a new launch.

The old one had proved to be too small for our needs and had been sold.

The new one was to be called The Judith—but there was something wrong with the attachments of the engine when it was first "set up" and the whole thing gave so much trouble that I rebelled and told Julius he'd better name it The Calamity Jane.

That was the Summer the Boy was with us. Just as the launch was finished the old Dominie came for a short visit to our Blessed Isle, and he, the Boy and Julius went off together for a launch-promenade down the Sound, anticipating a perfect voyage.

It was in August, and delightfully cool—the Sound all ruffled with little white-caps.

They had gone about three miles when all at once the engine stopped and refused absolutely to start again. They managed to reach the shore by throwing out the anchor and drawing on the cable—"kedging," I believe it is called—then they poled through the shoals. When the shore was reached the boat was tied to an old log and the three voyagers walked home at their leisure along the Beach. Julius was naturally furious; but his two guests were full of good-natured jokes about it all, and my point was gained—the boat's name was really, until she reformed, The Calamity Jane.

When the Old Dominie tried to remember it afterwards, in writing of the pleasures of his visit, he invariably wrote it "Crazy Jane," which was not at all surprising.

From the very first time that Foozle heard the sound of the engine's beat, he could never afterward be mistaken about our boat. To human ears there are dozens here on the Sound which are exactly like it. I could never tell whether it was our launch coming, or one of the others. But Foozle always knew, and sped frantically down to the wharf to receive it.

After a while the engine was fitted together so that it made no more trouble—I never understood just what they did to it. Something about a new "condenser"—and then Julius and the Boy used to go down the Sound and through the canal to our other place, for a stay of several days at a time. And no matter at what hour of night or day they returned, Foozle was always on the alert, hearing the throb of the engine miles away, and announcing their approach in unmistakable language.

After Van came, Foozle evidently told him about the boat, and together they listened for it whenever Julius was away—cocking up discriminating ears as each launch came within hearing and passed, never failing to recognize at once, and simultaneously, the first throb in the far distance of the one which held their Beloved Master.

Chapter Sixteenth.
Winnipete.

FOOZLE OFTEN reminded us of the fact that he was half pointer, though he had never received any training in that direction.

One morning when I came down to the dining-room the door of the glass-closet was ajar and Foozle stood, every muscle of his body tense and rigid, pointing at something inside. A hasty investigation showed Peterkin, encircled by tumblers which she had pushed from her on all sides (the fragments of one, belonging to our finest set, lay scattered on the floor) who looked up and mewed half in greeting and half in apology. Cuddled in the curve of her body were four tiny new-born kits. Her meek appeals to be left undisturbed in this chosen retreat were disregarded, and the two dogs showed a vivid interest in the removal of these intruders to the larger cat-room, and their bestowal in the bed where the careless stork should have put them in the first place.

Peterkin made several trips back and forth to convince herself that none had been over-looked or forgotten or dropped on the way, then she settled down contentedly to sort over her treasures and give them another breakfast. These babies had just got their eyes open when one morning a boat landed at the wharf of The Blessed Isle bringing Prudence's mother and Blair's mother with the two families of children for a happy morning with our various pets.

The mother of the new kits were charmed to show them to little Prudence, and extended a warm welcome to all the other children.

While I was greeting the mothers, their little ones ran to seek the kittens, and Jincy gave Peterkin's family to Blair in a small basin which they just filled to the brim.

The little man made a charming picture—his golden curls quivering with the joyful excitement of carrying these rare treasures, while all the other children followed eager to share the delightful burden. He set the basin on the floor where Peterkin, who had followed, went at once to inspect them, to make sure that they were being carefully handled. The children screamed with delight when she lifted them one by one out of the bowl and arranged them on the floor to partake of an extra repast.

After the kits had drunk themselves to sleep the children went for a run in the grove where General Bragg's two wives were sitting on nests they had chosen under two neighboring orange-trees, not yet quite ready to take the shell coverings off of the nineteen little turklets which soon afterward crept from under their wings.

From the grove of orange and lemon trees the children came back by way of the yard of guava bushes, where the Guinea-fowls live and stopped to admire the "big gray birds" and to pick up speckled feathers which had dropped from their wings.

Then into the other fowl-yard where Captain-Major stood before their house just announcing that it was time to gather the eggs with which his busy wives had filled the nests, and the children had the dear delight of filling their little skirts and caps full of fresh eggs which they must run in at once to show to their mothers, and go back to another interview with the kittens.

When I interrupted the conversation between Peterkin and her visitors to call attention to some oranges which had been chilling on the ice, Prudence's mother said, indicating the little people who were clustered around me:

"That's the only thing you lack here on your Blessed Isle, Mrs. Judith."

"Yes," said I. "If you would give me one of your little girls and Blair's mother could spare the youngest of her little men, then this would be Paradise indeed!"

The next afternoon I was on the other side of the Sound going to a reception when I met Little Winnifred. We stopped for a chat and her first piece of news was that a little black kitty had come to their house the night before from no one knew where, adding:

"It hasn't any Mamma and it cries all the time."

After I had expressed appreciation of the gravity of the situation, I told her to bring the little foundling right over to The Blessed Isle and Peterkin would doubtless make room for it in the nest with her new babies.

Winnifred was delighted with this idea and brought the kitty early the next morning, waiting to see Peterkin greet it with such motherly lickings and purrings that without delay the poor baby-kit began with enthusiasm to absorb the first satisfactory meal that it had been able to find for nobody knows how long.

After the first day Peterkin seemed to discover that this little black creature was in some way out of place among her own snow kits, and she carried it and put it in the bed where Pickaninny's babies had been. Then she began a daily routine of dividing her time and her supplies between these two nurseries.

Before long it transpired that Winnipete, as we named the little rescued wanderer, had won the lion's share of Peterkin's affection, and so when the white kits were large enough to begin to drink from a saucer they were given away, as there is always a lively demand for Peterkin's kittens for mousers, because their mother is celebrated as a mighty hunter.

As soon as Winnipete began to toddle around she told us plainly that she thought the most fascinating creatures on The Blessed Isle were the two dogs. At first this was a very one-sided opinion, for Van and Foozle were not at all enthusiastic about returning, or even accepting her admiration. In fact, the progress of sentiment on their side might be well described by the quotation:

"First pity, then endure, then embrace."

Only her helplessness saved her from utter destruction the first time she waked Foozle by trying to investigate the mechanism of his closed eye-lids.

He sprang up, giving a short snarl of disgust, and ran to leap into his big chair beyond her reach.

Winnipete, not a bit disconcerted by this rebuff, walked saucily out on the front gallery where Van lay asleep. She crouched, as if playing she were a lion stalking his prey, then bounced at him, catching one of his ears between her paws. He leaped up as if a live coal had touched him, and, giving a sidelong glance of suspicion and aversion at the bold little girl, walked solemnly out-of-doors where he took refuge in a hole he keeps digging out as fast as it fills, under the big mango-tree by the garden gate.

But gradually it dawned on the minds of both dogs that her friendliness was genuine—that although she was dressed almost exactly like White Slippers, they were not at all alike in temper or in manners. She showed such gentleness, and at the same time, so much lovely audacity, that she soon became as great a favorite with all of us as the departed Peter junior had been. And one day we had the surprise of finding Winnipete lying between Foozle's paws as he reclined on the floor, while he pretended to bite her little head between his side teeth as children crack small nuts.

He winked at me as he caught my amazed glance, then submitted with evident enjoyment to a dash the kitten made at him, hugging his big head between her arms while she nibbled at first one eyelid, then the other, and ended by chewing the loose bagginess of his cheek; he meanwhile, trying to watch her out of the tail of his eye.

As soon as Van discovered that Winnipete and Foozle had formed an attachment for one another, his jealous nature prompted him to make an effort to supplant this admirer in the little charmer's affections.

This was not difficult, for Van's manners were so gentle that they appealed naturally to kittens, inspiring confidence in the nervous little creatures, who are always more of less on guard against the attentions of an abrupt dog like Foozle.

It was a charming sight, these two graceful playmates, frolicking together, but Van could never endure our amusement at their funny antics. As soon as we began to laugh it was ever his custom to end the performance and walk away in high dudgeon. Then for so long as he saw that we were observing them, all Winnipete's coaxings were in vain. He was loftily oblivious of her existence until she, discouraged, went to play with Foozle. Then Van immediately relented and coaxed her back again.

Peterkin often called her little girl from these diversions and evidently gave her many lectures about playing with the dogs, though she herself was not above showing for them a dignified toleration—sometimes greeting them with a friendly "rub noses," and amicably sharing Van's dish of dinner, and again hiding behind the edge of the door and utterly demoralizing both dogs, one after the other, as they came in response to our summons, by reaching out to each a sudden flash of an unexpected paw bristling with claws!

When Peterkin interfered between her little daughter and her big playfellows Van and Foozle showed no little resentment, growling whenever she took Winnipete from them, and we were amused to see how the kitten evaded her mother with all sorts of ingenious tricks.

One day the two dogs gave Peterkin such a fright that for a minute things looked rather serious all around. Mother and daughter were having a frolic of their own, the two dogs lying at a little distance on either side, looking on. All at once Peterkin, in the excitement of the game, bit a little too hard, so that Winnipete gave a cry of protest. In a trice both dogs had leaped on Peterkin, and there was such a mix-up that I had to interfere, and was too much startled myself to see the humor of it until confidence had been restored all 'round. Peterkin has never entirely recovered from the shock. Ever since then she gives a nervous bounce every time either one of the dogs makes an unexpected move in her direction.

After a while we noticed that Peterkin had begun to ignore her baby, and that when Winnipete came coaxingly to partake of her accustomed food she was crossly driven away. Then the little creature began to follow us up stairs every night, and the next morning found her sometimes on the foot of my bed, sometimes with Julius, and again asleep on a rug between Van's paws with her little head tucked snugly under his cheek.

One morning Peterkin met us at the foot of the stairs, evidently waiting for Winnipete, to whom she offered the most affectionate greetings.

These so-long-withheld attentions were received by the kitten with humorous incredulity. She reared up on her hind legs and sparred playfully at her capricious parent, then galloped off at a tangent, returning to snatch her gaily around the neck and bite her ear, and again galloped off to reconnoiter from a safe distance.

When we followed Peterkin out into the big cat-room, there we found a nest of kits that she meekly claimed. So that was it! The new babies had opened her heart and filled it with renewed affection for the little discarded pet.

I lifted Winnipete up to see these mites, and there was not the least doubt about her opinion on the subject. She ruffled up her coat from neck to tail-tip, spitting viciously, her eyes dilated with lurid fury. Then she growled with deepest rumblings, and, wriggling from my grasp, she galloped off, speeding out through the two doors, and climbed up the nearest post of the grape-trellis, from there she leaped to the roof, where she entrenched herself until driven down an hour later by pangs of unendurable hunger.

Winnipete proved to be the cleverest kitty we have ever owned about slipping around and getting the best of everything. She learned from Van to hook her claws in the large screen-door of the back hall, and to open it by leaping back with all her tiny weight until it swung open, then to dart in, snatching her tail after her with a deft flourish, lest it be pinched with the door's slamming. Dearly bought experience had taught her that this is a thing to be expected and guarded against.

And so, oddly enough, this series of sketches ends as it began, with the tale of an adopted kitten.

History repeats itself; only with Catsie the baby-kit was sought, to fill an empty nest and heart, while with Peterkin it was that reaching out of the tenderness of universal motherhood to rescue the perishing.

Now that Peterkin's youngest babies are growing up, Winnipete has become reconciled to them, and she, with her mother and the babies, make a happy family.

This morning when I came down stairs I found the grape-vines that cover the south arbor had burst into full flower. The fragrance had attracted countless bees. The morning sunshine was making trembling shadows of flower, leaf and tendril on the ground underneath, and over these moving pictures, Peterkin, Winnipete and the younger kits were scampering, wrestling, biting, clawing and humping up their backs at each other—a picture of enthusiastic young jollity, drunk on the breath of sweet-lipped Spring.

Just beyond, to the Eastward, came flashes of light from the Sound, which showed in glimpsing wavelets between the palms—and from across the Sound came the ever-present rhythm of the breakers' roar on the Outer Bar.

END OF PART ONE.
March, 1904

Part Two.

Chapter First.
Changes.

WHEN JULIUS and I, with the harmonious companionship of the various cattles, sat together through the moonlit or starlit evenings, and talked with those long intervening pauses—thoughts audible melting into thoughts unspoken—which make evident that perfect harmony 'twixt soul and soul, our subject was often the kind fate that had led us to our Blessed Isle. Ever, in these talks, we expressed the hope and the expectation that we might never be tempted, or forced by any trick of Destiny, to move on. Often we reviewed all the circumstances—the paths revealed one step at a time—with many surprising turns and ambushes—that had led us to this haven of peace and reposeful delight; and coming, as did this home of happiness and of dreamy beauty, after so many trials and vicissitudes, it is no wonder that we accepted it as the conventional conclusion: "So they lived happily ever after."

We did so accept it.

And then came a tragic end to our summer dream. Life is not

meant to be a paradise here below—a garden of delight, where happy dreams never end—we may pause only long enough to find strength and courage. For it is an onward march to a definite goal. After wearying effort we rest, and after refreshing repose, we must again take up the line of march.

The illness which followed a severe accident left Julius with the kind of nerve-shock which can be treated only by a complete change of scene.

Some years ago I read a book, whose name now escapes memory, in which was portrayed a character—a woman—who, after any sort of wound from the hand of Fate, flew at her surroundings and began to change the relative positions of the furniture. The story was evidently what children call "made up;" but back of it somewhere was the real woman who had discovered the solace that is to be found in this shifting of inanimate things. To that some-where woman I mentally reached out encircling arms, claiming her as a soul-sister; for, to me, that is the cure-all for the turbulence of spiritual upheaval.

So, when Julius first began to sit up after his illness, I exchanged the pictures on his walls for those in other parts of the house and shifted all the movables of his chamber and study; but for him the only result of these changes was what he called a "mix-up." His trouble could not be reached by such simple treatment.

Fortunately, the warm weather was approaching, so we made all haste to prepare for an earlier hegira to the mountains, and chose as our destination a place that we had never before seen.

We stayed up on the Heights until cold weather drove us again southward, and we can never forget that home-coming. The sleeper-train brought us to the station within driving distance of our Blessed Isle—which rock-road and bridge had now made approachable otherwise than by boat—at an unearthly hour of the morning. The sun was just pushing his golden hat above the ocean waves. Dew-splashed tops of palms glistened with first day-glints, while shadows were in deep, wide sweeps of terra-verte and Vandyke brown, with here and there a hint of purple.

As we turned into the drive leading down from the rock road to the house of our Blessed Isle we saw Van, inside the wire fence enclosing the grove, rise from where he had been lying. It was at the point nearest our way of approach and he was evidently on the look-out. Had he been there, morning after morning, during all the long months of the summer's separation, eagerly awaiting our coming?

Later inquiries, made of Jincy and Jackson, were answered by the statement that they had always found him there; and he had worn himself almost to a skeleton with his ceaseless vigils.

As the carriage approached, Van stood, ears up and wide eyes fixed on us, until we were near enough for him to hear our voices. Then he pointed his nose to heaven and "lifted up his voice and wept." His howls and yelps of joy reached the ears of Foozle, asleep somewhere out of sight, and he came dashing through the trees to see what it was about. As soon as he saw us, he paused beyond Van, pointed his nose likewise to heaven and joined in the hymn of joy. Old Peterkin came leaping and bounding over the wet grass; and, by the time we were out of the carriage, all the other cattles had arrived from various directions and we were so set upon by a joyful mob that I later found my veil torn to shreds and my hat dew-drowned in the edge of the fern-house.

When I had dried my eyes and had got the lump out of my throat, I saw that Julius had sunk on a garden-seat that happened to be just where it was needed and had Van, who was still giving little gasps and sobs of quivering delight, in his arms.

That evening, as we sat together in the twilight, surrounded by all our happy cattles, Julius said:

"It seems to me that the end of life, as we are welcomed into the other world, could hardly be more overwhelming than this morning's reunion; only then, there will be more of it, with no anti-climax nor thought of future parting."

This last thought was, in its way, prophetic; for, as soon as the first effect of the joyful homecoming wore off, we found that while the change had been of benefit, it was to lose its power with the return to the scenes and memories of the illness that had followed the accident which had caused all the mischief.

Then we realized that our Blessed Isle must be left for a longer period; and, perhaps, for always.

Many reasons made it seem advisable to try a sojourn in Jacksonville where we had once lived, and which, since its baptism by fire, had become a new city. We gathered together our most personal keepsakes and belongings for a flitting which was like being pulled up by the roots and tossed over the fence.

I shall never forget a good-bye visit to the garden.

Over the gate leading into this home of flowers had always been inscribed—visible only to the mind's eye—"All who enter here leave care behind." No matter what perplexity or distress was hovering 'round, it ever paused outside the garden gate; and, as soon as it swung shut, I found myself greeting buds of promise and blooms of fulfillment with a heart so light that its joy spilled over in laughter and in snatches of childhood's flower and fairy songs. On this morning of leave-taking my feelings were of such a mixed nature that it was difficult to tell just which was uppermost. The roses, my especial friends, seemed to feel a premonition of separation. They reached out clinging arms to wrap their branches around me and to hook thorn-fingers so securely in my garments that, in finally escaping their embrace and turning away from the alluring touch of their petals on my face as they breathed sweet prayers not to be left, I found cheeks wet and blouse a wreck of tiny snags.

This garden ever haunts my dreams, and I hope to find, somewhere in Paradise, a corner just like it.

Chapter Second.
Winnipete and Van Prepare for a Journey.

WHEN OUR household gods had been transferred to their new setting and arranged in an experimental abiding-place there came over us such a hunger for the companionship of some of our dear cattles that we planned to go back to The Blessed Isle and choose those of them that seemed to be young enough and adaptable enough to bear the severe ordeal of being transplanted to a city life.

On our arrival there, behold a miracle!

We had thought our hearts to be left behind in this home of so many happy years; but when we entered the house—after the delightful exchange of greetings with our cattles, who, even after this two-weeks' absence, almost devoured us in the joy of reunion—we found there was a mighty change.

Instead of the home-spirit waiting just inside the door to greet us, as always heretofore, with an all-encompassing embrace of welcome, the indoor atmosphere suggested only the quotation: "Swept and garnished." It was no longer a Home; but simply a comfortable furnished house. There was everything needful for comfortable, even luxurious, living; but rugs, furnishings and such things do not make a home. The books, pictures, keepsakes and trifles—all the thousand and one suggestions that speak of heart-life—where were they?

The only place that seemed home-like was out-of-doors. The garden was there, waiting with joyful greeting and renewed coaxing. The fowls were as of yore, and all the happy, welcoming cattles. These were all the same—just as we had left them; but the home-spirit had migrated with our home-gods, and was now left behind in our temporary abiding-place of the city. There was both sadness and consolation in this discovery—in knowing that the home-spirit could be so easily transplanted. Julius had often said, jestingly, that wherever I take off my hat and open my work-box is home. We had laughed together whenever he had made this statement, both of us believing it to be just one of the pretty nothings with which he likes to please me. Now he recalled it with an I-told-you-so air; and yet, I could see that it was just as much a surprise to him as it was for me to find our old home bereft of the soul we had believed to be still haunting its deserted rooms.

With renewed courage, we hastened to make preparations for a return to what we now called HOME without a single mental reservation. There were many little matters that needed attention, so we decided to remain at The Blessed Isle for a week. We had brought only hand-baggage; but I never go anywhere, even for a day, without a work-box containing some bits of hand-sewing and a book or two. With these personalities we found it possible to arrange a corner of the library so it made an oasis in the bareness. All the cattles recognized this home-bit as promptly as did we and they gathered there, each instinctively choosing his or her position to complete the family picture.

After some discussion it was decided that Van and Winnipete, as the two most youthful, detached and adaptable of the cattles, were to be the chosen ones to accompany us back to the city. There were various perplexities and uncertainties in the contemplation of trying to transplant even these two docile and loving pets. Van had never in his life worn a collar; nor had we ever dared to attempt any sort of restraint with him, except to keep him inside the grove fence. He was obedient to come or to go at direction; but we had many misgivings in anticipating for him the restrictions and the confinement of a day of railroad travel—not to mention the terrifying motion and racket.

Julius got a collar and chain for him, and I coaxed him in position to adjust them by first making him leap to reach some sweet biscuit of the kind he best likes; then, when he was stretched up at full length, I caught his face between my hands and laid my cheek against the top of his head—this being the sort of caress that always put him in a tremor of delight. Julius slipped the collar on. Its lock snapped, and it was adjusted before Van realized what was happening. We expected to see him begin to struggle, trying to shake or paw it off; but once in place, he accepted it with no attempt at argument, so we began to feel less uneasy about his part of the journey.

Winnipete was then interviewed as to her intentions and preferences in the way of traveling.

One of our neighbors had a tragic tale to relate of another neighbor who had recently sent out on our same trip with a favorite cat confined in a slatted box. Before the train had got fairly in motion, it was remarked that the kitty seemed to be taking the journey more philosophically than anyone had dared to hope. Its anxious owner looked in to see if she found the situation to be too terrifying for outcries; or, if she had concluded to accept without protest the noises and the strange surroundings. There lay the poor little traveler in the box quite dead. Some of the by-standers opined that it was too closed and she had smothered. Others thought she might have been frightened to death because of not being able to see what was transpiring around her—that nothing in the noise and jolting was intended to harm her.

Discussing this event, and the comments there-on, we decided that a parrot-cage would be the ideal traveling-case for Madam Winnipete, and Julius went to the village on an exploring-trip to see if one could be found. Nobody there had one for sale; but he succeeded in finding a mocking-bird cage, and that was even better. The door was rather small; but I experimented to see if she could squeeze through by holding her before its aperture and poking a bit of tempting food through the bars on the other side so that the only way she could reach it was by getting into the cage. Winnipete slipped inside, ate her morsel, then squeezed out again. This point decided, the cage was left on the floor beside her favorite dozing-place, and all the nice bits intended as her share of the cattle-feasts were put in there that she might become accustomed to the cage before the start on her journey.

At last the day came, as crises have a way of doing. The cattles to be left behind us did not seem to be as much impressed by our preparations for departure as they had heretofore been. It looked as if they had conceived the idea that now it was to be a season of brief absences and quick returns. This made our good-byes less harrowing.

After those that were to be left behind had been enticed to the cat-rooms, where platters of tempting food had been placed, that they might be too much occupied to notice our departure, Winnipete was coaxed into her cage. Foozle had been hugged, and his attention drawn to a big bone, cunningly placed on the far side of the grounds behind screening walls and trees. We had sent to the village for an omnibus—a sort of "Black Maria," which belonged to one of the smaller hotels, thinking that this would be better than the carriage for the transportation of us and our queer collection of baggage. This was a happy thought; for it enabled us to have Van, the cat-cage and our hand-baggage all in a bunch, while the driver was not at all in evidence; thus still preserving for our nervous companions the fiction of a home-atmosphere. The motion of the vehicle, as we started on our way to the station, startled Winnipete so she began to yeowl and Van poked me and then Julius with a nervous and inquiring nose. I relieved a hysterical tendency by saying that Winnipete seemed to think her occupancy of the bird-cage called for an attempt to sing, which gave us an excuse to laugh. This eased the nervous tension of the situation and the remainder of the distance was accomplished in reasonable comfort.

There was a wait at the station, so that Winnipete had time to get her nerves again tranquil. I sat beside the cage talking to her, while Julius led Van around by the chain attached to his collar to let him have as much exercise as possible before the confinement of the all-day ride.

The approach of the train, with its ferocious clanging and snorting, completely demoralized both cattles. Van sprang up to hide his face against Julius and Winnipete began to caterwaul, wildly tugging at the bars of her cage. The conductor came out to help us on, and he looked with amazement at our menagerie.

The porter had taken our bags; Julius still led Van; and I had the bird-cage. This the conductor took from me and I followed close behind him so that Winnipete could see me and would feel that she was still with friends.

At the door of the car the bottom of the cage caught on some projection; the conductor gave a jerk, the bottom was wrenched off—there was a flash of disappearing black fur—and this was the last, so far as that trip was concerned, of Winnipete. The cage was carried back, in two pieces, and left on the platform. We had no further use for it.

Our bird had flown.

Chapter Third.
Van Travels in State.

WHEN JULIUS conducted Van into the baggage-car he was told that it was against the rules, without a special permit, for people to stay in that car. That, if it were necessary for Van to be personally conducted, a permit should have been secured in advance for his master to stay with him.

Here was a dilemma.

Van would no more have stayed among all those strange sights and sounds without one of us to keep up his courage than he could have spread wings to fly over the intervening miles to the city.

Julius led him back to the coach for people and was inspired to take him into the sitting-room at the end for smokers. There Van received a royal welcome—all admiring his beauty and his responsiveness. When Julius asked if anybody in there objected to the presence of such a fellow-traveler, the enthusiastic negative was most flattering; and there Van stayed all day, except for a run outside during a long pause we made about midway in our journey where there was a wait for orders.

From time to time, through the day, as Julius gave me the signal that there were no smokers in there to be embarrassed by my presence, I went to peep in at Van that he might be reassured by the knowledge that I was close by. Our pleasure in his joy at these glimpses and in his evident grasp of the situation, almost made us forget the fiasco with regard to Winnipete.

When we reached the city, Julius—having already arranged with the porter to put me and the bags in care of a station porter, who would bridge the gap from train to cab—tried to lead Van out by the shortest way; but this he found to be impossible. He resisted, dragging back and turning resolutely in the direction from which I had each time come to speak with him. He drew Julius along through the car, pausing to sniff at each chair, until he reached the one I had occupied. Then he hurried eagerly, nose to floor, until they both overtook me and the bags just as we were being handed into the cab. Van leaped in after me, and sprang up on the seat where he placed himself between us. As we drove along he took in the sights and sounds of the town which he now saw and heard for the first time—adapting himself at once to the clamor and confusion of the city—wagging an eager and impartial tail at cabs, wagons, automobiles, trolley-cars, gonging ambulances—everything that came along. This was, to us, a most encouraging sign. We had feared that it might take weeks, and perhaps months, to accustom him to seeing and hearing the city's bustle and roar.

When we stopped, Van leaped out as soon as the carriage-door was opened, seeming to recognize the place as if he had known it always. He hurried in with us, going the rounds of the rooms, sniffing at everything, then looking up at first one then the other of us as if he were trying to make us understand that he found the home-smell everywhere and was thereby "happified" to the ends of his toes!

At his sleepy-time a small bedside rug, which we had brought from The Blessed Isle furnishings, offered to him for a bed. This he accepted with evident satisfaction, and curled up on it to sleep the sleep of perfect rest until early morning. He was the first one up, and came as soon as he waked to see if we were really there—we three together—instead of all the past twenty-four hours of thrilling change and adventure being only a vivid dream which would fade in the light of sunrise. Satisfied that the dream was a reality, he explored all over again, from start to finish, then chose a commanding position on the front gallery where he might lie at ease and study the charms and intricacies of city life.

As soon as we arrived in the city home I wrote a note of inquiry about the fate of Winnipete. Several days of anxiety passed before the answer came; but when it did arrive it was eminently satisfactory. It had taken her just two days to find the way back to The Blessed Isle. On the morning of the third day after her spectacular departure she walked in tired, thirsty, dusty and hungry; but obviously overjoyed to be home again. Foozle met her as she approached "wow-wow"-ing a song of triumphant return, and they exchanged most loving how-de-dos. The other kitties of her tribe gathered around and licked her dusty coat while she ate and drank of the good things offered for her refreshment. Then she settled down to pass the remainder of her nine lives on The Blessed Isle. There was no temptation to re-open the question of moving her. She belonged there.

Chapter Fourth.
A Birthday Party.

IT WAS now mid-summer and dog-laws in the city, owing to a mad-dog scare, were very strict. Van accepted the license-tag with his usual docility; and, after a little bewilderment, he comprehended and submitted to the rule that in all his walks abroad he must be led by a chain or a cord. It was a choice between being led or wearing a muzzle, and we knew Van well enough not to try the muzzle; so he was initiated into the mysteries of tether-walks, and in a short time he learned not to tangle his feet nor to trip himself. These city promenades, where he was universally admired and caressed, soon began to be such delightful experiences for the country-bred dog that he formed the habit of teasing and coaxing for more of them than we could find leisure to give him. His requests were always so prettily and insistently made that we often yielded and put aside pressing occupations when it was far from convenient to do so.

Sometimes, when mild requests were disregarded, he would get his cord and bring it, jogging our elbows and interrupting every effort at concentration on the work in hand, so that nothing was to be gained by the attempt to keep at it. The only way was to yield and take him for a little run; and then, satisfied, he was willing enough to come trotting back home again, to lie on the front gallery and think it over.

The twenty-eighth of August approached, and, as it was the first time we had ever been with Van on his birthday—all the other anniversaries having come to him while we were up in the Heights for our summer vacations—I wished to celebrate for him. He had shown a distaste for the dogs of the city who had made advances to him; but he ever greeted, with the greatest cordiality, every friendly cat that came along. So I told him to invite all the kitties on his list of friends and acquaintances and we would have a birthday party. I don't know how many he asked; but, when the feast was ready, only one cat turned up to share it. That was enough, though, for "two's company," as everybody knows.

Their feast was placed on a tiny low table under the chinaberry-tree in the back yard. Van and his guest faced one another with the goodies arranged between them. There were two small dishes of cold soup, then each had a plate of cut-up beef and potato; after that came dessert of cheese and plain candy. Van and the kitty ate in silence with rolled-up eyes watching one another; and went conscientiously through with the bill of fare until dessert; then the kitty refused her share of the candy, which Van devoured for both. The feast ended, both sought the water-bowl, which had been placed, fresh-filled, near the table. Then Van sat gravely watching his guest while she made her toilet; from time to time reaching out a friendly tongue to offer assistance in the thorough licking she gave her coat from nose to tail.

Altogether, the party was a great success. Van was congratulated on having reached the dignity of "five-o'clock," and he gracefully accepted our wishes that he might live to see many more happy birthdays.

Chapter Fifth.
Van as Comrade and Protector.

DOWN ON The Blessed Isle, where Van had been one of a large family, he had distressed us by his superlative jealousy. It always put him in a state of distraction to see us pet any of our other cattles. We could never show affection for them except when Van was elsewhere—out of sight and hearing. Often when Foozle—who understood this perfectly—thought that Van was safely out of range, and came to either of us for an exchange of demonstrations, Van would mysteriously divine what was happening and come dashing in from some distant part of the grounds to throw himself in a fury of jealousy between Foozle and whichever of us was the object of his blandishments.

All this kept Van in a fever of excitement, and it had spoiled much of our pleasure in him.

But now in the city home where Van was the only pet, his whole nature seemed to change. His gentleness, docility, and overflowing affection, made him an ideal comrade. His beauty attracted universal admiration. The long hair of his coat was shaded in color from tan to seal-brown, with only enough white to give the idea of appropriate and spotless linen. He harmonized perfectly with his city surroundings, a fact which he seemed to recognize and appreciate every time he set out for a promenade. As the months went by the marked changes and development of his nature made him seem almost like another dog.

When Julius was called south again to attend to some business matters, Van and I stayed alone together with a feeling of perfect security in one another's protecting care.

During the nights that we were alone in the house he always came reluctantly when I called him at bedtime from his out-door bed on the front gallery; because he did not wish to go upstairs until the return of his master. Let alone, he would have watched there until morning, each moment hoping that the next would bring the sound of footsteps he was always so quick to recognize. But when I insisted, telling him that Julius would not come back for another day, he rose obediently and followed me up-stairs where he lay down in the hall just outside the bath-room door until I had finished my bath. As soon as I was in bed he always came to leap up and lie with his chin on my arm or shoulder until I had soothed and petted him for a few minutes. Then he slid down and went to his own bed which was arranged under a front window where the night breezes would sweep across him.

On the day I knew Julius would return I told Van: "Go watch for Julius. He's coming."

This was received with up-lifted ears and every symptom of lively joy. He hurried to take a position on the verandah which commanded a view of the corner around which Julius would first appear. And, at the first glimpse of the loved form, Van was off, hurling himself like a thunderbolt to lavish frenzied caresses, which Julius received as eagerly as they were offered.

Then we three sat down to talk over the trip, which sometimes included a glimpse of The Blessed Isle and messages from our cattles there. Van cocked up appreciative ears as the familiar names were mentioned and listened to news of all the dear animates and inanimates of that loved former home with apparent comprehension of everything.

We three, and our memories—tender, sad, or happy, that made a large part of our home-life—formed a complete home-circle with its outer circles widening in all directions.

The remaining summer weeks soon slipped away, and, with cool weather, the dog-laws relaxed. Van now found himself freed of his tether; and, when he took his walks with us, he could explore, to his satisfaction, all those alluring alleys and side-streets down which he had often looked so wistfully when he passed them restrained by his leading-string. In all ways he found the cooler weather to be a welcome change. Even the few weeks of weather that was really cold, which were scattered along through the winter months, were enjoyed by this thick-coated dog; and we often spoke of the difference, in this respect, that there was between Van and Foozle. Down on The Blessed Isle even the mildest of our Northers always prompted Foozle to come shivering into the house to coax for a warm corner by the fire. He could never have endured a Jacksonville winter. He was a child of the tropics, while Van was born on the chilly heights and his coat was of the texture that could have kept him snug and warm in an Arctic winter. The cold, frosty weather was bracing and stimulating. It prompted him to all forms of lively exercise and pranks. He insisted on long walks, which, for him, were composed of successions of short runs. The cold was all right for him; but not the dampness. As the season advanced and the time came when we began to expect warm spring days, we had nearly two weeks of blustering northeast winds with rain squalls at short intervals. I tried to keep Van indoors during this spell of weather; but just as it began Julius was called south again on a matter of pressing business and Van was unusually insistent about going out from time to time to look for him, so that his coat was almost constantly damp with chilly drops.

When Julius returned he remarked that Van seemed rather subdued, and asked if he had been taken out as often as usual for his needed exercise. I told him that we had been for short walks every day between showers; but that the weather had not been conducive to long, leisurely strolls of the sort to give Van his strenuous runs.

Van quieted down after his not very enthusiastic welcome to Julius, and went to lie on the hearth-rug as if the little blaze in the fire-place attracted him by its warmth.

Next morning the sun shone brightly and there was every indication that spring had come to stay. Van seemed like himself again and joyfully accepted the invitation Julius gave him to go for a long walk.

Chapter Sixth.
Van is Ill.

THE PLEASANT weather continued and we forgot our temporary uneasiness about Van. Julius had occasion to go for a day to Saint Augustine, and I was invited to go with him. The train left at a reasonable hour of the forenoon and it was supposed to return at twilight. I thought that a day without either of us would be lonely for Van; but Julius said he would be all right. We had made a little swing-door in the big door of the latticed porch on which the kitchen gave; and, with the kitchen door propped ajar, Van had the run of all the place. With him on guard it was perfectly safe to leave these apertures through which an able-bodied man could easily have squeezed himself. With a dish of food, a fresh bowl of water and with the presence of our clothes and other belongings to assure him of our return, a day's absence on our part could hardly be called a severe hardship. Then the kitty who had been the sole guest at his birthday party had formed a real friendship for Van and came for long daily visits. So, a little urging on the part of Julius demolished all of my objections, and, after assuring Van that we wouldn't stay long, we set off together.

The weather continued to be lovely, and we had a delightful day at Saint Augustine. When we reached the old city station toward sundown to take the train back to Jacksonville we found it to be a half-hour late. Having lost its place in the regular time-table, it had to side-track for trains from the other direction; so it was dark night when we arrived at our own door. The last block we had almost run in our eagerness to see what Van was thinking and doing there alone in the gloom. He heard us coming and was ready to greet us as soon as the front door was unlocked and opened. But he was strangely quiet as we hurried in to turn on the lights. It had seemed to all concerned to be such a good opportunity for our hand-maiden to go off for a long day with her own family that we had gladly offered her a full day's holiday; but our first thought now was a regret that we had not asked her to return before dark to have the house lighted up and livable on Van's account. It was too late for regrets, though, and we tried to make up for his long hour of darkness and doubt by coaxing and petting. Van responded with sweetness; but he seemed distrait, as if he had something on his mind which prevented him from giving us his whole attention. The next day he was strangely unresponsive, and Julius and I were more than usually concerned at the arrival of a telegram calling him from the city on a three-days' trip. Van always took it to heart when Julius left us even for a day, and it was doubly hard all around that he must go when Van was evidently either grieving about something or else ill. We had not yet determined whether it was illness or hurt feelings. For some time we had noticed that he had occasional spells of coughing—a cough that sounded as if he had strangled, or, as children say, had "swallowed the wrong way." More that than anything like a distemper or a cold.

Julius left before dark as he was to take a five-o'clock train. As soon as we had watched him out-of-sight Van came indoors and started up-stairs. I stood looking after him surprised at this change of his usual program in hastening indoors instead of the vigil on the gallery to see if Julius would not return before bed-time. Midway up the stairway he paused, staggered, then turned to gaze at me with a look of mournful appeal. I hurried up after him and sat down on the step. He rested his head on my knee for a few minutes, then toiled on up the stairs. I followed, and he went on through the upper hall to Julius' room where he went straight to the bed and leaped up to lie on the coverlet with his head on the pillow just where was still to be seen the dents made by Julius when he had taken a little snooze before dressing for the trip. I sat on the bed's edge, leaning over to stroke and coax Van, thoroughly convinced, from this sudden collapse, that he was really ill in some mysterious way. He responded with appreciation and lifted his paw to my shoulder while he feebly wagged the end of his tail. While talking to him I was mentally summing up the situation—facts and possibilities—and it did not take long to decide that we must have a doctor. This conclusion reached, I started from the bed to go down stairs to the telephone in the lower hall. Van objected as I started from him and reached over to catch my sleeve between his teeth and hold me beside him. This made me laugh; for it was a return, after four years of grown-up ways, to one of his baby-dog tricks. I coaxed him to let go and tugged the bit of sleeve from between his detaining teeth while I assured him I should be gone for only a minute or two.

Finally I freed myself and started from the room. Before I reached the head of the stairway I heard a jarring thud and there came Van, who had tumbled off the bed and was following me. In his weak state he had returned to that fear, which was a part of his baby-dog character of being left alone in the approaching night-shadows.

I tried to coax him back to the bed; but he insisted on going with me, staggering and tumbling down the steps until we had reached the lower hall, where he rested near my feet while I called—waited—and then talked with the doctor through the phone. When I hung up the receiver he raised his eyes with a look that said volumes and staggered through the archway to a lounge in the living-room in which he, after several ineffectual attempts, leaped—or, rather, scrambled—and curled himself among the cushions reaching out his paw to me with a heart-breaking gesture of apology and appeal.

All this confirmed my worst fears. Van knew that this lounge, with its tapestry cover and cushions, was not intended for his use, and in health he would never have thought of appropriating it. His matter-of-course way of going to it at this crisis showed that he realized that it was a serious situation—one where anything would be pardoned and accepted. I drew a chair up beside him, at which he flopped the end of his tail, and reached out both paws for me to hold.

When the doctor came he pronounced his patient to be seriously ill. The malady which had been creeping on by imperceptible degrees had taken a firm hold on the sensitive constitution of this aristocrat of Dog-dom.

After he was gone I sat beside Van as he lay dozing and faced a most serious situation. This dear dog was the joy and pride of his master, who was still so far from being a well man that even the smallest grief or crossing of his will was a more than possible cause of serious danger. There were not many humans in the world who meant so much to him as this dear little comrade who was so great a part of his daily life.

Even the gentlest man is not so submissive to Fate as is the average woman. Everything in life conspires to teach the lesson of patience to the feminine side of humanity. Woman soon learns to accept the fact that Providence either orders or permits everything that comes to pass; and that what is, is made right by the law of Compensation.

If Van's life—rounded out, complete and happy, as it had been— was now to end, I could reconcile myself after a sharp pang or two to the decree of Fate; but, for his master's sake, he must be cured, at all costs, if it were within the range of possibility. The doctor had said it would be more a matter of nursing than of drugs. I knew this to be a fact, and I knew, too, that I should have all the nursing to do. No one else knew him so well; even if Van were willing, which I knew he would not be, to have anyone to nurse him except the one who had been the joy and comfort of his infant days.

It would be a hard fight—three on one side, the doctor, Van and his nurse—three against Death.

It sounds like heavy odds—three against one; but, in this case, it was one against three. Death is a host in herself. Single-handed, she has power to rout armies. Her equipment is so complete that, when arrayed against her, neither number nor strength counts. Courage is something; but even courage cannot always prevail.

Courage I had, and I resolved that we must win, though I realized that it would be a struggle.

First, Van must be kept as quiet, as warm and as comfortable as possible. He was already very weak. I could not lift such a big dog, to carry him around. He must remain in the bed he had chosen; and, obviously, I must stay with him. Every time I rose from my chair, even to cross the room, he started wide awake, and watched to see if I meant to leave him. As the night advanced there began to be a chill in the air, and I went out to the back gallery for a basket of wood and kindling to make a blaze on the hearth. Van whimpered and whined as I went for the wood, then flopped his tail against the couch-cover to express satisfaction when I returned. I saw that he had no intention of letting me leave him, so I drew the most comfortable arm-chair the lower rooms afforded to the side of the couch with a hassock for my feet. I sat near for a few minutes while I thought over the situation, then I told Van he must be a good baby-dog and let me leave him for a minute. As soon as I started into the hall, toward the stairway, I heard him stir and begin to protest. I spoke to him, then went softly up the steps, still talking and raising my voice gradually as the distance between us was increased, that he might not realize how far from him I had gone. I gathered up his bed, with it denim sheets and denim-covered pillows, and brought it down-stairs. Van was eased along to one end of the couch and these things arranged on the other. Then he was eased along back onto his own bed, which he recognized, and showed that he appreciated. The tapestry couch-cover and pillows were carried up-stairs on another flying trip and I then brought back an armful of blankets and a pillow to line my own chair, which I realized must be, for the present, my bed. Van showed that he understood all these arrangements—that the couch was now really his bed and that I had camped beside him to stay. He reached out one paw for me to hold, his eyelids drooped, and we both went to sleep.

While the clock was striking four, Van awakened me by whimpering and beginning to struggle. I helped him to turn over on his side, then made up the dying fire. He kept on whimpering and whining, and I offered him water; then tried to see if he could be hungry. He refused everything; but continued his cries, so I drew my chair as close to the couch as it would go; and, taking both his paws in my hands, began to sing a foolish old song he had loved when he was a puppy, beginning:

> "The old red fox ran down the meadow.
> Long time a-go."

This, it appeared, was just what he wanted. With a contented sigh, he nestled his head against my knee, flopped his tail several times and again dozed off. He slept until the end of the song; then awoke and began again to whimper. So I sat there singing, humming, or whistling softly until dawn. There were three days and nights like this, and, as the malady progressed, it was constantly harder to see the little patient struggle for breath, and to help him fight the spasms that came to frighten and torment him.

Then Julius came home.

He was so upset to find Van in bed, and so aghast at the idea that I could not leave him day or night, that it looked as if my task of nursing was to be doubled.

Van hardly knew his dear master. It was strange to see how his illness had brought back all the puppy ways. He clung to me just as he had done in his infancy and regarded the presence of Julius almost with indifference.

Chapter Seventh, and Last

THE DAYS and nights dragged along. Endless hours of weariness or of pain for Van; and of ceaseless watchfulness for me.

Some days our patient seemed to be so much better and so happy in realizing that he had my exclusive care and attention, that we were all full of hope and began to believe he would soon be again on his feet.

Then would come a back-set and I watched beside him expecting that every spasm would end the pain and leave him lifeless.

Early in his malady the gentle patient had won the heart of his physician; and Van soon learned to watch for the coming of the kind stranger who was accepted as a friend to be greeted with a flop of the tail and an out-stretched paw.

During the third week pain and weakness took another form, which resulted in paralysis, and he began to lose consciousness.

Then he fell asleep.

As we brushed his coat for the last time—arranging the long wavy hair on the form now become so strangely large, heavy and unresponsive—the same question was in both our hearts. Where was not that gentle dog-soul so faithful, so loving and so devoted?

The clay we placed in the box was not Van. He was not there. Then, where was he?

Pondering these things, we arrive at the truth, old as human feeling, that the only realities of life are the things that do not exist.

What are called realities—life's necessities—these never quicken the pulses, nor choke the breath with hurried heart-beats.

But the intangibles—love, art, beauty, music, and again love; for love, in all its many kinds and degrees, is what gives meaning to art, beauty and music—these are the things that stir us to the depths— these are the things that grasp us with resistless power, dragging us up by the roots to throw us down quivering where we perish; or else take hold anew with our soul-fibers.

These non-existing realities make of earth a garden of delight; or a desert swept by simoons and scorched by droughts.

Nothing else really matters—or rather, everything else follows as the non-existing verities set the pace.

Adieu, Little Comrade, we made a brave fight; but we lost.

* * *

As soon as the carriage drove from our door taking Julius and a friend who had volunteered to go with him to convey the emptied shell, which had contained the loving soul of our little Van, to its last resting place in the sweet, quiet country under a wild olive tree; I realized, for the first time, that nights of vigil and days of ceaseless anxiety had left me in a state that approached exhaustion. I closed the house below, and went up-stairs to seek needed rest to be ready to assume again all the burdens that had slipped from my shoulders while every thought had been devoted to the little invalid.

I fell at once into a dreamless sleep; then, the first weariness past, entered through the Door of Dreams, memory-chambers that gave back a vision of that morning home-coming after our longest absence from The Blessed Isle. The scene was re-enacted; then surrounds changed, and it was the Happy Hunting Grounds. Van was just inside the flowery hedges that separate it from the Elysian Fields, keeping vigil for our approach. As we crossed the "swelling flood" he gazed with luminous eyes until sure of our identity. Then, as on that distant morning, he lifted his face, and began the hymn of joy that gathered around him all the cattles of The Blessed Isle: and then, hastening after them—Bruno, Rebecca and the others—all the faithful comrades of our happy years of HOME.

Magazine

Articles

Magazine Articles

In researching Byrd Spilman Dewey's writings, one of the most intriguing mysteries was her magazine writings. Several of her short biographical sketches, including those found in *Who's Who*, the *Review of Southern Literature* and the *Economy Administration Cook Book* mentioned that she did "much magazine writing." However, periodical databases and indexes failed to reveal any magazine articles written under the name Byrd Spilman Dewey. Biographies noted that she wrote under pen names, but no list of pen names was ever given.

A short fairy tale served as the key to unlock this mystery. In 1917, Mrs. Dewey published a children's fairy tale titled *Who Seeks Finds*. Upon examination, the printed copy indicated that it had been republished courtesy of the Century Company, a leading magazine publisher of the time. By researching a few of the story's key words, the entry was found, published in *St. Nicholas*, a children's magazine, in 1895. It was published under the name "Judith Ray." This brought to light again Mrs. Dewey's affinity for the name Judith.

A new search of periodical databases did not find any additional writings under the name Judith Ray. But just using the first name "Judith" her main pen name was revealed—Judith Sunshine. Using that name, entries were found in such publications as *Good Housekeeping* and the *Christian Union*. She also submitted letters and articles to newspapers using the initials J.S., or the name J. Sunshine.

She also contributed to the *Florida Farmer & Fruit Grower* magazine under the name Aunt Judith, which is also the by-line she used for her weekly column in *The Tropical Sun*, West Palm Beach's first newspaper.

These selections show her wit, good common sense, and ingenuity. In *At Other People's Convenience*, she relates an amusing tale of the minister's ill-timed attempts at a luncheon date; in *The Wall Furniture in our Perfect Home*, she tells how to make custom built-in furniture as she did in their first South Florida home, dubbed The Hermitage, tucked in the sand pine woods in the hills north of the present-day West Palm Beach, as told in *From Pine Woods to Palm Groves*. She also offers culinary advice to thrifty housekeepers in *On Toast*, how old bread can be toasted for quick meals.

Her story *The Tyranny from the Other Side* was reprinted in newspapers around the world, even found in a New Zealand newspaper and in tribal Native American newspapers; the reader will see what happens when housewives skimp on food for their family to save money for other things.

There exists yet a treasure trove of additional magazine writings, undiscovered under other pen names. These few examples bring to life the world of Byrd Spilman Dewey in the 1880s and 1890s.

At Other People's Convenience
"A Whole Week Put Out of Joint for a Twenty Minutes' Call."

B Y THE way, Judith," said Julius, one Monday evening at the tea-table, "I met Mr. Dominie in the post-office this afternoon, and he said that he and Mrs. Dominie had intended to come out to see us this forenoon, but they found, at the last minute, that the Deacon was intending to use his horse himself."

"Bless that dear old deacon," said I fervently. "I owe him one."

"Yes, it was lucky!" said Julius.

"I should think so! How any couple, in their senses, could ever think of making a surprise visit on Monday morning, I don't see! What did you tell him?"

"Well, you see, I didn't like to remind him it was wash-day—they have kept house, and know all about it; and they know we are doing our own work, for he asked how it agreed with you this weather, and when we expected 'Mandy back—so I just told him that they must not be discouraged, but must try again."

"And what did he say to that?"

"Why, he said they meant to try it again tomorrow."

"Tomorrow! and all the ironing to do, and nothing fresh baked!"

"Yes, I knew it wouldn't suit, but what could I do?"

"Nothing, of course. We will have to make the best of it. I will put off the ironing, and do some baking instead—bright and early before they get here."

So the next morning I got up betimes, set the whole house in spotless order, baked rolls and cake, got a chicken pie under way and made a salad. Then I dressed myself in a white muslin, with a ruffled apron, and gathered fresh flowers for all of the vases. Then I sat down and hulled a bowlful of ripe, dewy strawberries, which Julius had gathered for me. Mr. and Mrs. Dominie boarded in the village, and would, I knew appreciate our delicious country fare. He was preaching for us for six months "on trial." They were an elderly couple, whose children were all scattered, and they were fond of visiting. We did not feel very well acquainted with them, and wished to do them honor. At 11 o'clock Julius came in from the garden, to make himself presentable. He found me putting the last touches to the dinner-table, so that only the hot food would have to be added at "dishing-up" time.

"Haven't come yet!" he exclaimed.

"No," I said; "they seem inclined to be very fashionable. One would think the cool of the morning much pleasanter for driving this time of the year."

"Yes indeed; but they may be along any minute now."

A quarter past—half past—three-quarters—12. Still no minister, nor minister's wife. Julius paced between the front verandah and the gate, while I busied myself trying to keep the dinner hot, without drying it to chips. One o'clock struck; then Julius came in, saying: "We might as well give them up and have dinner. Something must have happened to detain them, and perhaps they will come this afternoon."

So we ate hurriedly, and Julius helped me to set all to rights; then, tired out, I sat down, with a new magazine and a basket of mending. At four o'clock, there still being no sign of our visitors, Julius came in and said: "It's time to go to the post-office; the mail must surely be in. Perhaps I'll meet Mr. Dominie, or someone from the Deacon's and find out what the trouble is."

When he returned, he said, in answer to my eager inquiries: "Yes, I met Mr. Dominie himself, the first one, and he said they 'did think of coming this morning, but Mrs. Dominie thought it looked like rain.'"

"Like rain! Why, I never heard of such nonsense. It has been a lovely day!"

"So I thought; but of course I couldn't contradict him. Then he said, if it was pleasant, they would come tomorrow."

I groaned: "Then I must put off all the ironing again."

So the next morning I again busied myself preparing good things for dinner and making the house as attractive as possible. When Julius and I a second time sat down to our belated dinner alone, I was fairly boiling with indignation.

"Do you know what I think of Mr. Dominie?" I exclaimed. "I think he is a first-class fraud!"

"I wouldn't say that," said Julius. "He may have had some good reason this time. Perhaps someone was taken sick and sent for him."

"Then she ought to have sent us word. It is shameful for them to be so rude!"

"So it is; and it has made you so much extra work, too."

"Yes, I have worked twice as hard as usual; and here, the week is half gone and not a piece ironed."

When Julius came home that evening he said: "I saw Mr. Dominie, and he said he was sorry they didn't get out this morning, but Mrs. Dominie thought that she felt one of her attacks of headache coming on, so he thought they'd better postpone it; but they will surely be out tomorrow."

"Indeed! Said I, then added, viciously, "I hope it will rain pitchforks!"

"Oh well, they'll come this time, and then it will be over, and we won't ask them again."

"They don't wait to be asked," I said, "but seem to think their visits are such treats to us that they put us to any amount of trouble, and it's all right."

Well, the whole program was again repeated, and still our visitors did not appear. It was fair all day until late afternoon, then a thunder-shower came up, preventing Julius from going after the mail, so we did not learn what trifle prevented their coming this time. At the tea-table I said, "Well, tomorrow is Friday, and, minister, or no minister, I am going to iron."

So, the next morning, I went to work on my belated ironing, in fear and trembling, starting at every sound, until I became so nervous I felt like flying—for fear they would come and catch me unaware in the short-sleeved Mother Hubbard I always wore when ironing. The day waned, but they did not come. When Julius started to the village, I took a book and threw myself into the hammock, completely tired out. He had been gone some time, when I heard voices. Looking out, there were Mr. and Mrs. Dominie coming up the front path. I met them at the door and tried to be cordial, but felt that it was a hollow mockery. It was impossible to keep the reproach out of my voice when I spoke of having expected them to dinner each day since Monday.

"Yes, we were so disappointed," said Mrs. Dominie; "but every time we planned to come, something would happen to prevent."

I think they expected an invitation to tea, but I forgot (?) it, and said, moreover, nothing about future visits. I suppose it was not very polite, but "the worm will turn."

Julius laughed rather grimly, when he came home and heard about the visit. "A whole week put out of joint for a 20-minutes' call," he said.

"Yes," said I; "and if Mr. Dominie remains here after his six months are up, it won't be my fault. A man who has so little regard for his own word, and other people's convenience, is a public nuisance!"

"Amen," said Julius.

A Suitable Christmas Present
What Happened From Not Having a Carving Knife.

DICK AND Maggie had been married only three months. As is often the case, some of their wedding presents were duplicates, while some other things, just as necessary, were forgotten altogether. The worst of it was, that, as they lived in a village, and the presents were all from dear friends or relatives, they could not exchange them, as we are told they sometimes do in the cities. However, Maggie being a sensible little woman, with the knack of making things do, they had got along very well.

It was the first of December, and Maggie, as she arranged the tea-table, was reviewing, mentally, her list of presents for Christmas. It had been a busy year—first, the endless preparations for the wedding, and since then, the setting to rights and making pretty of her little home—that she had not found the time for much "fancy-work," so she would have to buy the most of them.

She knew just what Mother and the girls would like—Father, too—in fact, her list was all complete and satisfactory, with the exception of something for Dick. "Last, but not least, oh, no!" she thought to herself with a happy smile. If he only smoked! To be sure, she was glad he did not; she thought it an untidy, expensive habit, but there were always so many pretty things one could give a smoker.

Here the click of the gate latch interrupted her thoughts, and she flew to open the door.

During the progress of their evening meal, Maggie was so unusually quiet, that Dick finally noticed it, and asked,

"What's up, little woman? Anything gone wrong today?"

"No. Why?"

"You seem so quiet."

"Oh, I've been thinking."

"That's nothing new. What about?"

"About Christmas. I can't think of anything to give you; you have everything."

"That's so. Don't give me anything. You have given me yourself; that will do for one while."

"What rubbish!" she said, with a pleased blush. "Anyway, I want to give you something; it would not seem like Christmas if I didn't!"

"Well, get something we will both enjoy—something we need about the house. That will do first-rate."

The next day, as soon as Maggie had finished washing the dinner-dishes, and had tidied the kitchen, she donned her stylish walking suit, and set out for one of the two hardware stores of the village. Not finding anything that suited her rather fastidious taste, she left an order with the proprietor, to be sent to the city and filled. Then, visiting some other stores to complete her list of presents, she turned her face homeward, with a feeling of satisfaction that the problem was solved.

The following week, Maggie invited her Mother, Mrs. Ripple, and the girls, Annie and Katie, to spend a long day with her. Pa Ripple was to come home with Dick at noon. It was an occasion when Dick and Maggie felt very anxious that their little establishment should have its "best foot foremost;" for, although the family had "dropped in" singly, time and again, at meal-time, this was their first attempt to have them all at a formal dinner.

The table looked very pretty in all the bravery of bridal linen, china and silver. As Maggie proudly surveyed it, she heard her father and Dick come in. The latter came hurrying out, his arms full of bundles. "See here, Pet." He began, in a pleased tone, "I saw them unpacking these grapes and oranges as we came along, and I thought they would give just the right look to the table. And look at this," opening a long package, "I remembered how I have had to carve with the butcher-knife all along, and thought it would never do with all our finery, today, and I saw this nice carving set at Hardy's, and I couldn't resist. Perhaps it was extravagant," he continued, answering an inexplicable look on her face, "but we will call it part of our Christmas in advance. Is it all right?"

"Yes, of course, you dear fellow!" she answered, swallowing a great many unspoken thoughts. "It is just what I was wishing for. Now go in, and make yourself charming, while I take up dinner."

"You are sure you are pleased? I thought it would just suit!"

"Yes, yes!" she said hurriedly, "go, or things will scorch!"

When all were seated around the glittering table, and Dick, with a flourish, took up the new carving knife and fork, Annie and Katie exchanged glances, and then looked at Mrs. Ripple.

"Something new?" asked the latter.

"Yes," said Dick, "I got them today; I was tired of carving with the butcher-knife."

Katie looked at Annie again, and both giggled.

"What's the joke?" said Dick.

"Nothing," said Katie. Pa and Ma Ripple were both smiling now, and Dick looked stupidly from one to the other.

"I declare, I don't see anything funny!" he said at last.

"Tell him!" "Tell him!" cried the two girls, now laughing outright.

"Yes do," said Dick.

"There, there, girls, don't be silly! They are laughing, Dick, because when we went to the city shopping, two weeks ago, we all settled on a handsome carving set as a Christmas present for you and Maggie; for we remembered you had none, and thought it would please you both."

"Did you! cried Maggie, "and only last week, I left an order for one at Steele's for Dick's Christmas gift, because he told me to get something we both wanted, and I thought we needed that most of all."

"There! I knew you were not pleased somehow, when I came with this! No wonder!"

"Ha! ha! ha!" "He! he! he!" "Ho! ho! ho!"

Long and loud, they all laughed, some one of them beginning again, and so starting the others, every time there was a pause. It was a merry meal.

As they arose from the table there were sounds of an arrival in front of the house—wheels, then the gate latch clicking, and voices. Going out, they found Dick's father and mother, just in from their home in the country. As soon as the confusion had subsided, they were told the "carving-set joke." They were not so much amused as had been expected, but looked at each other, and said:

"Well, did you ever!"

"Now what's the matter!" exclaimed Dick.

"Why, Pa and I," said his mother, "had sent for one, too. We noticed, when we were here last, that you didn't have one."

Here the old lady's voice was drowned in shouts of laughter. How they laughed, and laughed!

"I hope and trust," said Dick finally, wiping his eyes, "that nobody else has noticed that we haven't a carving-set!"

A Village Tragedy
Vindication for the Virtuous; Misfortune for the Gossip.

MRS. ROLY sat by the window shelling peas. She looked thoroughly at peace, and contented. A pitcher of "laylock" and snowball stood on the white-draped table. A tabby cat dozed on the window sill, and the bees sang musically on a tree in full blossom outside. A sound of footsteps on the back "stoop," and a middle-aged woman of lean and uninviting appearance entered. This was Mrs. Winklies, a near neighbor. She sat down in a rocking-chair, which Mrs. Roly drew forward for her, and fanned herself with her sunbonnet. "Dear me, how warm the days are getting!"

Mrs. Roly assented.

"I came over to borrow a cake of seed yeast. I am making new, today, and thought I had seed, but, come to look at it, it's all webby. I thought likely you'd have some fresh."

"Yes, I made new last week. I like to make it pretty often in warm weather, it rises so much better."

"Yes," said Mrs. Winklies absently. She sat silent for several minutes, after taking the packet of yeast Mrs. Roly had prepared and handed to her, and then spoke. "Do you believe all this talk that's going 'round about Lena Allen?"

"Talk about Lena Allen! What do you mean?"

"Haven't you heard anything of it?"

"Not a word; and I don't believe it either; I don't care who says it,

318

nor what it is."

"Well, I didn't say I believed it either, did I? But it does seem kind of queer. Nothing would do but she must go to the city to study music—music, indeed! and when she came back, didn't you notice how pale and thin she looked?"

"No, she didn't look any worse than I expected to see her after spending six months in that cooped-up, brick-and-mortar abomination." answered Mrs. Roly with some heat.

"Well, anyway, you must admit it looked queer for Mrs. Allen to go up there, soon after Lena came home, and adopt a baby that none of them can give any account of. I asked Lena, myself, whose child it was, and she got as red as fire, and said 'a friend's.' Friend, indeed!"

"Why, Mrs. Winklies, how can you suggest such horrible things. It is dreadful!"

"I'm not suggesting anything; I just said it looked queer, and don't it?"

"Not to me. I think the Allens have a right to keep their own affairs to themselves if they want to. Why should we want to pry into them? I don't doubt that the baby is the child of some friend or relative, and, if they have adopted it, they will not want it to know, when it grows up, that it is not really their own. Now, how could this be if everybody in the village knew its history?"

"Oh, well, think what you like, but I say it's queer, and I don't wonder folks are talking."

After Mrs. Winklies had gone, Mrs. Roly sat lost in thought. "She never comes here," she was saying mentally, "but she brings some piece of gossip, and leaves me feeling as if I'd rolled in a bed of nettles. I'm just getting tired of it, and half wish we lived miles away, where she couldn't run in so handy with her budget."

Such a piece of gossip was not long in spreading through the town. As might be expected it was received in various ways. The bold and honest thought it a "shameful calumny;" the timid and doubting said, "Most shocking, if true," while the malicious and envious received it complacently, declaring that "The Allens always have been above themselves," and "guessed" that "now they'd come down a peg or two, and not be so high and mighty."

In every village there is always at least one person who thinks it her—it is usually a woman—"duty" to let people know they are talked about. Lena had already noticed that she was stared at in an unusual say, in her comings and goings about the village, and had been sadly puzzled by this and many "trifles light as air." She was a beautiful and lovely girl, universally sought and admired, the only daughter of one of the wealthy families of the village. Many less fortunate envied the village belle, and delighted in her humiliation. The shock of the discovery that such unspeakably dreadful things were being said of her, stunned her with indignant horror. She shut herself in her own room, and fought the battle of her life alone. We will not pry into the bitterness of that hour. Angels must turn aside and weep at such a scene.

The struggle over at last, Lena came forth, dressed freshly in white, her curls damp from her bath. She sought her mother and kissed her, resting, for a moment, her cheek on the motherly bosom, then said, "I will live it down." Mrs. Allen tried to speak, but could not. No further mention was made of it between them until long after. It is not hard for a brave, high-strung nature to make a resolve of this kind, but the daily and hourly effort that must needs be, consumes the sensitive soul. Did she go abroad, she was met with coldness or aversion in some one or other of her former gushing friends; in others with such extreme kindness that she knew they had her humiliation in mind, and were making an effort to show her they believed her innocent. Did she stay at home, prying visitors came on all sorts of trumped-up errands, showing a maddening interest in the little one who had become so dear to them all. She would often see that they were examining its small features, and staring in turn at her own, as if in comparison. Afterwards she would grow hot and cold by turns at the remembrance of it. Her healthy young appetite failed, and her nights began to be long hours of sleepless horror. She tried to conceal her extreme dejection, and to pretend to eat; but it was evident that she was becoming thin and haggard.

At this time the baby, having reached the troublous period of teething, fell sick, and the whole family, with ceaseless anxiety, watched the little thing, battling for its life. After many sleepless nights, and long, painful days, the blue eyes closed for the last time. The whole family grieved sincerely, and Lena, who had seemed more like herself while absorbed in the duties of nursing, drooped visibly from the moment of return from the tiny heaped-up grave. She wandered about the house, languid and abstracted, trying to resume, with a show of interest, her old occupations. The gossips made great capital out of the grief the family, and especially Lena, had shown, and the fact that she and her mother had worn simple black dresses at the funeral, lost nothing in the telling. Lena felt this intuitively, and it added to her sufferings to see how many of the most vigilant gossips made errands to her home, she was sure, out of curiosity to see "how she was taking it."

"Now, Annie White," said Mrs. Winklies, at a chance meeting with one of Lena Allen's staunch girl friends, "I suppose you'll give in now that there's been something in this all along. Where there's so much smoke, there's sure to be some fire."

"No, I won't give in," said Annie. "It's not smoke at all. It's an unhealthy miasma from a bog of evil thoughts, and you'll see the day, Mrs. Winklies, when you'll be sorry you ever had anything to do with spreading it, if I am any prophet."

"Upon my word! That's pretty talk from a young girl to a woman who knows four times as much of the world. You might be in better business than standing up for that baggage."

"And you might be in better business than carrying gossip. You have daughters of your own, Mrs. Winklies; one would think that would make you more considerate of other young girls."

"It's because I've daughters of my own that I want to show up that doll-faced cheat."

Annie smiled grimly to herself, afterward, in recalling this admission. "You told the truth for once, Mrs. Winklies," she thought. "You are vindictive because your homely, ill-natured girls are outshone by sweet Lena Allen."

Lena made a brave effort to rally, but it is hard to be interested in the daily trifles that make up village life, when the heart is transfixed with a poisoned arrow. It was an unequal battle. The spirit was strong enough, but the flesh all too weak. Fasting, wakefulness, and constant heart-soreness at last undermined her naturally frail constitution, and, as Thanksgiving approached, the news went abroad that Lena Allen was going into a decline. She sank rapidly, and was soon too weak to leave her bed. One night she wakened out of a stupor-like sleep to see her mother "sitting in a mournful muse" by the fire.

"Are you alone, mother, dear?"

"Yes, darling," said Mrs. Allen, rising and approaching the bed. "Do you wish for anything?"

Lena looked at her with wide-open, sunken eyes, then spoke. "It's killing me, mother."

"Oh, no, my child, don't say that! You must get well."

"No, mother, it is better for me to die. If I get well, I will always be 'a girl there used to be talk about.' If I die, they will soon forget."

"Oh, no, my own! I have already told them about little Blossom, and if you will only get a little stronger we will go far away, and live among strangers. Anything, oh! Anything! If you will only come back to me the bonny, light-hearted little girlie that made life so good to live!"

"No, mother darling, it is too late. Oh, the world is so cruel—so cruel!"

They buried her in the frozen ground the week before Christmas.

When the story went around that Mrs. Allen had said that the baby was her brother's, by an ill-advised private marriage, and she had wished to keep the secret, as the mother had died at its birth, and to raise the child as her own, some of the villagers felt such pangs of remorse that they sifted all the old rumors, and succeeded in tracing them, every one, to Mrs. Winklies. In every instance she had started them by asking each one privately if they "believed all that talk about Lena Allen." This recalled so many other rumors that she had, in similar ways, and equally without foundation, started, that Mrs. Winklies found the village becoming too hot to hold her, and was obliged to move away.

This is a true story, and was recalled by a sentence in a letter received a short time ago. It was this:—

"I had a letter not too long ago from Cousin Sue, saying that Mrs. Winklies is living in a village not far from them, and just to think, Judith, she is miserably poor, and utterly friendless. She has suffered one misfortune after another ever since Lena Allen died."

Verily, "The mills of the gods grind slowly, but they grind exceeding small."

"You Ought to Know"

A Gossip May Learn to Make Kind Remarks about Her Neighbors

OUTSIDE THE flowers bloomed, and the chickens cackled and sang in the bright sunlight. Inside, the white window curtains swayed slowly in the breezes entering the open windows. The morning work was all done, and I sat at my sewing, at peace with myself and all the world, when there came a sound of footsteps on the back porch and a shadow on the floor.

"Good morning, Mrs. Sunshine!"

"Good morning, Mrs. Green!" I answered; not very cordially, I am afraid, for my peace of mind fled at the sight of her, knowing as I did from sad experience that she had come to gossip.

"I told Angie Kate I was coming right over to tell you, because I thought you ought to know."

"Did you?" I said dryly.

"Yes. Mrs. Glib was over at our house last night to borrow our 'weekly'-she is too stingy to take it herself, and always comes for ours before we have half read it, and she says 'I think Mrs. Sunshine is dreadful stuck up, never runs in in a neighborly way, but always primps up, and comes mincing to the front door, and knocks like a stranger.' And I told her, says I"-

"Mrs. Green," said I, rudely interrupting her, "why did you think I 'ought to know' all that rubbish?"

"Why? Why because, I think folks ought to know who their real friends are."

"You think she is my enemy then?"

"No-I suppose she likes you well enough." came the hesitating answer.

"You thought it was your duty to tell me, though?"

"Yes," looking brighter, and evidently making ready to proceed.

"I suppose then you think it is my duty to tell her that you said she was too stingy to subscribe for the 'weekly' and always borrowed yours before you had read it?"

"My goodness, no! she would be as mad as hops. I wouldn't make her mad for anything."

"Why not? You have risked making me 'mad as hops' at her. What is the difference?"

Mrs. Green fidgeted in her chair. Her face slowly reddened, and she rolled and unrolled the strings of her sunbonnet. At last she spoke.

"I declare, I never thought of it that way before."

"I thought not. You remember how angry you were at Miss Pry for telling you that Mrs. Gray said your tongue was too long?"

"Yes. I thought she had better look at home; and I think yet she only told me to see what I would say."

"Is not that one of the reasons you have told me that Mrs. Glib thinks I am 'stuck up'? Very likely I do seem 'stuck up' to all of you. I never lived in a village until I came here, and have not been accustomed to back-door visits; but I feel very kindly to my neighbors; it is only that our ways are different. Now confess, you thought there was a grain of truth in Mrs. Glib's criticism of me, and you wanted to see what I would say."

Mrs. Green looked distressed.

"I will not be angry," I said. "It was only a misunderstanding."

"Well, I have thought so, I never will again," she said at last.

"I hope not…Mrs. Green, do you know you have repeated a great many such criticisms to me?"

"Why no, I didn't think I had."

"Well you have. You have reported something from almost every lady in the village. Do you think they expected you to repeat their remarks?"

"I suppose not."

"What would you think if I were to repeat all you have ever said to me about them?"

"I would think it was real mean." she said quickly. "And you would be right. It would be 'real mean.' Now it is not barely possible that what is 'real mean' in one woman is—well—not exactly kind in another?"

Mrs. Green began to cry.

"I did not mean to hurt your feelings." I said: "but gossiping does cause so much heartache and unhappiness, I wanted you to see it as I do."

Mrs. Green, still crying, arose to depart.

"You will not be angry when you have thought it over." I said.

"I'm n-not m-mad."

"Well, sit down again then, and let us talk of something pleasanter."

She stood irresolute a minute, and then said, "I think I'd better go."

"Not until I have given you something pleasant to think of. I heard someone speaking very kindly of you the other day."

"Did you? Who was it?" she said eagerly.

"It was Mrs. Sweet. She was saying what a kind neighbor you are, and that she never could forget what a comfort you were to her when her little Ernest died. I tell you this," I added mischievously, "because I think you 'ought to know'."

"You are a funny woman, Mrs. Sunshine; I don't know how to take you more than half the time."

Without replying to this, I continued, "There is trouble and heartache enough in this world at the best, and I think we ought to repeat pleasant remarks, or none."

"I know it," and then irrelevantly, "I always did like Mrs. Sweet. I hear kind things said of you, too; shall I tell you some?"

"Never mind. I am not fishing for compliments, but I admit I would rather hear them than the other kind. I have been made uncomfortable for days by hearing some unkind speech repeated."

"I am sorry; I will try not to do so any more."

"Then we shall be good friends."

"I hope we shall."

The Tyranny from the Other Side
Of the Firm of Husband, Wife & Co.

THE MAN who stints his family in order to indulge himself, has for so long been held up to the scorn of the reading public, that the other side of the subject has been entirely lost sight of. Some time ago, I was calling on an acquaintance, who had a number of new purchases to display, articles of furniture, decoration, etc., and some lovely tableware. Knowing her income to be no larger than my own, I asked:

"But how can you afford such handsome things? I cannot even think of making such purchases."

She gave me an intent look, then, dropping her voice, confidentially said:

"I save it out of the housekeeping. For a long time I have saved, at least, half of my monthly allowance, and this month I will save more. I want to buy me a new silk—something really elegant."

"But," I said, "can you save so much and still make your family comfortable?"

"I suppose they are comfortable enough," she said, as if offended. "I'm sure what's good enough for me, is good enough for them!"

She had detained me so long bringing out one thing after another to display, that tea-time approached, and her little boy, a child of nine or ten years of age, came dashing in, saying, "O Ma! I'm so hungry! Is there anything for supper to-night?"

"Certainly, my son, we will have the supper we always have."

"O-o-o Ma! Nothing but cold corn-bread and milk! Oh!"

"Hush! If corn-bread and milk is good enough for me, it ought to be good enough for the rest of you," she answered sternly.

"Yes, but Ma, you like it and all of the rest of us hate it. Why can't we ever have anything the rest of us like?"

"That will do. If you are not hungry enough to eat what we have, you can go without."

I hastily took leave, and as I shut the front gate I heard the poor little fellow burst into a perfect storm of sobs. I no longer envied her the beautiful things she had bought. She had paid too dearly for them. After that I used to watch her children passing by on their way to school. Their once ruddy faces grew sallow and pinched, while deep scowls of discontent and discomfort became habitual to them. In a few weeks, the mother returned my visit, arrayed in the "really elegant" silk dress. As soon as there was an opportunity, I asked:

"And how are your children?" she frowned.

They were such healthy babies, and their father and I, too, have always been strong—I don't understand it—I suppose I shall have to take them somewhere for a change, but it seems an awful extravagance!"

May not such a woman be, without exaggeration, likened to a vampire, draining the life blood, or its equivalent, from the family to indulge herself! I never returned the visit, and could only think of her afterwards with loathing.

A friend I used to have lived a short distance from town, on a fruit farm. One spring day I heard she was getting ready for her usual summer trip, so I, thimble in pocket, went out to spend the day, and help with her preparations. She received me joyfully, and we were soon deep in the mysteries of ruffles and gores. Though not intimately acquainted, I had loved her dearly. That night I went home thinking her a selfish little beast. At dinner time her husband came in tired and hungry. She had left me sewing, and gone out half an hour before to the kitchen and now called us out to dinner. The table was set with beautiful china, and there was a dish of squash and a small plate of bread and butter, and a pitcher of water, nothing else. She made no reference to the scanty fare, but seemed to think it was all as it should be. I did not care for myself, knowing I would be at my own bountiful table at tea-time, but I did pity her husband. I knew he could have eaten every mouthful on the table and still be unsatisfied. The bread plate was soon emptied. He looked hesitatingly at his wife, and then said:

"My dear, is there any more bread?"

"Yes," she said, without moving. "I only cut what I think will be eaten, it gets so dry."

"The plate is empty," he said. "Perhaps Mrs. Sunshine would like some more."

"Would you like some more, Mrs. Sunshine?" she said turning to me.

Of course I said no.

He waited several minutes, then said,

"If it isn't too much trouble to get it, I would like another piece."

She looked unsmilingly at him for several seconds, then arose and cut him one little piece. He ate it, looked around wistfully at the empty dishes, sighed, and folded up his napkin. I knew him to be the kindest, most indulgent husband, and I felt indignant to see him so imposed upon. When we returned to our sewing, I dexterously led the conversation to the subject.

"How tired and hungry Mr. Walters must get, working as he does, out of doors all day!" I said.

"Yes, I suppose he does," she answered carelessly.

"I should think you would take a great deal of pains to have things nice for him, he is so thoughtful for you!" I ventured further.

"Oh, no! He doesn't expect me to exert myself. He knows how frail I am."

This uttered at the sewing machine, in the pauses of stitching a sixth ruffle on a "summer silk," did not impress me as being very consistent.

"Besides," she continued, presently, "we must economize. My

outfit is costing a great deal and my trip will be expensive. I cannot afford to spend much on our home living. I don't have any appetite myself, anyway, so I bother just as little with housework and cookery as I can."

This was so manifestly selfish, it fairly took my breath away and I worked several button-holes before speaking again. Then I said, "I wonder if you are willing to go away and leave him here alone all summer. Supposing he should get sick?"

"Well, I would rather he had some one here with him, but he will not be able to afford it. I must have money to spend while I am away. There are always little unlooked-for expenses. I can't go empty handed, and I will go. Jack promised me before we were married, that I should always have a summer trip and I mean to keep him to it."

These are not fancy sketches. They are drawn from life, and many more might be added. In fact, I have known more wives than husbands who took the lion's share of the income and used it for selfish pleasures in which the others had no share.

One woman I know whose husband has broken down from over-work. Her house is a perfect museum of useless pieces of furniture and finery, hideous chromos, "ornaments," silks, laces, etc., etc. She bores every visitor she has showing these, and bewailing the "better days" when she constantly haunted bargain counters, and ends by saying, "I little thought I would one day have to take boarders for a living!" as if she, instead of her poor broken-down husband were the aggrieved one. It is evident that she really thinks she is. Even now, she stints her family in every possible way, that she may save for fresh "bargains."

Some years ago, when we were younger and less wise, my husband and I resolved to cut down our living expenses in order to purchase a set of books for which our souls longed. We did so, and enjoyed the possession of them as only book lovers can, but all at once our days began to be languid and nervous, and our night filled with trouble dreams. The symptoms increased until alarmed, we "called the doctor in." He looked wise, asked questions, then prescribed tonics, and a nourishing diet! How we laughed when he had gone! It was such a joke on us! When we viewed the condition of the family purse, after paying the doctor and druggist bills, we realized that it was useless to try to cheat nature. But how much better I felt than if I had privately cut down the table expenses to indulge some selfish "fad" of my own, then ascribed our feebleness to a "mysterious dispensation of an all wise Providence!"

On Toast.

TOAST IS the housekeeper's best friend, and is the foundation of numberless appetizing dishes.

Comparatively few housekeepers have discovered that, if made properly, it will keep for weeks—even months; therefore always ready, and enabling the "lady who does her own work" to prepare apparently elaborate dishes on short notice, and without overheating herself; especially if she be so happy as to own a kerosene stove.

The bread should be cut as thinly as it will conveniently handle, and browned over live coals quickly and evenly. Then, arranged in a large dripping-pan, it should be slowly dried in the oven, with both doors open, or on the hearth. It should not take on more color in process of drying, but should become very brittle.

When perfectly dry, place in paper bags or boxes, and keep in a dry place. In damp, rainy weather, it should be looked at occasionally, and if it is gathering dampness, should be dried again.

When wanted for use, the toast should be warmed on the hearth or in a moderate oven.

Young onions, peas, asparagus, etc., are delicious when stewed until tender, seasoned with butter and milk, and served on slices of toast.

Stewed chicken, and all stews, minces, hashes, etc., are improved, and "go further," when so served.

Poached eggs on toast, and cream toast, are dishes of established reputation, and many other dishes will suggest themselves to the housewife who has a store of toast laid by for emergencies.

A loaf of bread about to mold or dry up cannot be put to a better use. It is very convenient, when there is sickness in the family, to have plenty of toast ready, so that the invalid—proverbially impatient—will not be kept waiting when the bit of dry toast, cream toast, egg on toast, etc. is wanted.

Our Perfect Home
(Suggested by "What I Covet")

ANY YEARS ago I was subject to the feelings so aptly described in "What I Covet." They were always more intense as the time for spring or fall cleaning approached, and when the dreaded ordeal was over, leaving me with empty purse and exhausted energy. I no longer doubted if life under such circumstances were worth the living—I was sure it was not. I, too, imagined a tent life would solve the problem—until I tried it. We camped out one summer, and I do not care to repeat the experiment. It will rain occasionally, even in the best-regulated climate, and although a good tent will not leak, there is a dampness about the inside air that can not only be felt, but smelt, and also tasted. Its flavor is like mildewed mold.

But I have solved the problem of housekeeping without dirt and without the semi-annual siege, and as "What I Covet" must have struck a responsive chord in many hearts, I write that others may also be benefited by our perfected home.

First, there is not a carpet nail in the entire house. The floors are all stained, and so covered with rugs that it is never necessary to step on the bare floor, both the noise and feel of the bare boards being disagreeable to many. The rugs are very handsome, and too heavy to wrinkle or curl, but were not expensive, considering. The one in the library is of velvet, and covers the entire center of the room to within eighteen inches of the walls. I picked this up "at a bargain" many years ago, and it will last a lifetime.

The other rugs are made of remnants of the best body Brussels stair-carpeting, cut in lengths to suit, the ends hemmed, and a home-made fringe sewed on them of imported yarn, the colors matching those in the carpet. No one who has not seen these rugs can imagine how handsome and durable they are; and, by getting the remnants, quite inexpensive.

Next, the furniture of "Our Perfect Home" is all built in the walls, with the exception of beds, chairs, and tables. In the library, which is also drawing-room, sitting room, and parlor, the book-shelves are built in between the windows and are so neatly finished as to be very ornamental. In one corner is a sofa extending along the walls under the windows in each direction. Built under this sofa, is a shelf, concealed by the upholstering of the sofa, where slippers and such comforts can be ready for a few minutes' relaxation without having to be sought in remote bedrooms. In dining-room and kitchen the sideboard and safes, etc. are built in the walls; and in the bedrooms the only movable articles of furniture are beds and chairs; dressing cases, washstands, wardrobes, etc., all being built in the walls. The beds, tables, and heavy easy chairs are all on well-oiled casters, so there is no heavy furniture to move.

Any bright morning all the rugs in the house can be hung out on the clothesline and dusted, and the whole house be perfectly cleaned. Stained floors never have to be scrubbed. The stain fills and closes the pores of the wood, so that dirt or grease cannot be absorbed. A damp cloth takes off everything; and with a bucket of clean water, in which is mixed a teaspoonful of carbolic acid, in which to dip the cloth, the floor can be made "surgically clean." The floors are all dried, and the rugs back in place, while the sun is still in the east. An occasional sweeping down of the walls with a clean bag drawn over a broom keeps them nice, while the windows can be washed with a weak solution of household ammonia without disarranging anything. Only a few choice pictures and ornaments are to be seen in any of our rooms. The rest are awaiting their turn in the attic closet. There is a threefold advantage in this—the rooms look better, it saves dusting, and makes a pleasing change.

There is a law in our home against the accumulation of old clothing, etc. If worth giving away, they are given at once; if not, they are destroyed; therefore we have no moths or other insects, and no large chests of trumpery to be periodically aired and dusted.

The wall furniture in our house was all built from my own designs, and I will give detailed descriptions of it if desired.

Our home is comfortable, artistic, and complete, and, rarest of all rarities, I have attained my ideal.

The Wall-Furniture in
Our Perfect Home

I T MAY not be generally known that legs or supports for tables, etc., can be purchased or will be made to order at any planing mill or cabinet makers' where there is a turning-lathe. The expense is regulated by the kind of wood used. We paid twenty cents each for very neat ones of yellow pine. Walnut, ash, etc., would be more expensive, and white pine, which can be stained to imitate hard wood, probably cheaper.

Moldings, half-rounds, quarter-rounds, etc., can be purchased at any planing mill, and are sold by the foot, from a few cents up, according to material and design. Also wide boards planed on both sides, and the kind of ceiling used for wainscoting.

If white pine is used, the stain for it can be had at a drug store or paint shop by describing the effect to be produced—i.e., the kind of wood to be imitated, and whether or not a gloss is desired. If a very high polish is wished for, a coat of varnish should be put on after the stain dries.

We have found that the best material for upholstering—all things considered—is jute. It is handsome in appearance, durable, not easily soiled or defaced, and not expensive.

It is fifty inches wide, and ours—a very handsome pattern—was seventy five cents per yard.

Cretonnes and all other cottons are a "delusion and a snare." As

338

soon as their first freshness is gone they have a limp, draggled effect that is very depressing.

CORNER SOFA.

Three legs or supports will be needed for this: one in the corner and one at each end to support the front edge of it. The back rests on two long cleats nailed or screwed to the wall and meeting in the corner, which is the center of the sofa. The corner shelf underneath rests on two cleats, nailed or screwed to the wall, under the sofa. This shelf may be of any size, or may be omitted.

The legs which support the front edge are secured to the floor in the same way staircase banisters are fastened.

A frame or railing of planed scantling connects the legs with each other and with the cleats at the back. This is well braced with crosspieces.

On this framework, ceiling sawed to fit and mitered in the corner is nailed as neatly as possible.

If the sofa is built against a plastered wall, a board back must be added.

Let this be narrow at the ends, sloping up to meet in a point in the corner. It is firmly screwed to the wall and wadded (a worn-out blanket or bed comfort will do nicely) and covered with the upholstering goods. Tack this at the bottom and draw it up smoothly, fasten at the top with common tacks, turning under the edge of the cloth to prevent raveling. Finish with a row of furniture braid put on with gimp tacks.

The pillows or cushions for the back are covered with jute to match the rest, and bound around the edges with a cord which is sewed on so as to form a loop at each corner, which makes a neat finish.

The mattress, made to exactly fit the seat, is covered and ornamented the same way, and has a box-pleated flounce to hand from the edge, deep enough to conceal the shelf and contents beneath.

The side of this sofa must be regulated by the dimensions of the corner in which it is to be built, or the taste of the builder. Ours is twenty-two inches deep and forty inches long each way, measuring from the inside or back to the ends. The seat is sixteen inches from the floor; the shelf, six inches below the seat and ten inches from the floor.

BOOK CASES, SIDEBOARDS, ETC.

Two book-cases, built one on each side of a large mullioned window, give it the effect of a bay-window. These would also look well on either side of a door or archway.

Each consists of two boards five feet long and ten inches wide, with shelves the same width, fitted into grooves made to receive them. The top projects slightly all around, and is finished with a cornice molding. The edges of the sides and shelves are finished with a bead molding.

The bottom shelf is six inches from the floor, and the other shelves at distances to suit the size of the books, the wider space being at the bottom.

These book-cases may be curtained or not, according to taste.

Between two windows where there is a space four feet wide a third book-case is built, which is a combination of book case, reading desk, and shelves to hold files of papers, magazines, etc.

This piece of furniture is five feet high; the upper part is seven inches deep, and the lower part eighteen, making a shelf eleven inches wide, thirty inches from the floor, which holds the reading lamp, etc., with two shelves, each eighteen inches deep, underneath to hold the aforesaid papers, magazines, etc.

These are concealed by a curtain, box-pleated, and fastened under the edge of the shelf with furniture braid and gimp tacks.

The ends are built solid. One seven-inch board reaches from the top to the floor, and shorter boards are fitted neatly to it, to form the extension below.

Grooves to receive the shelves are made in the boards at distances to suit, and all of the edges are finished with half-round molding.

The top is finished with a cornice molding like the others.

The plan for this combination book-case has been used with success and satisfaction for a sideboard in the dining-room and a table cupboard in the kitchen.

The sideboard is six feet long and four and a half high.

Two shallow shelves above hold the most ornamental dishes, etc., the table part extends out two feet, and underneath are two deep shelves (heavily curtained doors may be used), where are kept those canned and bottled goods which need to be kept in the dark, leaving room for dishes, etc., not ornamental enough to be displayed with advantage.

The top shelf is the top of the sideboard, and at each end the top of the board, instead of being sawed off straight across, is slanted back, beginning to saw in front just above the groove cut to receive the shelf, and slanting up five inches at the back; this makes a unique finish and gives variety.

The kitchen table-cupboard is larger still, filling one whole end of the room.

The table part is two and a half feet deep, and is covered with enameled cloth, drawn over the edges and secured with tacks on the underside.

The shelves above and below are curtained with Turkey cotton, with a row of shoe buttons sewed on the lower edge to prevent fluttering. The shelves underneath do not extend the whole length, but a space is left at one end for the flour barrel. This stands on a platform fitted with casters, so it is easily drawn out when needed, and pushed back out of the way when not in use.

Shelves on each side of and behind the stove, and broad boards added to the window-sills, complete the wall furniture of the kitchen.

These shelves are easily put up, and save many steps. At any hardware store iron brackets, with screws to fasten them, can be had for a small sum. A planed board completes the shelf, which may be of any length.

Several of these shelves, placed one above the other, with a curtain hung from the edge of the topmost one to conceal and protect the contents of the others, make a very convenient cabinet to hold the many small articles that would "clutter" the rooms. If the cabinet is intended for medicines, etc., it should be placed quite high to be out of reach of little fingers. A single vase or statuette on the exposed top adds to the appearance of the whole.

BEDROOM FURNITURE

Where two persons occupy the same bedroom it is desirable to have two closets or wardrobes. From this idea a combination of wardrobes and dressing-case was evolved.

It is eight feet in length by five in height, and eighteen inches deep.

It is divided into three sections by vertical partitions.

The two sections at each end have each a shelf eight inches from the floor, the full depth and width of the section, to hold shoes, etc.

On three sides at the top are rows of hooks for clothing.

The top is finished on the outside with moldings.

The middle section is the dressing case. The lower part has three deep shelves for linen, and the upper part recedes to form a table, on which the mirror stands, with shallow shelves above, for small toilet articles. The wardrobes and shelves are curtained, poles and rings being used.

The washstands are built in the corners.

A piece of scantling thirty-six inches long is nailed to the floor, cutting off a corner two feet deep; a corresponding piece is nailed across, about two feet from the floor. Two upright pieces are nailed each side of the middle where the door will be.

Each side of the front is then ceiled, and the door hung in the middle.

The top, being well braced on each side, is ceiled over and a round hole cut in the middle to receive the bowl.

The slop jar sits directly under, so the bowl can be emptied without trouble, and the jar kept concealed. A little corner shelf above holds the bottles, tooth-powder, etc.

In another bedroom, where the walls are more cut up with windows and doors, corner wardrobes are built like the washstands, but taller and supplied with hooks and shelves; the dressing-case in this room is built like the combination book-case, altering the dimensions to suit, and is fitted between two windows.

All of the rooms have the cabinets of shelves described above.

This furniture was easy to build to our walls because they are ceiled. Still, it can be built in a plastered house, by using screws to fasten it to the walls.

If the plastering is broken in the operation, it can be mended with a little moistened plaster of Paris, applied with an old case-knife.

No hiding-places for dust or insects should be left.

Our furniture was all home-made, the "good man of the house" having a taste for such work. To those who must depend on outside skill I would like to say, do not have any dealings with those mechanics who will tell you that a thing is impossible because unusual.

Who Seeks Finds

ONCE UPON a time there was a wise queen who reigned over a country so beautiful that she ought to have been perfectly happy. And she would have been happy but for one thing: the lords and ladies of her court were always quarreling. All through the long bright days they would come to the queen with ill-natured complaints of one another. In order to remedy this state of things she called a secret council of the wisest men of the kingdom.

When they assembled before her, she told them her trouble. Then, one after another, they spoke; some advised severe punishments, and others suggested that the discontented courtiers should be sent away, and new lords and ladies appointed in their places.

At last the eldest was called. He was bent nearly double with age. He walked with a staff, and his white beard almost swept the ground. He said, "Oh, queen, live forever! Thy lords and ladies are like naughty children. They quarrel through envy, and because they try to find one another's blemishes. If thou, oh queen, canst teach them, by some parable, how ignoble such feelings are, they will be ashamed, and repent, and be freed of their fault."

After the queen dismissed her wise men, she pondered awhile, and then she called her seneschal, and bade him to summon all the lords and ladies, and she also directed him to see that there should be two pages waiting in the anteroom.

When all were assembled, the queen arose and said:

"I am about to send forth two pages on a quest so full of interest that I wish you all to witness their departure and their return." Then she said to the seneschal, "Summon the first page!"

The page entered and knelt before the queen, who said to him: "I wish you to mount a trusty steed, and, keeping always to the right, to go entirely around the kingdom, visiting in gardens and plucking here and there the sweetest flowers. Then hasten back with them to me."

The page bowed, and left the queen's presence. After a moment they heard the clattering of his horse's hoofs on the pavement without. When these sounds had died away, the queen commanded:

"Summon the other page."

When he had knelt before her, the queen said, "I wish you to take a trusty steed, and, following the roads to the left, to go around the kingdom, visiting its gardens, plucking here and there the bitterest, most harmful of the weeds; and then hasten to return with them to me." The lords and ladies exchanged puzzled glances, as this page, also, departed.

But the queen, without explanations, gave orders that a watch should be set in the palace tower, and directed that word should be brought to her whenever either of the two pages was to be seen returning from his quest. Then she dismissed the lords and ladies.

Several days passed, and then the seneschal came one morning to tell the queen that both pages could be seen in the distance, approaching the palace from different directions. The queen bade him call all the lords and ladies, and admit the pages separately. Just as the courtiers were assembled, the first page entered.

His arms were full of flowers that filled the whole palace with the sweetest perfumes. Some of them had withered, but all were yet fragrant. As he laid them at the queen's feet, she asked: "Well, what did you find on your journey round the kingdom?"

Smilingly he answered, "Oh, Queen, I found a kingdom filled with flowers! Not only were the gardens all a-bloom, but even the hedge-rows, fields and forests. And as I looked beyond the boundaries of the kingdom, I saw flowers beyond—I have ridden through a world of flowers!"

"Were there no weeds?" asked the queen.

"Your Majesty, I do not remember any. There may have been, but

I saw them not." Then the queen rewarded the page with a purse of gold, and dismissed him.

When he had gone, she told the seneschal to put all the flowers out of sight, and then to admit the other page. He came in, his arms filled with rank and poisonous weeds—some so full of acrid juices that he wore thick leather gauntlets to protect his hands from them. As he laid them at the queen's feet, she asked: "Well, what did you find on your quest?"

"Your Majesty, I found a kingdom overrun with weeds. Not only were the hedge-rows, fields, and forest full of them, but even the gardens also. And beyond the boundaries of the kingdom I saw weeds, weeds, weeds!—the world must be full of them! I noted them even inside the palace gate, as I returned."

"What!" said the queen; "did you find no flowers?"

"There may have been flowers, your Majesty; indeed, there must have been, but as I looked only for weeds, I saw only weeds."

The queen rewarded and dismissed the second page.

Then she lifted her eyes and looked around her at the lords and ladies. All were abashed, and could not return the gaze of the good queen. Some of the gentler ladies were trying to conceal tears of penitence. The queen had thought to speak words of loving reproof to them; but she saw no words were needed. The courtiers had learned their lesson; and they gathered around her, and one of the ladies-in-waiting said:

"Dear Queen, forgive us, and we will no longer sadden your loving heart by seeking only weeds. We will bring you flowers, and trouble you no more with the weeds."

Then the queen was very glad, and they were all happy ever after.

Short Stories

Short Stories

Byrd Spilman Dewey self-published most of her short stories in pamphlet form. *A Lake Worth Romance* was originally produced in the 1896 *Lake Worth Historian*, a literary magazine published by local women as a fundraiser for the Royal Poinciana Chapel.

As a prelude to the story, this warning was given: "The 'old-timer' is warned that it will be a waste of 'grey matter' to identify the characters in *A Lake Worth Romance* as the writer informs us that each one is a composite photograph." This is, to the best of our knowledge, the first published work under the name Byrd Spilman Dewey. She later self-published the work with some photographs in 1914 under the title *Romance of Old Lake Worth Days*.

One particular phrase used in *A Lake Worth Romance* requires some explanation. In the story Mrs. Dewey wrote "A man never 'makes love' to a woman...". The term "makes love" in 1896 had a very different meaning than today's connotation of intimacy. In Victorian literature "make love" meant "pay attention to;" our modern meaning would have had no place in a church fund-raiser publication!

A Lake Worth Romance also mentions something called an "Aeolian Harp" which is a type of stringed instrument placed in a window and played by the wind. They were popular in the Victorian era after being mentioned in many books and poems, most notably Henry David Thoreau's "Rumors from an Aeolian Harp."

Many of Mrs. Dewey's other short stories such as *Flying Blossom* and *Peter, The Tramp* were self-published. *Peter, The Tramp* is particularly noteworthy as it takes place during the 1894-1895 Great Freeze that almost ended Florida's citrus industry.

The Tale of Satan returns us to The Blessed Isle, where we hear the tale of the handsome black cat that was admired by all the Lake Worth settlers. It could be said that the *Tale of Satan* is Chapter Nine of *From Pine Woods to Palm Groves* as it picks up the story at about where that book ended.

A Lake Worth Romance

SOME PEOPLE there are who live always in the reflected glory of "The light that never was." Others there are who see it only in faint and fitful gleams, while to the great mass of the people it does not exist at all, and those matchless words, as beautiful as a strain of music—"The light that never was on the sea or land. The consecration and the poet's dream"- are to them as meaningless as the unsyllabled croakings of our night-frogs.

This "light that never was" may be freely translated as romance. Practical people often deride it, but by so doing, they only show ignorance of its charm. It is a priceless gift. One who possesses it goes through life keeping step to music unheard by others. Little wrecks he if they call him a madman—or worse. He knows he possesses "The inalienable treasure"—a treasure that makes his whole life an altar flame.

The home where most of the following events occurred is illuminated always by "The light that never was."

Some people feel its radiance as soon as they enter the door; but alas! many are as oblivious of it as is a blind man of the matchless beauty of a rainbow.

There were three old hotels then, but no matter. It was at the old hotel.

In those primitive times any excuse served to draw the people together. They were glad to meet and exchange news, experiences, and so forth. So we all went, from babies to grandmothers.

Although it was midwinter, the air was soft and balmy—the lake like a mirror—with that oily surface seen only on salt water.

We went early, not to miss any of fun. As we landed we saw that the piazzas and the lighted rooms beyond were full of guests, while others strolled aimlessly about.

We joined a group on the front piazza, and at once began felicitating all concerned on the charming weather.

Presently I saw Teddy Banks approaching. He saluted us both in his usual cordial manner, then said to me: "Come, there is someone I want to show you." As we went along the piazza, he went on to say. "I suppose you have heard that a Miss Milson, friend of the Wilders, is coming."

"Yes," I answered, "I have heard nothing else for days from you boys." "Well, there is a girl I want you to see."

We had paused at a window, showing the well-lighted room filled with groups of chatting people. Opposite where we were standing, I saw a most charming picture. A group gathered around one who would have been noticeable in any company, but there where beautiful strangers were then at a high premium, she was ravishing.

Her eyes were of that melting softness that the initiated know only comes from long, thick lashes. An occasional gleam of fun lighted their brown depths. Her hair of the same color, her snowy brow and throat, made charming contrast with scarlet lips and rosy chin and cheeks. As she turned her head to speak to someone beyond, she showed a faultless profile, and presently standing up to greet an elderly lady who approached, she showed a slender form which carried with matchless grace the small, deer-like head.

For a few seconds I was speechless with delight: then murmured: "Is that she? The Miss Milson we have been expecting?"

"No," he answered in a tone of deep disgust, "and that's what's the matter. Do you see that little fright over there in the corner reading a magazine? That's the wonderful she. Come over here where we can sit down and I will tell you all about it. I've been watching for you, because I wanted to tell you. If you hadn't come tonight, you'd have seen me landing at your wharf at all sorts o'clock in the morning."

After a disappointing glance at the girl so gallantly indicated in the corner, I followed him to a seat on the end of the piazza.

"But who is that lovely creature?" I impatiently asked, before we were fairly seated.

"Isn't she though!" he rather irrelevantly exclaimed "She's enough to make a man want to hang himself."

"But why? I think she ought to make you glad you're living—she does me."

"But she doesn't; she makes me half wild! You see it's this way, she and Miss Milson were in the party that came Saturday. I was off down the Lake on Tom Barrow's sloop. We didn't get in till midnight. You know the wind was north all day Saturday, and we had to beat back. I was late to breakfast Sunday morning so the first glimpse I had of the strangers was in church. I was late there too, of course, and had to take a side seat. The first thing I saw after I sat down was that lovely profile between the two heads in front of me. I was sure at once it was the Miss Milson. All through the service I watched her; once I thought she caught me staring, but I wasn't sure. By the time church was out, I was fathoms deep. All through the last hymn I was swearing I would win her or die in the attempt."

"Fine devotional attitude for church!"

"Yes, wasn't it? Well, like the bad little boys in the Sunday school books, I was promptly punished. After church I was presented to her—and her husband."

"Her husband!"

Yes. She is a bride on her wedding-trip; did you ever hear of anything so disgusting??"

I was speechless.

"There is just one consolation." he went on moodily, "there is an old lady in the party, who has always known them both. She tells me it was a family arrangement, and any one with half an eye can see they are not in love with each other. He spends his time fishing while she is off with the women. That's a comfort."

"Oh, for shame." I cried. "You want her to be unhappy because you are disappointed. I don't believe it."

He hung his head in sullen gloom.

"I'm no China angel," he growled, "I'm a man."

"Yes; but you are not a bad man."

He only grunted at this, so I could not tell whether or not he assented.

"Her name's Natalie, too" he said after a pause. "Natalie. Miss Milson's is Sara Anne. Oh thunder!"

I smothered a laugh. Before I could control my voice so I dared to speak, the music struck up a march, showing the ball was about to begin, and we joined the crowds of merry-makers who were gathering from all directions toward the dining-room, where the fun was to be.

All through the dance I feasted my eyes on the beautiful stranger. I was glad to see that Teddy did not show her any attention. He was lively as usual, helping all the girls enjoy the occasion. I noticed, with secret amusement, that he even led out the despised Sara Anne, who proved to be a pleasant enough little girl, though to compare her with Natalie Craig was like placing a field daisy with a damask rose.

All too soon the evening sped.

When we had donned our wraps and had come out into the night, we found that the wind had begun to blow gently and the lake suggested a scene from the Inferno. It was one of those matchless nights, when the surface of the water is covered with phosphorescence. Every darting fish was a meteor, every oar dripped molten gold, each wave was tipped with fire.

After one is really launched on such a sea of glory, the sensations are indescribably weird. As we sped along we were awed into complete silence, feeling like a part of some strange dream, which would presently dissolve.

Three days after the dance, as I sat on the side piazza sewing, I heard the snapping sound which sails make when brought, as the sailors say "into the wind."

I looked out and saw it was a sharpie, with the Blue Racer in tow. It had come about, and as I looked, I saw a man get into the tender and cast off. I knew it was Teddy Banks. The Blue Racer, so called from its speed and color, was his boat. I was glad to see him, for I had thought many times since the dance of his tragic state of mind, and had feared it would get him in some scrape.

I met him at the door, and was not reassured by his look of gloom.

"Well?" I asked when he had sat down without speaking.

"It isn't well, though," he said, with a sort laugh. "It's ill."

"You haven't done anything rash!" I exclaimed in alarm.

"Oh, no. I haven't spoken more than three words to her, if that's what you mean; and you are the only one who knows I'd like to."

"That's right," I said, heartily relieved, "I thought you would be a good boy."

"Well, it's confounded hard," he almost whimpered. "I sit and look at her from dark corners, and wish from my soul I cared less, so I could dare to go sit near her and make her talk to me."

"But don't do it," I coaxed, "You'll be sorry if you do. All women like to know they are admired, but in a case like this of yours, it would be unwise."

"That's queer talk from you."

"What is?"

"Why to say all women like to be made love to."

"That isn't what I said. It's the exact opposite."

"How's that?"

"I said all women like to be admired. A man never 'makes love' to a woman who is not free to be won if he admires her, quite otherwise."

"Will you say that again, and say it slowly? I don't catch on."

"I see we aren't speaking the same language, so I'll explain. When a man admires a woman who is already appropriated, he shows it by treating her with great respect. When he is thrown in her company, he listens when she speaks, and he talks to her as if she were a reasonable being. He may say pretty things of her in her absence to someone who is kind enough to repeat them to her; and if he has no wife, or mother, or sister near, he may even go to her for advice and sympathy when he gets into scrapes." I paused to laugh, and waited for his answering grin. "On the other hand, the worst left-handed compliment a man can pay a married woman is to make love to her. He says, in effect, 'I am a weak idiot, and I take you for another. I see nothing in you to respect or admire. You are only a weed to be plucked up by the roots and tossed aside.' Do you call that admiration?"

"Well, hardly. You always give a fellow new ideas. I suppose, too, you have some new explanation for the thousands of sins committed for love."

"No such thing has ever happened since the world began, and it never will."

"We certainly aren't speaking the same language. Will you explain again?"

"Just think a minute," I answered, "you will see for yourself." True love is unselfish. It longs above all for the happiness and well-being of the beloved. The woman who commits any sin, no matter what, for the sake of her lover, does him a deadly injury. She destroys his high ideal of womanhood. A man who lets a woman sin for him does all that and more. The so-called sins for love are generally errors in judgment on the part of the woman, and sins for self-love on the part of the man."

"Huh! You make love to be too good for common mortals."

"No, it isn't; but it is the best thing in the world, and I don't like to hear it slandered. Nobody ever loved yet, without being nobler and better for it. The trouble is, that so few people understand what love is. Many will look embarrassed when it is mentioned; their only idea of love is physical attraction, which isn't love at all, and no more than smoke is fire. Love is what Boyesen calls 'An enthusiastic congeniality of soul;' you know we sometimes recognize that at a glance. The same writer goes on to say, 'More than half of its joy consists in the feeling of being completely understood in one's noblest potentialities.' Is that a thing to blush for or to sin for? No; anyone who says he sins for love is far from the truth. He sins because he does not love. You think now, a great misfortune has overtaken you, but it is not at all unless you weaken and make it one. Love is always a gift of the gods. Live up to it and your whole life will be better for it—who knows? It may be the means of your doing great things in the world."

He pondered deeply for a few seconds, and then spoke:

"The question is, what am I to do now?"

"What do you think? You know yourself better than anyone else does."

"I think I ought to go away. 'Discretion the better part,' you know— 'He who fights and runs away,' and so on."

"If that's the way you feel, the sooner the better."

"I seem to hear music; do I, or am I going daft?"

"No. You aren't daft—that is. I think not. It is the harp—the Aeolian—in the window. It has been singing all morning. These gentle east winds make sweet music. When I am here alone, with all the doors open, I can hear it all over the house. It is full of memories for me— some sad and some sweet. Your trouble has added another to its list- whenever it sings again, I shall remember."

He rose, and walked to the window. I busied myself with my sewing, which I had forgotten, knowing there was a reason why even one so full of sympathy as I felt I should not look into his eyes just then. Presently, to help him out, I began to talk of the approaching yacht race. "A month ago," he said, turning 'round, "I wouldn't have missed it for a farm. Now I have lost all interest in it."

"Of course," I answered, "that is natural. While you were crying for the moon, earthly matters are as if they never existed."

A short pause, then:

"I'll tell you good-bye now," he said, "a steamer leaves Jupiter tomorrow night, and I will have time to make it if I hurry. 'If 'twere done, 'twere well 'twere quickly done', you know."

"Yes, I do know. We shall miss you, but you are doing just right."

I went out on the piazza with him. When he turned for a last handshake, "How that thing squalls!" he exclaimed, referring to the harp. "It sounds like a Banshee."

"Oh no. Listen, it is playing the 'Wedding March'—a good omen. The next time I see you, Mrs. Banks will be there too. That's a prophecy."

He listened intently. A puff of wind raised the tone so that if one "imagined a great deal" it did sound a little like the "Wedding March." As he caught the strain, his face relaxed, and he smiled brightly.

"It is a good omen to take with me. I feel better already."

I watched him embark at the wharf and paddle off up the lake, the sharpie which had towed him over having gone on down stream. Once he dropped an oar to wave his hat to me, and I felt greatly relieved to see him go off in such good spirits.

I find I have not described Teddy Banks, but no matter. It makes no difference how a man looks. To be loveable, he only needs cleanliness of soul which is godliness, and a sufficient supply of moral and physical courage.

The years sped by.

Great changes took place in our community.

The people began to come in great crowds and old friends were— well, not forgotten, but they necessarily filled smaller corners in our hearts.

We heard with a comparatively small thrill of surprise and sympathy that Natalie Craig's husband had been drowned before the end of their first year of married life, while they were stopping at one of the summer resorts of the North. We wondered vaguely where Teddy Banks was, and if he knew of it, then were engrossed with other matters.

One day in early spring as I sat at my desk, I heard a launch come buzzing down the lake. By this time launches had become so numerous with us that they ceased to excite interest. Engrossed in my writing, I did not look out until I heard the engine stop. Then I saw it had tied up at our wharf, and two stylish looking people had debarked.

You have already guessed who they were—Teddy Banks and his bride. I was not sure till I met them at the door. Then I knew. He had not changed much; but she!

Still beautiful-in fact, more beautiful, though the brilliant color was now more delicate, and the dark brown hair snow white. I heard later that it turned during the first few months following her husband's death, and did not wonder, poor child alone among strangers with such trouble.

She spoke at once of the many changes at the lake.

"I was here about five years ago," she said. "Teddy says he was here then, too, and I will try to think I remember him, but I am afraid I really don't. It's too bad, for he says he remembers me perfectly."

"Yes, I dare say he does," I said dryly, with a glance at Teddy who sat gnawing the ends of his mustache, and looking rather foolish. "I think we all remember you."

"Do you? How kind! Teddy told me you were one of his best friends in the old days. He said you used to give him motherly advice."

"Which he never took," laughed I.

"Oh yes, I did, sometimes," put in Teddy.

"I think that is one reason I failed when I tried to 'place' you," Natalie babbled on. "When he said 'motherly advice' I thought at once of a stout, elderly lady. I couldn't recall any one living here who filled my ideal of "motherliness" to a big boy like Teddy."

When we were done laughing at this sally, I said:

"We don't expect you to remember any of us. We were all strangers, and you were meeting them everywhere. It is no wonder we seem to be only a blur."

A puff of wind just then brought a strain of music from the harp unusually sweet and tender. Teddy and I exchanged glances and I saw his eyes were suffused as he 'rose and walked to a window, where he stood looking out, while I, knowing what it was saying to him, covered his retreat by explaining to Natalie whence the music came, and the construction of the wind-harp.

Julius came in while we were still talking about it, and when Teddy spoke about the way our trees had grown, he proposed a stroll outside.

Natalie and Julius went first, and while he was explaining to her the nature of tropical fruit trees I had the opportunity for a word with Teddy.

"So the harp and I were true prophets, weren't we?" I began.

"True prophets," he echoed, feelingly.

"I congratulate you with all my heart. She is lovelier than ever."

"Yes, isn't she? And the strangest thing is this: I used to think I wouldn't marry a widow for anything: I thought there would be no romance about it; all sort of things, don't you know?"

"Yes, I have often thought myself if I were a man, I wouldn't marry a widow; not if she were the last woman in the world,"

"Yes? Well now, do you know, I am glad she was a widow."

"Glad! Why?"

"Why you see it's this way: You know all young girls have romantic notions about us men. They think we are half angel and half fairy prince; but you know we aren't." I gave a laughing assent. "Well it stands to reason then that when a girl marries, all those notions get knocked into a cocked hat. Do you believe a woman ever quite forgives the man who kills those precious illusions?"

"I'd rather not argue that question," said I, much amused.

"Oh, I know what that means; that's all the answer I want."

"Look here! You mustn't talk that way, it's high treason."

"Oh well, consider it unsaid. But let me finish my point. You know when a woman marries a second time she knows what she's about. No illusions there. She and her husband make an even start and their chances for happiness are 'way up', don't you see?"

I saw—and yet—but I did not try to disturb his serenity.

Flying Blossom

IF ONE of the scarlet hibiscus-blooms had let go its mooring from the parent bush and gone fluttering across the lawn—pausing from time to time to rest a moment on tree-bough or palm-stem—Flying Blossom would have recognized it as his twin. The resemblance would have been exact—all but the song.

One June morning, just at dawn, the song scattered my dreams. From the first notes, I knew it to be my favorite of all dawn-choir, and hastened to the window for nearer glimpses and cleaver notes. His tiny body—a vivid morsel against the morning sky—rested on the top-most leaf-spine of a cocoa-palm, while he whistled:

"Teebo; teebo; sweet; sweet; here we are; here we are; teebo!"

He whistled it all through once before I reached the window; then he fluttered his wings and repeated the crystal-clear notes:

"Teebo; teebo; sweet; sweet; here we are; here we are; teebo!"

At the end of the phrase, I cried:

"Well! You are the first little bird I ever saw who sat down to sing!"

At the sound of my voice, off he darted, flashing through the greenery, and disappeared.

The next morning he was there again.

I hid behind the window-draperies and answered his whistle.

He listened, cocking up a bright eye toward the sound; then answered, and lifted his scarlet crest till it stood up on his head like a little cap.

I whistled again, keeping out of sight, and moved from window to window till he had followed the sound to the other side of the house, and so discovered the bird-table. He saw from the actions of the busy guests already gathered there, that its rule was: "Good cheer for all at the price of a song." He dropped to its edge, then I understood why he sat down to sing. The little fellow had only one foot. When he tried to stand he balanced himself by keeping both wings a-flutter.

When the wings became weary of the effort, he dropped on his breast—or "sat down." The fluttering wings, with the single slender leg as support, made the bird look exactly like a wind-swayed hibiscus flower.

I noted that after eating and drinking he carried away food in his bill, which told that his nest was built and occupied. Later in the day he came again, bringing this time, his mate—a pale reflection of himself. She made herself at home; first sorting over the dish of grain—cracking the wheat-kernels, and choosing the plumpest oats; then she drank from the water-dish, and dropt in the middle of it, fluttering her wings and making a great splashing. Then out again, to spread the wet wings to dry, and finally to gather up all she could carry, and dart off more quickly than the eye could follow.

I knew their nest could not be very distant, for I found, after they had accepted my friendship, that I could whistle them back at any hour of the day; and she would hop from twig to twig, while he twirled and balanced his gay little body, both evidently curious about the captive bird which whistled to them and seemed to be a prisoner shut up somewhere just out of sight.

After a while of visits together or singly, one day the sound of much confused twittering called me to the side-door, and there, on the bird-table, were Mr. and Mrs. Flying Blossom, with a row of fledgling Blossoms fluttering oddly like their little father, on the edge of the table between them. The parents were feeding the little ones, with much of the sweetest bird baby-talk, and encouraging them to help themselves to the good things so bountifully provided.

The birdlets showed a lively interest in the game; and from the moment of their introduction to the Blessed Isle bird-table, were numbered among its regular patrons. Their parents often fought pitched battles with the other birds—usually the quarrelsome Florida jays—while the children busied themselves with the food and water.

One day a bachelor, who lived several miles down the Sound, came to The Blessed Isle on an errand and something was said in his hearing about Flying Blossom and his little family.

"A one-legged red bird?" he cried.

Then he went to the window and looked out.

"Why, that's my bird" he exclaimed. "I wondered what had become of him. It's one I caught in my possum trap and broke off his leg. He stayed 'round my shanty a long time, then he disappeared. I've wondered about him."

After awhile Flying Blossom and his little mate came alone together to the bird-table, as at first; so we knew the children were grown up and had flown away to make nests of their own.

Many red-birds are still our friends; and, whenever one stands up on its tip-toes and flutters his wings, without apparent reason, we say:

"Oh look! That must be one of Flying Blossom's babies!"

Peter, The Tramp

PETER WAS a tramp cat who brought himself to us for a Christmas present. True, he arrived three days before Christmas; but that was unavoidable. If he had waited until Christmas Day he would have starved. It was rather a narrow squeak as it was.

We always thought and spoke of him as one of our Christmas gifts.

It happened this way.

We had closed the house on our Blessed Isle, and had gone to pass that winter in a little city much further north, up in central Florida; because Julius said he was beginning to hunger for what he called "A little smell of winter."

He got it.

It was the year of the Big Freeze.

The cottage we took was in a pleasant neighborhood. We carried a few things with us, and bought a few more in the way of furnishings. The three front rooms had picturesque open fire-places, and when we had hung fluffy white draperies in the windows, and arranged the few pictures and other trifles we had brought in our trunks, and scattered a few rugs on the stained floors, some easy chairs and two or three book-littered tables gave the rooms just the atmosphere that we adore. On the evening of the twenty-second it was just chilly enough to give us the always-wished-for excuse for a little blaze in the hearth. We had drawn a table in front of the fire to hold the reading-lamp. Julius sat on one side of it with his papers, from which he read aloud whatever happened to strike his fancy, while I sat on the other side listening to him and answering his comments, all the while busily engaged on some Christmas stockings I was making of gay tissue paper, with an interlining of thin cloth, to hold candies for some children I had on my list. All at once there was a soft thud on the outer door, followed by a scratching sound. I sprang to open it, thinking it was one of the children from over the way. There was a sound of scampering, and something fell from the edge of the porch. I ran for a candle and searched all about; but nothing was to be seen. This happened again. Then I drew my chair to the door and, at the next sound, I opened it softly.

Just outside was a small object which turned to flee as soon as the light fell on it; but I had spied it—a miserable-looking little kitten. After coquetting for some minutes it allowed itself to be coaxed inside. Rain had been falling earlier in the evening and the poor little creature was shivering with the combined misery of wet, cold and hunger. I never saw a more pathetic little object. It reminded me of those remarkable cats I used to draw on my slate when I was a child—all acute angles and knobs, with a few sparse hairs bristling in all directions at once. It made an eager dash for the saucer of milk I placed on the hearth, and after licking the dish to be sure of the last drop, it crept as near as possible to the blaze and began to purr with a queer clicking sound like winding up a Waterbury watch.

At bedtime I brought another saucer of milk, which was as eagerly devoured as the first. Then I warmed a bit of flannel to wrap the little creature in, and Julius held the lamp while I put it to bed in one corner of the wood-box in the kitchen. It was still asleep when I went to look at seven o'clock the next morning; but awoke as soon as I uncovered it, looking so bright that I began to hope it had not been seriously injured by the hardships it had endured.

After breakfast, I announced that our tramp must have a bath. He was so dirty it was not possible to determine his exact complexion. I made great preparations for his toilet, preparing a basin with a jug of warm water, that he might be washed and rinsed with as little discomfort as possible. Everything necessary was placed on the rug before the open fire; then I put on my largest apron, a combing sacque to protect my waist, and even pinned a handkerchief over my hair, thinking the little fellow would be sure to act like a small whirlwind and scatter soapy water in all directions. Julius was full of misgivings for fear I should be badly scratched or perhaps even bitten; but to our surprise and relief the little mite submitted like a lamb. When I had lowered him into the basin he rested his chin on my fingers, shutting his eyes while I washed his face, spreading his feet wide apart to try to brace himself while I scrubbed his back; and when, after the water had become the color of ink, I lifted him in my hands while Julius hurriedly emptied the basin and poured in fresh water, he even tried a feeble little purr.

As soon as he had been thoroughly rinsed I rubbed him in an old bath towel, then wrapped him in a bit of flannel which had been heating on the hearth. I held him snugly until he ceased to tremble, then gave his hair a thorough brushing with a small scrubbing-brush I had found in the kitchen. When his coat had become dry and fluffy, the smut and general stickiness all washed away, the change in his appearance was wonderful. We found his hair to be soft and white with a gray spot on one side of his head which gave him the roguish air of wearing a cap tipped up sideways.

While he was enjoying the saucer of cream which was the reward for his patient endurance of the bath, Julius said:

"I believe he will turn out to be one of our handsomest pets, and I want to name him myself. You've named all the other cats we've ever had."

"I like that," said I.

How does it happen that I have named them? I always thought it was a case of mutual agreement—that we named them together."

"Well, so it was. You have suggested the names and I have agreed to them; but this time I want to choose the name and let you agree to it."

"Very well. What shall it be?"

"Let's call him Peter."

"Why 'Peter'? What sort of a name is that for a kitten?"

"It's a good name, "said Julius. "You'll see he'll like it. Here Peter!"

Peter, who had just finished his cream, turned to look at Julius, then leaped to his knee and struck with coquettish grace the finger Julius held out to him. It was the first playful sign he had given, and we both laughed heartily.

"You see he likes the name," said Julius.

"Yes," I answered, "he likes it, and you like it, so of course I must like it, too."

Peter grew so rapidly that by Christmas Day his bones had all disappeared, and he looked as round and chubby as if he had never known what it was to be hungry and miserable. He took part in our holiday festivities, showing especial enjoyment of the Christmas party we had on the afternoon of the Day-of-days for all the little tots of the neighborhood. It was a delightful party; but space will not permit it to be described in this story. This is about Peter.

It was on New Year's Eve that Peter first began to disclose his talent as an entertainer. Julius was preparing to enjoy the newspapers he had just brought from the post office. He tore the wrapper off the first, and, crushing it absently in his hand, tossed it in the direction of the waste-paper basket. Peter scampered after it, and after a little struggle got hold of it with his teeth, then trotted back to Julius with it.

"Well, did you ever!" exclaimed Julius. "Look here, Judith: Peter brought this ball of paper back to me. I do believe he is a retriever-cat!"

"Impossible!" said I; "I never heard of such a thing!"

"Neither did it," said Julius; "but he certainly did it."

"Try him again;" said I. "Take it from him and throw it back."

Julius took the ball of paper from Peter and tossed it across the room.

The little fellow scampered after it, picked it up, trotted back to Julius, and placed it triumphantly in his hand.

Julius was delighted. He repeated it again and again, Peter seeming to enjoy it just as much.

From this time "playing ball" became a regular amusement for

Julius and Peter. Every night there was a performance, and often between times; for all who came to call on us heard of our accomplished pet, and when they looked incredulous at the idea of a retriever-cat, Julius always called Peter, who would come scampering in, not at all reluctant to prove that we had not been exaggerating his accomplishments. The children were always especially delighted, and kept on crying, "Do it again!" until Peter was exhausted, and would throw himself on the floor, panting open-mouthed, and switching the floor with his tail, exactly like a little dog. Julius was perfectly devoted to him, and Peter returned his affection with the utmost enthusiasm.

It became necessary to make a bed on the back porch for Peter, because as soon as he began to feel well and frisky, he liked to go on little prowls in the night, and if he waked to find himself shut up in the house, he howled. At dawn each morning, Peter would scratch and mew at the back door. Julius always awakened at the first sound and hastened to open the door for him. Then Peter dashed into the room, and leaped on the bed. Reaching my face in two or three jumps, he would gently bite the end of my nose to awaken me. I soon learned to cover my face before he could reach me; then he would jump on the pillow and pull my hair.

He was a cat of the most original ideas!

As soon as he heard me begin to laugh, he sprang to the floor and galloped around in a frenzy of delight until he had made himself dizzy. Then he would sit on the hearth and talk about breakfast until we were dressed.

At last, one morning we awoke to find our water-pipes all frozen, and ourselves chilled to the bones. Before we had finished dressing, one of the neighbors was knocking at the door to say that it had been the coldest night within the memory of the oldest inhabitant, and the oranges were all surely killed. When we opened the outer doors we found that he had not exaggerated. There were several orange trees in the back-yard loaded with ripe fruit. We had been feasting on them all the weeks since we had taken the cottage, without seeming to diminish the supply. That morning we finished breakfast, with a dessert of orange-ice fresh from the trees. Cut open, and eaten out with a spoon, the frozen oranges made a dish fit for the gods.

But what a scene of desolation around us! All of our neighbors had orange groves from which came their livelihood. In one night they changed from a condition of comparative wealth to the pinch of poverty. We could not help sharing their distress; and, when the cold began to develop rheumatic symptoms in joints which Julius had forgotten he possessed, he said:

"I tell you what let's do, Judith; we'd better give up this cottage and fly back to our nest in the tropics."

I thought so, too; but what about Peter? That was where the wrench came. We had two changes to make, and one stop-over on the way home, so it would not do to try to take him with us. As soon as we spoke of our plans, one of the neighbors begged to have him; and, after many discussions, we decided it was the only thing to do. There was a dog at the stop-over house on our way home that had been trained to chase cats; because his owner disliked them. We dared not risk Peter in his sight.

We and Peter were to part.

He had been with us not much more than two months; but it seemed as if we had always owned him.

The parting was a real grief.

All through our packing Peter seemed to understand what was coming; and the morning we left the house he sat on the front steps, after we had told him good-bye, watching us as long as we were in sight. We spoke constantly of him as we journeyed, and as soon as we were settled at home on our Blessed Isle, Julius told me to write at once and ask for news of Peter.

He felt better when the answer came telling us that while Peter seemed to miss us, he was reasonably happy, and was beginning to feel at home in his new quarters.

Julius sat thoughtfully silent for some minutes after reading the letter; then he sighed and said:

"After all, Peter was the jolliest little cat we have ever owned."

And of course I agreed with him.

The Tale of Satan

WE NAMED him "Robert, le Diable," for Mr. Bobs, a young neighbor who was musical, and who showed a whimsical interest in the orphaned kit.

No kitten could be expected to answer to so much name, and "Satan" being a free translation of "Diable," it seemed natural to condense his name to "Satan." We had never heard of a cat by that name, and thought it quite original; but Satan-cats seemed to spring up in all directions as soon as his fame began to grow.

As he developed, the sweetness of his temper, and his bright amiability, made the name not as appropriate as it might have been; but the blackness of his coat, and his great luminous yellow eyes that flashed and flamed, evened things, in a way. "Satan" was a good name for him. He accepted it and, as soon as he was old enough, he answered to it just as a child does to its name. A single call brought him galloping from near and far, wherever he happened to be when the sound reached his alert ears.

To begin at the beginning:

Satan was one of a family of four kits that ended the list of the long line of young felines born to Kitty-Winks and Catty-Meow.

Kitty-Winks and Catty-Meow were The Hermitage cats, and the tale of their lives begins in "From Pine Woods to Palm Groves." When they were moved from The Hermitage to The Blessed Isle, which happened in Chapter Six, of that history, there were so many other things to tell about, that not much was written of the cat-family after the arrival of their first nest full of kits.

They liked the change of residence. It suited them. The hunting was as good as in the woods around The Hermitage, and fishing was soon added to their program of joys.

Cats are known to detest water; but they adore fish. After Catty and Kitty had watched the cast-net being thrown into the Sound, and had devoured the minnows which were the results of the throws, they thought things out for themselves and soon learned to go a-fishing on their own hook. They seemed to know that I couldn't manage the net—that it took the long arms and the strength of a man to handle it with any hope of success so, when Julius was gone, and cats and I were alone on The Blessed Isle, they went fish-less till the craving got too strong for them, then braved the dangers of the deep. Not very deep, along the edge of the shore; but wet and frightsome. It took courage to rush into the waves; but courage was, as usual, rewarded. The little fisher came out dripping of breast—head held high to keep the captured minnow free of the water—and brought it triumphantly above high-tide mark where it was devoured with enthusiasm. Gradually, the fear of the waves, and the distaste for the wetting, were entirely overcome, and fishing became more fascinating than going a-field on a dry chase. They hunted the shore and the wharf.

One blowy day all the family—Catty-Meow, Kitty-Winks and the kits—it was their third family—were down at the water-edge, both parents tired out with fruitless attempts to get a sea-dinner. The waves were so roughened by the wind, that the fishes had all gone to take refuge in deep water. Catty and Kitty had watched faithfully for minnows in each shore-rolling ripple. Not one had been glimpsed. Finally, all started up the bank. Catty leading, the kits following and the little mother bringing up the rear. As the top of the bank was reached, Kitty turned, her quick ear caught by the sounds of splashing. Then she sat down to watch. It was a fish-hawk hunting a dinner for her own young in some tree-top away over in the Everglades. She dived several times without result, then again, desperately, and came up laboring with a heavy burden. It was a big fish. They struggled, the fish flapping, trying to escape, the hawk making all efforts to hold and lift it. Finally, as they were only a few yards above the waves, the hawk began to sink. The burden was too great for her. As they descended, she swerved and landed on the wharf with the fish. They struggled together for a few seconds, the hawk evidently occupied with freeing its talons from their grip in the body of the fish.

Kitty-Winks had grasped the situation and was running down the bank—out on the wharf—and reached them just as Mrs. Hawk had freed her talons and spread wings for flight. She snatched the fish, and lifting her eyes in gratitude to the big bird now hovering over her and her booty, she galloped gaily up the bank where she was met by Catty and the kittens, who had watched the climax and had raced to join Kitty-Winks.

Then, Oh, what a feast!

It was more than they could manage, I thought; but they kept at it—now and then, one of them stopping to rest—lying a while on the grass—then up and at it again. The darkness hid them, still busy, and next morning not a scrap was to be seen.

While watching the fish-and-hawk struggle, I had recalled an incident related by an old-timer.

He said, once, when he was throwing his cast-net, during very low tide, he brought up a queer-looking mess. He investigated, and it proved to be two skeletons locked in a death-grip. A hawk and a fish. The hawk had fixed her talons in the fish, which had proved too heavy for her to lift. She could not withdraw her talons. The fished dived for deep water and drowned her. They perished together. The hawk's talons were clinched in the fish's backbone, and could only be loosened by breaking the spinal column.

Catty and Kitty had chosen an ideal nursery for their kitten-families. They were cradled in a most romantic nest under the over-hanging leaves of a young palm-tree.

This was chosen for reasons. It was not too far from the house; it was snug, yet roomy, and it was concealed from view, as well as shaded from too much sunlight, by the palm leaves. Only those in the secret could have found it.

As each family of kits had reached the age of lively antics and scampering, it was the custom of their parents to bring them to the porches for games and races. Moonlight nights ever drew them to the front gallery where they raced up and down, round and round, in games that made their thumping little heels sound like snare-drum selections.

Rainy days also brought them to the porches for their larks; but pleasant afternoons always found them either along shore; on the wharf; or else playing in the grass in front of the porch.

One day I was upstairs at a front window, busy with some writing. All at once, I heard a queer confusion of sounds, and looking out, I saw Kitty-Winks and her little family, surrounded by Mr. and Mrs. Bob White, and a big covey of half-grown Bob Whites. Kitty was crouched for a spring, which amazed me, for she and Catty never disturbed the quail. They came constantly to eat and drink in the fowlery and the cats showed that they accepted them as members of the chicken families. I dropped pen, and went dashing downstairs—out the door—shouting to Kitty—crying shame that she should offer to hurt a little quail.

She took no notice at all of me; but kept the crouching attitude, with fixed eyes and lashing tail; and the parent birds went on twittering in a strange, alarmed manner. As I went close, not one moved till I was upon them. Then, as I stooped, with a loud SWISSH! A chicken snake made off. Kitty-Winks had been helping the parent birds to defend the little quails from the snake.

When it had quite disappeared, Kitty turned toward me, reaching up her head to be stroked and making a queer little throat-sound, at once questioning and re-assuring. The parent quails called their little flock together, and hustled them in the opposite direction from the one taken by the snake, and, as they disappeared in the undergrowth, Catty came dashing in from the woods, where he had gone alone on a hunting excursion, having got wind in some mysterious way a message brought him, probably by some of our winged pets' that his family were having some excitement which he was missing.

Another time, at that same window, I looked up absently from my work, searching the mental store-house for just the word to fit an elusive thought, and noted Kitty-Winks out there alone, lying on the bank just like a dead cat. Idly I gazed—half unseeing—and then attention was arrested by a buzzard swooping. To and fro it flew, swooping lower each time it passed over. Finally, its wing brushed the dead-asleep cat and there was a mutual surprise as she started up in a panic and scampered away to hide under the house; while the equally startled bird sailed off at a tangent.

The little scene was amusing, and more. It was the final argument, or rather proof, that settled a question we had been discussing, which was started by one of the scientific publications. One of its writers had raised the question of the way buzzards find their food; if by sight, or the odor. An incident which happened near the Blessed Isle just as we had read the discussion had seemed to prove it was by odor. Buzzards had been noticed gathering in a thicket and some of the men had gone to investigate, thinking some animal had perished there, or that it might be even a murder. When the bushes were parted, a stifling odor greeted the investigators, which was found to be from a patch of red fungus— the Trellised Clathrus. Its sickening odor had fooled the buzzards. Then, after seeing Kitty-Winks fool one, which had followed only his sense of sight, the question was really settled. They depend on both senses smell and sight—to lead them to the scenes of their orgies.

Thus Catty, Kitty and their various families furnished us with constant entertainment, and their enthusiasm in all things that went to make their daily life—food, frolic and affection—gave added zest to life for us.

After two years of successive kitten-families—one set barely weaned and provided with homes before there was another little nest full to be welcomed—the family of which Satan was a member arrived. There were four. Satan alone had the little mother's inky coat. Two were tiger striped, and the other, like Catty, white with grey markings.

They were still tiny kits, their eyes just open, when very early one morning I was awakened by hearing strange sounds of distress which seemed to have been haunting my dreams, growing always more insistent.

I slipped on shoes and dressing-gown and followed the sound. It brought me to the cat-nest, and there I found evidence of a sad and strange little tragedy.

Kitty-Winks had evidently realized her fate. She had climbed to the top of a vine-draped stump which was close by their nest, to die where the kits could not get to her; because instinct—the same instinct that warned her the death she was to die—had told her the kits would be poisoned too if they got to her body and tried to nurse. She was quite cold, and the cause of her death was discovered on the ground near the nest, the eye being led to it by green flies which circled and buzzed round. There is a sluggish, mottled fish which frequents the salt waters of warm climates. They are not plentiful along the Sound shores; but we have seen them, and knew that they carry a deadly poison, which seems to be all in the head; and by some naughty trick of nature, the head is especially attractive to fish-eating animals. The little mother had caught one of these toadfish—or maybe Catty had got it and brought it to her!—she had devoured its head, and then, feeling that she was doomed, she had climbed to the top of the stump which was just wide enough to hold her. It was evidently a painful death. Her eyes were half open, and also her mouth.

Poor brave little mother! Even in her death-pangs her one thought was to protect the baby kits.

The nest under the palm-leaves was a scene of misery. One kit lay quite dead, on the edge of the nursery, as if he had, in desperation, started to try to find the mother who failed to answer his cries. The others had cried themselves hoarse, so their voices were unnatural and they were exhausted with hunger and misery. For the first time in their brief lives, no mother had responded to their cries.

Catty was trying his best to quiet them; but he too was evidently puzzled and full of dismay.

They scrambled and staggered to me as soon as I spoke, begging for food and comfort.

I gathered them in my skirt and carried them to the kitchen where milk was poured into a saucer, and each little nose was pushed gently to it.

They were too young to lap; but they managed to get some satisfaction by dipping in their little muzzles and licking what stuck, meanwhile making little growly cries of satisfaction.

By the time all were fed, they were sticky with the spattering caused by their unskillful motions, which covered themselves and each other with flying drops.

I wet a sponge, and squeezing it nearly dry, went over each little coat with it, then wrapped them in a bit of soft cloth and put them to bed in a box, where they nestled together, and were all soon fast asleep.

Then the little mother was carried out to the edge of the garden, where her last resting place was made under a wild sweet bay tree, while Catty was diplomatically kept from seeing what was going on by the tempting dish of cream with biscuits crumbled in it, which he ate with relish after his troubled night with crying babies, and the so-strangely unresponsive mother.

That evening there was a full moon, and it was warm, so the box of kits was set outside the kitchen door, on the back porch.

Early next morning, when I came down to feed them, I found only two left. Catty had not stayed with them. He had seemed to be so demoralized by the way things had gone he disappeared, and returned no more for many days.

We could not imagine how one of the kits could have vanished in that way, leaving no sign. The sides of the box were too high for a kit of that tender age to climb over. And yet, it might be. The little thing might have waked and have made heroic efforts to go find its mother.

So, I made a thorough search in all directions. No sign of it was to be found. That evening the box with the two lone kits was again set on the porch; but closer up in the sheltered corner. We sat inside with our books beside the shaded lamp and as bedtime approached, there came suddenly a kit-scream of dire pain and terror. We rushed out, and there in the moonlight was a 'possum making off with a kitten in his mouth.

Julius caught up a broom which was hanging near the kitten-box, and slammed it at the 'possum. It leaped high, dropping the kitten, and made off in the shadows.

The kit lay where it was dropped, quivering and kicking evidently in death-throes. It was soon motionless.

We looked in the box. There was the little black kit, squirming round, hunting his little bed-fellow. I lifted him from his lonely bed, and carried him indoors, finding a small basket which was nearer his size. This was warmly padded with a folded duster, in which he curled up and slept till dawn.

Busier people than we were then, or those less devoted to dumb creatures, might have thought the only way to meet this situation was to put the lone kit painlessly out of life; but in the leisurely long days of that epoch, and with the devotion to animals which was characteristic of The Blessed Isle, the only thought was how to best rear the little orphan and make of him a fine cat.

So I found myself committed to the exacting task of bringing up "by hand" a baby-kit so tiny I could hide it between my two hands like a cake of toilet soap.

It showed a liking for the warm nest made by the two palms shut together against its sides, and when hands were otherwise occupied, it squirmed and complained unless snugly wrapped and sheltered among the folds of sewing work; or with one hand resting on him in his snug covers, while the other held book or pen. All sorts of ways were invented for working that made room for the baby-kit's comfort. Writing paper was held with weights, and various other expedients became the rule, that little Satan might not feel himself neglected. He slept sweetly most of the hours of both day and night, for the first few weeks. He was fed often, the time gradually lengthening between eats as he grew large enough to take bigger supplies at a meal. Very soon he could toddle and it was both touching and diverting to see him try to follow me about. Whenever he felt himself to be left too far behind he lifted his voice in the most ear-piercing wails—sounds out of all proportion to his size. Julius declared he could plainly distinguish words like "I wan my Marrrrrr!" in the cries which followed me as he scrambled along making heroic efforts not to be left behind. Kitten baby-hood being the briefest of periods, one could well afford to humor the lonely little fellow. As long as he was so helpless as to need constant looking after, he was ever first thought. Soon the helplessness began to be a thing of the past, and little Satan became the most frolicsome of kits, scampering around and ready for any sort of a lark.

It was as he approached this stage that Jack came for a short visit to The Blessed Isle.

Jack was a setter. His master wished to go on a cruise, and it wasn't the sort of trip for a dog to enjoy. We were already his friends, as his master had done some work for us on The Blessed Isle, bringing Jack with him. This was when Satan was a wee baby, always indoors, so when Jack's master asked us to let him stay on The Blessed Isle during his absence, one of my problems was to keep the little cat out of his way.

Jack seemed glad to be with us again, and I kept Satan's box on the little screened porch where Jack was never allowed to go. It was Satan's room, and used for no other purpose.

Every morning when I fed Satan and gave him his bath, Jack was allowed to look on; but I never left them alone together. Jack had watched me with a lively interest, when I went over the kit's coat with a squeezed out sponge then glanced from the kit to me, with a funny look that seemed to say: "I know a trick worth two of that." But I didn't trust him, and had no doubt that it would be the end of Satan, if I ever left them alone together.

The kit evidently didn't find my amateur baths very satisfactory; but it was the best I could do, and the bath, of some sort, was certainly a necessity after each spattery feeding. Flecks of rich milk—the evaporated, from the cans—splashed and dabbed all over the little fellow's black coat in his eager and awkward efforts to get as much cream absorbed as he could in the fewest minutes.

One morning I made haste to feed and bathe Satan, and put him out on his little porch for his morning nap, then gave Jack his bone to enjoy on the grass. It was sweep-day, and I was in a hurry to get things out to sun while the rooms were being freshened. I carried everything out to hang in the air on the east porch. As the last armful of draperies was being spread on the railings, I noticed that Jack down on the grass was apparently chewing something that I mistook for a small black shoe. I spoke to him, and he looked up, cocking his ears, and turned his head inquiringly. While he looked, the supposed shoe began to squirm. Could it, by some evil chance, be little Satan he was devouring? Down the stairway I rushed, and out on the grass, meanwhile shouting reproaches to Jack. He stood up, surprised and puzzled as I flew at him, and I stooped all a-quiver, to look at the kit, which rose up and came toward me. I snatched him up. He was unhurt, and very much alive; but dripping wet. Then I began to laugh. Jack had tried to help me out. My problem of giving Satan his daily baths had seemed an easy one to him. He had watched the chance of me being too occupied to interfere—had managed to open the screen door to Satan's room—had lifted the sleepy kit from his bed, where he was docilely taking his morning snooze, and had carried him unhurt to the soft grass. Then had gone at the bath as he had seen, somewhere or other, a mother-cat attending to her off-spring. It wasn't a complete success. The difference in the cat and dog tongue being that Madam Kitty's is rough, and leaves the coat dry as if brushed, while the dog's tongue is smooth and leaves anything he licks very wet. I was so relieved when I saw the kit was unhurt, and so tickled at the way Jack had tried to help us both, that I praised him, telling him he was a good dog, and a fine kit-nurse. Then I got Satan's towel and gave him a good rubbing.

Next morning I left it to Satan. Jack stuck close to us when he saw me making the usual preparations. I dampened and squeezed the sponge, held it out to Satan, and waited for him to come to me as he had learned to do. He stood looking at the sponge for a few seconds, then tuned to Jack, and ran to meet his lowered muzzle. That decided it. From that time, my part in the daily baths, was only to rub Satan dry when Jack had finished his part. And as he matured, he learned from Jack, to do his own licking. Jack now became Satan's protector and comrade. When Catty returned, as he did when Satan was about two months old, it took but little coaxing to make him accept Jack's friendship too; so the three friends—big cat, little cat, and dog— formed what we call "The High Jinks Club." Such acrobatics and games of all kinds were never before seen. It was a perpetual circus. And when Jack's master returned from the cruise, and came to claim his dog, Catty was so demoralized, that he again disappeared for a long absence.

In the meantime, Satan kept on growing; it seemed as if he would never stop. He grew till he was as heavy as a child to lift. He was big and chunky, like a bull-pup; but graceful and agile. On seeing him for the first time, people always exclaimed at such a splendid cat, asking what kind he was. They were always surprised to hear he was "just a cat." No particular breed. He was afraid of nobody, and would walk right up to a stranger, ready to meet more than half way and "shake-hands," or any other courtesy or endearment. His gentleness and playfulness was remarkable. Everybody wanted him. He could remember nothing of his own mother, he always thought himself to be absolutely mine, and he loved me accordingly. The tin milk diet had made him robust and full of vigor, his only weak point being his teeth. Something was lacking to make his teeth what they should have been, and he often suffered with tooth-ache. This gave him little appetite for meats, his favorite food being fish.

One afternoon Julius and I were down on the wharf fishing. The little sail boat was fastened to the wharf by its painter, and swung with the current. It made a shadow in the water which drew small fish to its shelter. They had been biting, and Julius had caught little ones, giving them to Satan, who always followed us, especially when there was fishing on the program. Finally the fish seemed to be done biting, and Julius tossed the piece he had been cutting for bait, to Satan, telling him he could have it, when suddenly there was a strong pull at the line, and the end of the pole curved to meet the waves. Julius began playing the fish, which was big and lively. Meanwhile he said to me over his shoulder; "Take that bait from Satan, I may need another piece." I turned to Satan; but he had heard, and was too quick for me. He ran to the edge of the wharf and gave a wonderful leap. He landed ker-plunk on the deck of the sharpie and ran to the stern, where he laid down the bit of fish and looked triumphantly at us before beginning to eat it. We were astonished. So much so, that Julius, when he saw what had happened, forgot all about the fish, which slipped from the hook, and escaped. We sat and laughed and looked at Satan—the wise—the uncanny, in his knowingness.

Catty came back after awhile, and he and Satan were again comrades. Games of the gayest engaged their time, till both were exhausted. Then they piled up together in a tangle for good snoozes, then more food, and then strolls together in the forest. Catty had seemed to us to be a gigantic cat; but Satan was so immense, that Catty was dwarfed by him.

They made a handsome pair.

One thing about them seemed to us almost uncanny. Catty had been a great fisherman before the tragic end of Kitty-Winks; but after that happened he never went into the water again. Both he and Satan preferred fish to any other food; but the fishes had to be caught for them and given to them, otherwise, they would have gone without.

End of the tale of Satan.

Newspaper Articles, Essays and Poems

Newspaper Articles, Essays and Poems

Byrd Spilman Dewey was a frequent contributor to newspapers around the nation. She submitted philosophical essays such as *O Youth Eternal*, which appeared in the Maysville, Kentucky *Daily Public Ledger* in 1910. *Back Home* is a sentimental piece she wrote in 1909, her first time back in her childhood city of Maysville in more than thirty years. In it she alludes to her father, Jonathan Edwards Spilman, who preached there for more than a decade. Bittersweet it must have been, as Maysville was the site of her mother's untimely death in 1866 aboard a steam vessel that caught fire.

As a modern woman ushering in the twentieth century, she took her stance in favor of women gaining the right to vote in a stylish and nonthreatening way in an essay published in several newspapers. Mrs. Dewey was 64 when she was first able to vote in 1920.

Housekeeping was always a passion for Mrs. Dewey. She did not think of it as drudgery, and cooking took center stage in many of her early newspaper columns. Her friendship with Mrs. Woodrow Wilson, first wife of the 28th President, resulted in her selection as a participant in the *Economy Administration Cook Book*. Mrs. Dewey contributed fruit recipes that showed her ingenuity and creativity in the kitchen.

Very few examples exist of Byrd Spilman Dewey's poetry. *Glimpses and Echoes* looks at a day at Pitt's Island (now Munyon's Island), a popular picnic spot for the Lake Worth pioneers.

Finally, *The Beach* is a short essay on the ocean's power to affect emotions and the awe she had for the beauty and sounds of the waves breaking on the shore.

O Youth Eternal

O N THE shores of the Infinite towers the glorious city of achievements. Its slender spires glisten in the morning sunlight—for there is always morning and always Spring. Each mortal who has a spark of the divine fire in his soul has helped to build this city inspired by life's twin angels of construction—Hope and Love.

As the old year dies the New Year is born.

The hour of passing from old to new is one of vigil—of remembrance—of hope. From a dawn sky, gilded by the sun's first ray, comes the glad new year—a boat sailing wing-and-wing loaded down to the water's edge with gifts. It speeds us—wards dashing up the spray with its golden prow, leaving in its wake a ruffled track of sparkling light. Turquoise and emerald set in dancing points of gold and silver. Onward, at a merry clip it comes.

Welcome new year! Thy packages are so enfolded in mystery we cannot divine their contents; but we fearlessly receive and unwrap them knowing all to be gifts with a purpose; some will charm us at first glimpse, others set us guessing what they may be—what may be their meaning and mission.

New Year is a re-birth—a fresh beginning. The heart stirs—goes out to its new gifts. Life has yet something to offer. We hold upturned hands—perhaps feel misgivings—tempted to let fall some of the offerings; or, reach joyfully to take those that please the eye; but all are good, whether or not they seem acceptable to finite limitations of understanding.

Life's joys are cumulative. Maturity is better than immaturity. Young-in-years has only the present, tumultuous and happy though it be. Maturity has both past and present, each supplementing the other—balancing, explaining, reflecting—the present experience, a mirror of what is, reflecting what was, the two blending to make new joy which partakes of both and is more than either. "The tender grace of a day that is dead" is ours again. We laugh, we weep, we glow, responsive to the voice of memory. The bright never fades—the sweet is never lost. Any joy once grasped is ours forever. In nightwatches—in twilight musings—memory prompts recollection to search for and bring us all the flowers which in the past have bloomed for us; and they come with all their tender fragrance. Dreams bring them, without waiting memory's invitation. We awaken from sleep with fingers still tingling from the warm clasp of what was only a dream-hand. It has reached out from the past throbbing with vital magic to claim the unbroken—the unbreakable—tie 'twixt soul and soul. The darkness is peopled with dream faces, and a radiance—not of earthly light— glorifies the silence. An angel whose name is Youth, is beside the couch, holding in her hand the torch of memory—of vibrant life. Oh, Youth, Youth! In thine other hand is the horn of plenty which ever pours out and is never emptied! Give us again that faith, and that innocent trust, Youth's sword and shield!

But, says doubt, will not the world rob us of all we possess if we enter the lists armed only with faith and trust?

Nay, why question? The strong man, filled with the conqueror's pride, armed for victory, stalks the beast of the forest. Aggressive strength is met with cunning, the beast springs out to tear him limb from limb, staining the earth's brown bosom with his life-blood. The straying infant wanders through the forest of dangers, fearlessly brushing the serpent, the ravaging beast, the prowling marauder. It finally stumbles into the lair of the tigress. Fearless, it reaches out tiny hands in gleeful greeting, approaches the ferocious mother with joyful babblings. Does the beast fall on the youngling to rend and devour? Hear her purring to the fearless innocent! See her curve out the velvet paw of mute invitation, as the human babe nestles down to join the wild cubs in their sheltered nest. Knowing no fear, it passes all dangers guarded by the lion of its own disarming trust. This is life. Attack, and the whole world threatens; trust, and all nature purrs. Then is there nothing in life to fear? Only our own unfaith. If we become as little children, we are safe. 'Tis only untrusting age, with fear in his heart, which sees danger everywhere, and is there-by conquered. Youth—gentle, gay, and trustful—passes by unharmed, not knowing there are teeth, claws, and venom.

In welcoming the fulfillment of maturity, we lose not the garment of youth. We hold fast, with loving trust, to the joy of living. Youth of the year—youth of life—youth of the heart—trinity of happiness. Everything gilded by life's sunshine, which is power to love, a happy trust in The Angel of Destiny, a loving tenderness for all created life. And this is the spirit of youth—unfading youth—the guardian angel leading us through life's mysterious mazes to the draped doorway which opens into that vast region beyond peopled with our loved ones—a country glorified with the radiance of Youth Eternal.

Back Home

TO COME back, after an absence of more than thirty years, to a home town, hallowed by memories of early childhood and youth, is an experience to move the soul.

More than a quarter of a century passed in a growing country where young cities are mapped, then spring up in a few months to thriving business centers where only wild growth and wilder creatures of earth and air had dwelt, makes it the more striking to come home to a conservative old town like Maysville, to find so many landmarks and so many old friends left.

The little old schoolroom in the back room of the Third Street Methodist Church, where Mrs. Pears used to hold restless little girls and boys at their books for five mornings and afternoons a week, from September to June of every year, is still here. The Church has been painted, but it is, in all other respects, the same.

The McGranaghan home, where the Doctor had his office on the first floor, and the family—from Grandma Ellis to little Lou-Amy-lived upstairs, is just East of the Church, where the "dame school" was, and looks as it did more than thirty years ago, the most marked change along there being the disappearance of the late Mrs. A.M. January's exquisite flower garden between the January mansion and the East wall of the McGranaghan home.

This garden with its roses, heliotropes, pinks, tuberoses, baby lilies, and many other delights, is now only a memory, and as a memory, is immortal. So live we all in the hearts that love us!

The old Church opposite the January home is so little changed that it is difficult to realize the thirty-three years of absence; and one sees, with the spiritual eyes, that silver-haired Clergyman who stood up in its pulpit that many years ago, to preach the farewell sermon to the beloved flock he had so faithfully led for thirteen changeful years. Though he is no more—though his body has for years reposed in the cool, silent earth-like that hero, whose memory is embalmed in song, "His soul goes marching on," and still leads upward those he loved when he was here in the flesh.

A second and even a third generation now gives back those who are gone to return no more. They look at us with the eyes and speak to us with the voices of those who have passed on "with the ceaseless tramp of marching feet" to the Beyond.

A few of the older generation yet remain, looking still so youthful that the years between seem the dream of a night.

It is bewildering.

The dear old friends, seen through the rosy haze of youthful memory, seem the same age as their children and children's children.

And those who, in the old days, were a few years older—belonging to a "grown-up set" and looked up to with childish reverence—have, by some magic, waited by the way, and are now the same age, or even younger, than the children they used to pet or tease or instruct.

As the old town was approached, at the close of the day, just a week ago, there were tremors of fear that the beautiful hills so dear to childhood would be shrunken in size and less beautiful than the treasured mental pictures of long ago, but these were needless fears. The fondest memory could not exaggerate the beauty of the fair hills that encircle the town—a green rosary of charm.

All is more beautiful—more "happifying"—than fondest memory's dream. The only note of sadness in the glad coming is that so many

"—names we loved to hear
Have been carved for many a year
On the Tomb!"

We are Ready for Vote

THE OBSERVER is constantly reminded of the power of the vote. Each one with a vote to give or to withhold is hedged round with a magic importance that makes him a factor to be reckoned with in every question. The candidate, or those who back him, and will benefit by his election, has a respect for the vote-wielder of which we daily and hourly see proofs.

Many of us women do not feel the need of this power, because we are surrounded by those who look after our interests, and who see that we are not imposed upon; or that we do not lack for protection when any question rises which threatens us; or our interests. But, for the sake of those of our sisters who go out among strangers fighting alone and unprotected, hampered by laws framed by men who are unscrupulous in exploiting their helplessness, we are willing, even eager to right cruel wrongs by taking upon ourselves the responsibility of the franchise.

Any human being who has the sense and the courage to administer a home and to bring into the world human beings to train them for this life and for eternity, has surely the sense and the nerve to take hold and help father, brothers and sons to attend to the public housekeeping.

Some alarmists say we shall neglect the home if we take to the vote; but have we ever yet attempted anything we couldn't do? Many mothers have to be business women, have to run farms, or have to do other rough work which nature seems to have intended for masculine strength and still they have found time to keep the little garments mended—to see that there is wholesome food a-plenty always ready for hungry little mouths—to find time to make the home the happy center of life, and to train the budding minds and morals, bringing up all around good young citizens to take their places in the game of life.

The vote does not interfere with a man's other business; then, why should it be an interruption to the life of the house-mother, who has always shown herself to be equal to any emergency?

In those countries and states where women now have the franchise, we know they have made good. First of all, they have looked to the welfare of the weak, and the helpless. Children, unsheltered young people, invalids, abused animals—all the helpless little ones cared for—protected, both from the cruel greed of others and from the consequences of their own young foolishness.

It's up to the men to show their alertness in grasping the trend of things. Let them offer the franchise and let women accept, giving man the credit for showing both the good sense and his gallantry.

Surely he can trust an equal share in the government to those hands which in his first helplessness have pressed his tiny form against the bosom of comfort and tenderness, and will be solace when that same bosom will be his dying pillow!

Recipes of Mrs. Byrd Spilman Dewey

Pink Fruit Sauce

Like many other good things this discovery came accidently. A grocer boy late, and company till the grocery was closed, and company for next day's luncheon, with morning engagements which made the preparation of sauce the night before imperative. Then the discovery that cranberries were so soft, only a cup full was fit to cook, and that the pretty little red apples which had been chosen to help out the dessert had not been sent, but instead some big, ugly, mushy specimens, devoid of flavor. It all ended with a sauce made of the apples, with the cupful of cranberries to give flavor and color, and the dish has ever since been a standby, preferred to either cranberry or apple sauce "straight." By various proportions it can be made more or less red, and more or less tart. Sugar to taste.

Crystallized Pineapple

Peel and slice. Measure as much sugar as fruit. Place in agate or earthen saucepan a layer of fruit and a layer of sugar, till all is used, then set in a warm place for the sugar to melt. When a syrup is formed put to stew briskly till fruit is clear. Dip out with a silver fork and drain on a tipped platter. When dry roll in sugar and set in the sun, or on the back of the range, or in the warming-oven with the door open. If still wet, after a few hours of drying, dip out again and roll in fresh sugar. When perfectly dry, pack in boxes with dry sugar between the layers. The same recipe makes delicious candied bananas.

Glimpses and Echoes

A GLORIOUS morning after days of storm.
A white winged boat speeds towards the wharf.
She pauses; friends disembark.

"Get your hat!"

"Never mind the lunch!"

"Plenty on board!"

"Picnic!"

"Come along!"

"Hurry up!"

All talk at once. Bread butters itself. Gloves and hats are found to be already on. Everything does itself.

"All aboard!"

"Cast off!"

Flying up the Lake.

Pausing for more picnickers.

Greeting passing boats with friends on board. Everything and everybody glad of the inspiring weather—drunk on sunshine.

Flying past the Inlet.

"Where to?"

"The Island."

"What Island?"

"The island of palms and flowers!"

We disembark. Flowers, singing birds and happy people, bright dresses, warm welcome, laughter, everybody talking at once.

"Dinner time!"

"Spread the cloth!"

Bread and butter-fish-chicken, potato salad-

391

"No cake?"

"No cake."

"No pie?"

"I thought you had brought the cake."

"I thought you had."

"Never mind; who cares for cake, anyway."

"Not I."

"Nor I."

"I adore bread and butter."

"And I."

"Good bread and butter."

"Yes, indeed."

"Mh-hm."

"Pass the jelly."

"Have some more chicken? salmon?"

"Good coffee."

"Yes, splendid. Another cup."

"Cucumbers?"

"Yes and bananas."

"Everything but cake and pie."

"Unique picnic."

"Gather up the dishes. Let the birds have the fragments."

Long paths and avenues of palms, rubber trees, and all queer vines and shrubs. Hermit crabs.

"Oh, he bit me, the horrid thing! I want his pretty shell."

Laughter-jokes-conundrums.

"Inlet?"

"Yes, come along."

Lying on the sand. Point of rocks, with spray falling over it. Woman in a red shawl watching steamers plowing through white waves. Tide coming in.

"See that shark!"

"Where?"

"There he goes."

"Sand fleas."

"How funny, where do they go?"

"Time to go back on the boat."

"Come on."

"What a lovely conch shell."

"Phe—-ew, he's dead!"

"What a funny fish! There see it?"

Homeward bound.

"How lovely!"

A silvery moonrise on one side, a golden sunset on the other.

"Oh, for eyes all around like a spider!"

"How beautiful the cocoanuts, on that point against the sunset! Their leaves, 'each alone in feathr'y grace, against the tropic sky.'"

"That was written about the pine trees."

"Yes, I know; but it fits the cocoanut even better."

The afterglow dies swiftly. The beautiful moon! We sail through the pathway of silver.

Home at last.

"Good night!"

"Good night!"

"Tired?"

"Yes."

"Sleepy?"

"Oh no."

Sunlight. Moonlight, laughter, fish, steamers, winds, waves-the pillow is full of them.

The day is gone; but its echoes linger.

The Beach

I SCOOP out a nest in the sand, and cuddle down on the breast of Mother Nature, to feel her soft breath on my cheek, and to listen to her whisperings. How close Heaven seems! Lying so, and gazing upward, nothing else is in sight. I close my eyes, it seems to descend. I feel its benediction over me. The beauty, the silence, the peace, the blessing, bring the quick tears to my eyes. I sit up to brush them away, and thus spy, far out on the horizon, a pair of white wings, bearing northward its burden of hopes and fears.

What fascination there is in the never-ending ebb and flow of the waves! One seems to hear all the harmonies of the universe in their murmurings. All the petty strivings of life seem but a troubled dream. Only high, noble thoughts could live in such surroundings. Is that true? See those people coming down the beach…watch them. Never once a glance at the majestic scene spread out before them. Every faculty absorbed in poking up the debris, to find—shells. The lucky ones triumphant; the unlucky, disappointed—envious—cross.

The ocean frightens me. No, not that, it awes me. It is awe-full, so relentless—powerful—cruel. Trembling, I sink back into my nest, and look again to the Heavens—they are always kind.

Epilogue

Epilogue

Fittingly, the last piece to appear in this collection is Byrd Spilman Dewey's last published work. It appeared in a 1927 issue of the *Florida Naturalist*, published by the Florida Audubon Society, and appears here by courtesy of the Society.

In this article, we see the true passion of Byrd Spilman Dewey's life brought together—the love of animals, protection of the environment, and a devotion for her adopted state of Florida. She could see what the incredible growth rate and population explosion was doing to the state's natural environment, and offered this timely warning: "If we who now hold the world's law-making in our hands, do not give attention to conserving our natural resources, then the children coming after us, will inherit a looted estate." She said these words decades before environmental protection was even a thought for most people, and sadly her prophesy has come to pass in many parts of Florida.

Some Bird Notes

AS I go to and fro among Florida towns and neighborhoods, also in other states, I am constantly asked to speak in schools and various sorts of clubs, along my chosen lines. Of these, I have three favorite "jobs": Bird Protection, Forestry and Humane. The three interlock. Trees need animals and birds, and they need the trees. We can hardly speak of one without including the others.

When I get up to talk to an audience, I like to make it understood that I'm not to do all the talking. That they are to ask questions and to make it more a discussion than to have the idea that they must "take it as it comes." That old sailor who said he liked the Episcopal church best of all, because there he could "jaw back" instead of letting the "preacher" do it all, had the right idea.

One question I am often asked is, why I give so much time to birds, other animals and trees, instead of devoting all the time and thought to the needs of children. My response, of course, is that all of it is for the children. If we who now hold the world's law-making in our hands, do not give attention to conserving our natural resources, then the children coming after us, will inherit a looted estate. We know the world is held by us "in entail" for our heirs. Then, is it not a point of honor with us to pass it along to them at least in as good shape as we ourselves have inherited it from our forbears? I find when it is so put to those who have thoughtlessly suggested that we are neglecting the children when we give our attention to forests, and to the conservation of our animal life therein, they are quick enough to realize that it IS for the children we are working when we give attention to conservation of what they are to inherit.

My greatest hold on the interest of those to whom I speak is that my stories of birds, trees and beasts, great and small, are not what the children call "made up." They are true, and are from my own experience and observation. One needs to love them in order to understand, just as it is in our contacts with humankind. When we understand the birds we find they know very much more about us and what we are doing than we know about them. I whistle them in, and they come trustingly to me showing that they have no fear of me, because I speak their own language. They even turn their backs, cozily going on with eating, drinking, splashing in their basin, and preening their feathers, close to where I am working among the flowers, now and then looking at me over a turned shoulder as I whistle or speak to them; in all ways showing perfect confidence in a tried friend; but let a strange voice be heard, or an unknown visitor appear and they are gone in a second.

One mystery about birds and all animals is their way of knowing when and where they are safe. I can never forget the first time I wintered in a town which was a bird sanctuary. In some mysterious way all bird-dom was informed when the open season was to begin. Three or four days before the fatal date, coveys of quail began to assemble in my grounds which were inside the city limits. They came, and came, and came—parents followed by grown, or nearly grown youngsters, and all "camped" right there till the open season ended, when they promptly returned to their runs in the surrounding forests. It was a most thrilling experience.

A thing which could only be believed by seeing. Those wise little fellows fleeing to their City of Refuge, and staying fearlessly until the time of banging guns in forests round-about the city had ended. They were as tame as domestic fowls, fearlessly gathering to eat the food and to drink at the constantly refilled basins placed and replenished for their refreshment. Other birds came also; but in some way, that seemed less remarkable. Quails are so very shy, as a rule, that having them come and stay and show such wonderful confidence gave one a real "lump in the throat."

At a down-state settlement—a settlement so new people there still believed it fair to kill for food every eatable creature, regardless of any other side of the question—birds of all sorts were being ruthlessly slaughtered—even the robins who had migrated there from lands where winter reigned. A tourist who was a bird lover, happened to sojourn there long enough to see what was happening, and he at once started a petition to make it unlawful to shoot any creature within a two-mile limit in all directions from the town center. He soon got enough signatures to have it made a law; and in a miraculously short time the wild creatures of all sorts had discovered their haven of safety. Inside those imaginary lines it was especially noted that all birds which had been so wild, were now gentle and approachable.

I went there, not knowing myself just where those limits were, but one afternoon a party of neighbors all gathered for a picnic to sail up to the Inlet and see the full moon rise. We started about three and as we sailed along ducks and other water birds gathered and followed the boat, begging for food. We fed them from our picnic baskets, and they followed right along, greedy as a flock of hungry children. We held bits over the boat-side for them to snatch from our fingers. So eager were they and so many other birds kept on joining the hungry throng that one of the party laughingly predicted they would get all the picnic supper we were supposed to enjoy at the Inlet.

I was leaning over, holding a bit of biscuit at which two wild ducks were snatching, each trying to get it all, when suddenly both desisted and turned to swim away, even spreading wings to help in the quick retreat. I drew back from the leaning position to look around and see what had frightened them but could see nothing to explain it. The captain was nearby and I called to him to ask what had happened to frighten all the birds, as I could see the others were all rapidly beating a retreat. He turned and answered, "Why, don't you know. We have just crossed the two-mile line!" I didn't know. None of us but the captain knew where the two-mile line was, but every bird that had been following us knew and understood its meaning.

Among our picnickers was a young man who had lately arrived in the town from a visit to a game preserve further up-state. We were all excitedly discussing the miracle of the birds knowing so well what we had not even suspected, and he, as soon as there was a pause, began to tell us about the way it was in the game preserve, as told him by the men in charge of it. It was that every bird (and indeed all the animal life) inside the game preserve was just as tame as are domestic animals, but as soon as any of them happened to get outside the line of safety it at once became "wild as a hawk." We cannot understand why or how this is but many witnesses testify to its truth. They do know, but how?

Postscript

In examining these stories of more than a century ago, set in an untamed paradise long since lost, it might be asked if these works still matter; they do.

Byrd Spilman Dewey's stories can still touch the soul because she taps into emotional areas we so treasure—the need for adventure and the need for companionship. No adventure is fun alone, and Mrs. Dewey had husband Fred and her menagerie of cats, dogs and birds at her side. She chose to pioneer in America's last frontier, South Florida, at a time when the harsh sub-tropical climate and environment was an untamed tiger. But that wildness is what attracted her, and inspired her to write of what she saw and experienced. As the decades passed her into obscurity, our rediscovery of her writings was the spark that served to uncover Byrd Spilman Dewey and invite her "children"—these writings—to a grand reunion for all to enjoy.

Byrd Spilman Dewey knew that one day South Florida would be home to countless thousands. She said, "In our isolation so remote and wild—so denuded of all the luxuries of life's centers—the world had come to us, just as we had dreamed it would, bringing everything we lacked and completing what Nature had so perfectly begun."

She captured that place and time and shared its charm with us, which now is preserved for the ages. We hope these stories have enchanted you as well.

—The Editors

Further Reading

Brownstein, Ted. (2013). *Pioneers of Jewell: A documentary history of Lake Worth's forgotten settlement (1885-1910)*. Lake Worth, FL: Lake Worth Herald Press.

Curl, Donald W. (1986). *Palm Beach County: An illustrated history*. Northridge, CA: Windsor Publications.

Drake, Lynn Lasseter & Marconi, Richard A. (2006). *West Palm Beach—Images of America*. Charleston, SC: Arcadia Publishing.

Hofman, Charles (2004). *Letters from Linton*. Delray Beach, Florida: Delray Beach Historical Society.

Kersey, Harry A. (2003). *The Stranahans of Fort Lauderdale*. Gainesville, FL: University Press of Florida.

Linehan, Mary C. (1980). *Early Lantana, her neighbors—and more*. St. Petersburg, FL: B. Kennedy.

Linehan, Mary C. & Watts Nelson, Majorie. (1994). *Pioneer days on the shores of Lake Worth*. 1873-1893. St. Petersburg, FL: Southern Heritage Press.

Marconi, Richard A. & Murray, Debi. (2009). *Palm Beach—Images of America*. Charleston, SC: Arcadia Publishing.

McIver, Stuart. (1976). *Yesterday's Palm Beach, including Palm Beach County*. Miami, FL: E.A. Seeman Publishing.

Metcalf, Guy. (1891). *The Tropical Sun*. Juno Beach FL: Author. Available: http://ufdc.ufl.edu/UF00075915/00552.

Myers, Ruby Andrews. (Ed.). (1896). *The Lake Worth Historian: A Souvenir Journal*. Palm Beach FL: Ladies of Palm Beach for the Benefit of the Royal Poinciana Chapel.

Oyer, Harvey E. III (2008). *The American Jungle: The Adventures of Charlie Pierce*. Fort Lauderdale, FL: Middle River Press.

—(2010). *The Last Egret: The Adventures of Charlie Pierce*. Fort Lauderdale, FL: Middle River Press.

—(2012). *The Last Calusa: The Adventures of Charlie Pierce*. Fort Lauderdale, FL: Middle River Press.

Palm Beach Post. (2009). *Palm Beach County at 100: Our History, Our Home*. West Palm Beach, FL: Palm Beach Post.

Pedersen, Ginger L. & DeVries, Janet M. (2012). *Pioneering Palm Beach: The Deweys and the South Florida Frontier*. Charleston, SC: The History Press.

Pierce, Charles W. (1981). *Pioneer Life in Southeast Florida*. Miami, FL.: University of Miami Press.

Robinson, Tim. (2005). *A Tropical Frontier (Pioneers and settlers of Southeast Florida, 1800-1890, a comprehensive history)*. Stuart, FL: Port Sun Publishers.

Root, Susie & Rhodes, Grace Porter Hopkins (1913). *The Economy Administration Cook Book*. New York: Syndicate Publishing.

Smith, Patrick D. (1984). *A Land Remembered*. Sarasota, FL: Pineapple Press.

Tuckwood, Jan & Kleinberg, Eliot. (1994). *Pioneers in Paradise: West Palm Beach, the First 100 Years.* Atlanta, GA: Longstreet Press.

Tuckwood, Jan. (2000). *Our Century featuring the Palm Beach Post 100: The people who changed the way we live.* West Palm Beach, FL: Mega Books/Progressive Publishing.

About the Editors

Dr. Ginger L. Pedersen, a native Floridian, grew up in South Florida among the palms and pines in Jupiter, Florida. Her interest in Florida history was sparked through her grandparent's theme park Africa USA, a 1950s roadside attraction in Boca Raton, Florida.

Dr. Pedersen is an administrator at a state college in Lake Worth, Florida and holds a Doctoral degree in Educational Leadership from Florida Atlantic University in addition to Masters and Bachelor's degrees in Psychology.

In 2012 she wrote, with co-author Janet M. DeVries, *Pioneering Palm Beach: The Deweys and the South Florida Frontier.* In this book she presents an incredible, inspiring story of pioneer life in early Palm Beach County that was hidden for more than a century.

Dr. Pedersen continues her research on Palm Beach County history, specializing in pioneer history and the acquisition of historical documents, maps and photographs for museums.

She serves on a local historic preservation board and conducts history tours in locations throughout Palm Beach County. She is currently finishing research for two books, and writes a history blog at www.palmbeachpast.org.

When not doing historical research, Janet M. DeVries loves being near or in the Atlantic Ocean and enjoys swimming, snorkeling, and boating. She earned a Bachelor of Arts in History from Florida Atlantic University and is completing a Master's degree in Library Information Science at Florida State University.

She is author of *Images of America: Sport Fishing in Palm Beach County* and *Vintage Postcard Series: Around Boynton Beach*. She co-authored *Images of America: Boynton Beach* (with M. Randall Gill) and *Vintage Postcard Series: Delray Beach* (with Dorothy W. Patterson). She has also written articles on South Florida history and Girl's Series Books for various publications.

Her last book, *Pioneering Palm Beach: The Deweys and the South Florida Frontier* with Ginger L. Pedersen, uncovered Palm Beach County's hidden history. A resident of Palm Beach County since 1987, DeVries is the archivist for a South Florida library. A member of the American Association of State and Local History, the American Association of Archivists, the Society of Florida Archivists and the Gold Coast Archivists, and the Historical Society of Palm Beach County; DeVries is President of the Boynton Beach Historical Society.

DeVries credits her passion for research, treasure hunting, adventure and clue seeking to the fictional pop icon, Nancy Drew, whose suspenseful adventures captivated her as a youngster. Janet is a charter member of the international club of Nancy Drew Sleuths. She is currently writing several other books, including her first historical fiction novel for juveniles. Her history blog is found at: www.boyntonhistory.org/author/jdevries/

Pioneering Palm Beach

Palm Beach's sunny and idyllic shores had humble beginnings as a wilderness of sawgrass and swamps only braved by the hardiest of souls. Two such adventurers were Fred and Byrd Spilman Dewey, who pioneered in central Florida before discovering the tropical beauty of Palm Beach in 1887. Though their story was all but lost, this dynamic couple was vital in transforming the region from rough backcountry into a paradise poised for progress. Authors Ginger Pedersen and Janet DeVries trace a remarkable history

of the Deweys in South Florida from their beginnings on the isolated frontier to entertaining the likes of the Flaglers, Vanderbilts, Phippses, Cluetts, Clarkes and other Palm Beach elite. Using Mrs. Dewey's autobiographical writings to fill in the gaps, Pedersen and DeVries narrate a chapter in Florida's history that has remained untold till now.

GOLD MEDAL WINNER—Florida Publisher's Association – Best Florida Non-Fiction Book, 2013

Critical Acclaim for Pioneering Palm Beach: The Deweys and the South Florida Frontier:

"Long before Henry Flagler and his railroad thundered through South Florida, a pioneering husband and wife set down humble stakes in Palm Beach County. Arriving by boat in 'the Lake Worth Country' in 1887, Fred and Byrd "Birdie" Spilman Dewey were the little-known first settlers to build a homestead on sugar-sand surrounded by swamp and sawgrass." —*Doreen Christensen, Sun-Sentinel*

"The authors bring us on a delightful journey into the history of that part of Florida defined largely (in the 19th century) by the borders of Lake Worth. It truly was a frontier. Sketchily populated and without much of a commercial or transportation infrastructure, this beautiful but isolated region appealed to only the hardiest souls. Fortunately for the authors, they found a magnificent focal point in the lives and writings of two such pioneers, Fred and Birdie Dewey, providing readers with a general story of the region's gradual development anchored by a specific, personal story." —*Phil Jason, Florida Weekly*

"If she'd wanted it, Boynton Beach might have been named Dewey Beach or Deweyville. After all, Birdie owned and platted the town more than a century ago. After decades of believing that Major Nathan S. Boynton, a distinguished Civil War veteran and hotel developer, founded Boynton Beach, Birdie's portion of the story has come to light. The history of Birdie and her husband, Frederick Sidney Dewey, is told in the recently published *Pioneering Palm Beach: The Deweys and the South Florida Frontier* (The History Press, 2012), by Ginger L. Pedersen and Janet M. DeVries." —*M.M. Cloutier, The Palm Beach Daily News*

"This was an absolutely fabulous book. It was short and sweet, with wonderful photographs. Information about the Deweys was not well-known, until now. The authors also painted a vivid picture of early life in South Florida, naming familiar landmarks to enable the reader to compare between today's Florida and yesterday's Florida. Highly recommended!" —*Rosa Sophia, Author*

Read the complete biography of Byrd Spilman Dewey and Fred S. Dewey—available at local bookstores and online through Amazon.com and other book sellers.